Chicana Liberation

WOMEN, GENDER, AND SEXUALITY
IN AMERICAN HISTORY

Editorial Advisors:
Susan K. Cahn
Wanda A. Hendricks
Deborah Gray White
Anne Firor Scott, Founding Editor Emerita

*For a list of books in the series, please see our
website at www.press.uillinois.edu.*

Chicana Liberation

Women and Mexican American Politics in Los Angeles, 1945–1981

MARISELA R. CHÁVEZ

© 2024 by the Board of Trustees
of the University of Illinois
All rights reserved
1 2 3 4 5 C P 5 4 3 2 1
∞ This book is printed on acid-free paper.

Portions of Chapter 1 appeared previously in different form as "'We have a long, beautiful history': Chicana Feminist Trajectories and Legacies" in *No Permanent Waves: Recasting U.S. Feminist History*, edited by Nancy Hewitt, 77–97. New Brunswick: Rutgers University Press, 2010.
Chapter 3 appeared previously in different form as "Pilgrimage to the Homeland: California Chicanas and International Women's Year, Mexico City, 1975" in *Memories and Migrations: Mapping Boricua and Chicana Histories*, edited by Vicki L. Ruiz and John R. Chávez, 170–95. Urbana: University of Illinois Press, 2008.

Library of Congress Cataloging-in-Publication Data
Names: Chávez, Marisela R., author.
Title: Chicana liberation : women and Mexican American politics in
    Los Angeles, 1945–1981 / Marisela R. Chávez.
Other titles: Women, gender, and sexuality in American history.
Description: Urbana : University of Illinois Press, [2024] | Series:
    Women, gender, and sexuality in american history | Includes
    bibliographical references and index.
Identifiers: LCCN 2023041742 (print) | LCCN 2023041743 (ebook) |
    ISBN 9780252045707 (cloth) | ISBN 9780252087813 (paperback) |
    ISBN 9780252056567 (ebook)
Subjects: LCSH: Mexican American women—Political activity—
    California—Los Angeles. | Chicano movement—California—Los
    Angeles. | Activism. | Feminism. | Los Angeles (Calif.)
Classification: LCC E184.M5 C439 2024 (print) | LCC E184.M5 (ebook)
    | DDC 979.4/940046872—dc23/eng/20230912
LC record available at https://lccn.loc.gov/2023041742
LC ebook record available at https://lccn.loc.gov/2023041743

Caminante, no hay puentes, se hacen puentes al andar.
(Voyager, there are no bridges, one builds them as one walks.)
—*Gloria Anzaldúa,* This Bridge Called My Back

Contents

Acknowledgments ix

Introduction 1

1 Bridging Activism: Mexican American Women and Political Leadership from the Postwar Era to the Early Chicano Movement in Los Angeles 15

2 Forging a Chicana Feminist Praxis: The Comisión Femenil Mexicana Nacional, 1970–1976 43

3 "We Would Go There and Be Part of a Great Audience": California Chicanas and International Women's Year, Mexico City, 1975 69

4 "The Right to Govern Their Own Bodies": Chicana Body Politics in Los Angeles, 1969–1981 95

Epilogue 121

Notes 127

Bibliography 159

Index 179

Acknowledgments

This book has been a very, very long time in the making. Along the circuitous path that this book journey has taken, I have been privileged to be able to count on many people for their unwavering support, encouragement, and guidance because they believed in the importance of Chicana feminist histories. I am immensely grateful.

First and foremost, the women who shared their stories and experiences and who preserved documents, letters, newsletters, and photographs, are the foundation of this book. These women shared their time, welcomed me into their homes, and allowed me to probe their memories, ask a multitude of questions, and at times, bring up difficult experiences. I thank Lilia Aceves, Hortensia Amaro, Grace Montañez Davis, Anna NietoGómez, Celia Herrera Rodríguez, Yolanda M. López, Yolanda Nava, Connie Pardo, Isabel H. Rodríguez, Corinne Sánchez, Dolores Sánchez, Sandra Serrano Sewell, and Patricia Córdova Vellanoweth. In addition, I am grateful to other scholars for their interviews, housed at various institutions, including Maylei Blackwell, Phillip C. Castruita, Virginia Espino, Marcie Miranda-Arrizón, Michelle Moravec, and Carlos Vásquez. Writing this history knowing that those who literally made it will be able to read and critique it has been a daunting task. The analysis and conclusions are my own, but I hope that these women will be able to both recognize their experiences and find value in the telling.

While writing this book I have received wisdom, guidance, and encouragement from many scholars, some of whom were my teachers, some whom I've been lucky enough to have as family, and some whom I've met along the way. Two historians have been absolutely instrumental in this book's coming to fruition: Vicki L. Ruiz and Ernesto Chávez. Since I met her as a young undergraduate, Vicki has believed in me and taken me under her wing. Vicki guided my entry into the historical profession and has been a consummate mentor. For this book, she provided me with reassuring and critical feedback that challenged me to develop a deeper analysis of how women's individual experiences collectively forged a type of Chicana liberation. She has been a constant in this journey, encouraging me every step of the way, even when I thought at times that this process was impossible. This book exists because of her mentorship and unwavering support. Ernesto Chávez, my uncle, has been a lifeline throughout this project. I recognize how extremely fortunate I am to have an uncle-historian who generously gave his time to read draft upon draft and provided insightful and honest critiques to help refine arguments and the larger story I was trying to tell. Vicki and Ernie helped me navigate the complicated nature of the publication process, offering many contacts and resources to help me finish this book. Mere words cannot convey the depth of gratitude that I hold for them. At Stanford University I benefited tremendously from Albert Camarillo's and Estelle Freedman's sage but tough guidance. They challenged me to continuously think beyond the obvious and to seek out the broader historical significance of this story. At Arizona State University, in addition to Vicki, Susan Gray, Gayle Gullett, Edward Escobar, and Asunción Lavrin encouraged my historical interests and generously nurtured a budding graduate student. During my undergraduate years at Occidental College, Arthé Anthony first introduced me to oral history and to Vicki Ruiz. Norman Cohen and Lynn Dumenil planted the seeds of my interest in history. I feel extremely privileged to have worked with such wonderful scholars, teachers, and mentors, who have shown me that excellence in research, teaching, advising, and mentoring go hand in hand. I am grateful for the lessons and examples that I have learned from them all.

In the years that this book has been in progress, my colleagues at California State University, Dominguez Hills have been supportive writing partners and consistent sounding boards for ideas. Anne Soon Choi, Donna Nicol, and Laura Talamante have held me accountable for writing for the past five years. Ericka Verba also supported this project through a previous writing group. They have all read drafts and provided important feedback to make this book better. Others who have provided counsel and support include Corina Benavidez López, Siskanna Naynaha, Helen Oesterheld, and Keisha Paxton. Alfredo González helped me crunch census data. Dana Ospina has been instrumental in clarifying questions regarding permissions. I am grateful for the larger community at CSU Dominguez Hills, past and present, for supporting this project, often behind the scenes, including Ellen Junn, Mitch Avila, Cheryl Koos, Tim Caron, and Natasha Alexsa Garcia.

Acknowledgments

In the long life of this project, I learned the value of editorial guidance. Cecelia Cancellaro and Christopher Lura provided much-needed direction in how to develop a solid book proposal and refine my writing. Shanon Fitzpatrick was instrumental in helping me develop a stronger and clearer narrative. Dawn Durante first saw this book's promise and Dominique Moore then shepherded the process to the publication stage before handing it off to Tad Ringo, Roberta Sparenberg, and other staff at the University of Illinois Press. Jane Zanichkowsky was helpful in clarifying and streamlining the writing.

Along the way, I have also benefited from crucial financial assistance from the Stanford University School of Humanities and Sciences, the Mellon Foundation, the Woodrow Wilson Dissertation Grant in Women's Studies (now the Institute for Citizens and Scholars), the Irvine Foundation Doctoral Fellowship at Occidental College, and the Ford Foundation/National Academies. This project has also been supported by the Research, Scholarship, and Creative Activities Grant and the College of Arts and Humanities at CSU Dominguez Hills.

I also owe special thanks to several librarians who helped in the research process. At the California Ethnic and Multicultural Archives at the University of California, Santa Barbara, Sal Guereña and Alexander Hauschild allowed me access to previously unprocessed papers and interviews. They were extremely helpful in guiding me to collections that would be useful in my research and always answered my questions. Roberto Trujillo and the staff at Special Collections at Stanford were also very helpful with research materials and quick turnarounds on research requests. At the Southern California Library for Social Studies and Research, Alexis Moreno was most helpful with finding obscure materials. Daniel Hernandez, librarian at the Chicano Research Center at the East Los Angeles County Library, helped with access to difficult-to-find periodicals. Three students aided me in research: Cynthia Tamayo transcribed various interviews; Anna Aguilar made trips to California State University, Los Angeles, to track down crucial articles and make copies; and Diana Madrigal scanned materials. I also thank Emy Gregor for her assistance with citations and permissions.

This work has also been buoyed by scholars working in the field of Chicana studies and Chicana feminisms. I thank Maria E. Cotera for her close reading and generous comments and suggestions for making this book's arguments stronger and more cogent. Special thanks go to Virginia Espino, who through her work at the UCLA Oral History Center conducted extremely important interviews that I relied upon as I revised this book. I am thankful for Virginia's generosity in providing contact information for many women

I interviewed as well. Maylei Blackwell and Dionne Espinoza have also been extremely supportive of this work.

I have also received important support from colleagues who I am lucky to call friends. Shana Bernstein, Margie Brown-Coronel, Elizabeth Escobedo, Virginia Espino, Gabriela González, Shelley Lee, Dawn Mabalon, Monica Perales, Gina Marie Pitti, Maythee Rojas, Kim Warren, and Mary Ann Villarreal have been part of this project in some way, shape, or form since the beginning, and I am thankful for their friendship and guidance through the years.

I could always rely on a group of friends, some of whom I've known since junior high school, to remind me that life existed away from my computer. Tonantzin Rodríguez (who is also my cousin), Nicole Presley, Elizabeth Payne, Christa and Brendan Wagner, and Lisa Mauricio have supported this endeavor with their optimism and generous hearts.

Acknowledgments of family support come last, but certainly not least. No words can express my gratitude for my family, the Chávezes, Rodríguezes, Aridas, and Mejías. My parents, Isabel Hernández Rodríguez and Carlos A. Chávez, taught me to question, to look critically at the world, to be proud of who I was, and to believe in the possibility of social justice. My mother taught me about the importance of knowing the past. It was her experience, and that of women like her, that first inspired me as an undergraduate to explore this topic. I could always count on my uncles Arturo Chávez and Jorge Rodríguez to put me in contact with someone I needed to interview. My mother-in-law Alicia Arida and my own mother provided crucial childcare along the way. I am saddened that my grandparents Isabel Hernández Rodríguez, Bertha González Chávez, and Alberto Chávez are no longer here in this world to see this book come to fruition, but I am thankful for the strength, wisdom, and ideals that they imparted. It was their stories that inspired me to search for the past in the first place.

I thank my husband Luis Arida and my children, Sabina and Avery, for their love and patience throughout this project. With his humor and generous spirit, Luis has supported me through the ups and downs of this process, whether it was accompanying me on research trips, shouldering the running of the household when deadlines loomed, or lending his ear for the joys and the disappointments that are part and parcel of the research and writing process. I am eternally grateful.

Chicana Liberation

Introduction

One day in 1953, soon after the birth of her second child, Lilia Aceves opened the latest issue of *Parents* and read about cooperative nursery schools. She was in her early twenties, and as a stay-at-home mother whose husband had been drafted into the Korean War, Aceves was drawn to both the community childcare and parent education aspects of these facilities. Aceves immediately began to inquire around her Boyle Heights neighborhood of Los Angeles and learned about such a school at Ramona Gardens, a public housing development within walking distance of her home. She enrolled her toddler, and along with the other mothers began to volunteer at the co-op and attend the parent meetings, as required. She recalled, "We got some education there and that was my first encounter with spreading out a little farther than my home at that point." Although she did not know it at the time, this action marked her entrance into Los Angeles's Mexican American political scene, where she would remain an active participant for many decades. She later described this move from informal cooperative work at the neighborhood level to involvement in city and national political action organizations as "kind of natural."[1]

Some twenty years later, the Chicano movement of the Vietnam era would provide Corinne Sánchez an entrance into politics. Sánchez was born and raised in the Inland Empire, east of Los Angeles, and her introduction to activism took a different path; she became politically active during her college years, when she transferred from San Bernardino Valley College to California State University, Long Beach. As a student at public schools in Colton, California, Sánchez recalled, "I really realized, once going to junior high, the segregation. I mean, it was discrimination. I just really became aware I was Mexican." Sánchez aspired to attend college but was tracked into homemaking and clerical courses. Although her parents supported education, "they saw it [as] important [only] to the high school [level]." She was, however, also an athlete, competing in gymnastics and track, and a member of the Girls Athletic Association, which she credits with keeping her "going in terms of excelling" and providing a space where she was seen as equal. Sánchez aspired to become a physical education and history teacher in order to change the dynamics that she had experienced in her schooling. When she transferred to CSU Long Beach, she recalled, "That's where everything happened. The movement—it was the peak of the movement. I was there in '68 in the summer, and the movement was in the full force and the farm workers, the Vietnam War, Católicos por la Raza."[2]

Despite their vastly disparate backgrounds, experiences, and paths to political activism, Aceves and Sánchez were both part of a political and social movement dedicated to the empowerment of Chicanas and their communities that spanned decades. Centered on Los Angeles, a city that, due to its large number of Mexican-origin peoples, has long been an epicenter of Mexican American politics, this book reconstructs the history of this movement and the women who shaped its transformations over the course of more than thirty years. While most accounts employ a framework of generational radicalization in describing how and why the Chicano movement evolved over time, this book foregrounds an alternative approach that highlights different movement dynamics. By tracing the lives of Aceves, Sánchez, and other women, as well as the organizations they joined or even created, I focus on the ways Los Angeles Chicanas continuously bridged different realms of politics and approaches to activism to create generational, organizational, ideological, and transnational interlinkages that enabled them to effectively advocate for Chicanas as Mexican Americans *and* as women. Through what I call "bridging activism," the women featured in this book helped create a flexible, resilient, and sustainable liberatory praxis centered on Chicana empowerment whose influence impacts us today.

The concept of bridging activism sharpens the focus on and helps elucidate the connections between four historical trends that emerge in reconstructing the biographies and accomplishments of those who propelled what from the mid-1940s through the early 1980s became the Chicana liberation movement in Los Angeles. First, regardless of generational differences, ethnic Mexican women in Los Angeles began their political journeys in their own communities, whether in a local neighborhood or on a college campus. They thus brought a wealth of knowledge that linked their personal experiences of both liberation and oppression to broader structures; simultaneously, they also understood the importance of creating change within communities, which required the continued building of bridges between formal and informal activist arenas. Second, women worked to change the conditions of their communities by drawing from a variety of ideologies and their associated political tactics—including but not limited to communism, unionism, Chicano nationalism, feminism, third-worldism, and Marxist-Leninism. In bridging these ideologies, they often created new synergies between them. Third, women political activists were so committed to their communities that they participated in various organizations across the span of their activist lives, moving from one to another, founding new initiatives, or being members of several organizations, all simultaneously. This built densifying webs of interconnection between organizations, with some women serving as bridges that brought others onto new activist paths. Finally, across different generations and regardless of political leanings, these activists, who faced overt sexism in the organizations to which they belonged, sought to forge spaces for themselves that acknowledged their reality as ethnic Mexicans and as women, the primary identities they bridged. Their experience in a variety of organizations led them to advocate for themselves and other women *as women* within their respective organizations, sometimes forming women-only groups to further the goals of bettering their communities. Bridging activism was not necessarily a conscious strategy, but rather a modality of activism shaped by the historical circumstances in which Chicanas found themselves, including their relation to the contemporary Chicano and feminist movements, and the capacious visions of change they hoped to enact.[3]

Aceves's and Sánchez's lives illustrate bridging activism in action and show some of the generative outcomes produced by Chicana practices of community and political engagement. In 1957, Aceves's activism continued when she moved to the City Terrace neighborhood just east of Boyle Heights and enrolled her younger child at the Heights Co-op Nursery School, a new facility. Although the expansion of the Los Angeles County General Hospital had forced Aceves and her family to relocate, moving to her new home and joining the co-op nursery school opened new political opportunities for her.[4] She soon became involved with the nearby Wabash Coordinating Council and subsequently became a member of the Los Angeles Human Relations Commission and the Mexican American Political Association, founded in 1960.[5] Six years later, after about a decade of working within Mexican American and coalition-based organizations that were broadly male-dominated, Aceves decided to join the League of Mexican American Women (LMAW), a nascent organization founded in Los Angeles. What distinguished LMAW from other groups of the era is that it both claimed and created a space for

Mexican American women's leadership. Aceves was drawn to the league as an alternative to the male-dominated atmosphere of the other political and community organizations to which she had belonged. For Aceves, LMAW also affirmed that Mexican American women could and should advocate for themselves as a group within the larger Mexican American community in Los Angeles and within the burgeoning Chicano movement. The league unapologetically asserted the necessity for an organization that would develop Mexican American women's leadership. Using networks and connections with like-minded women, it created its own space to achieve this goal.

Aceves's trajectory makes clear that Chicana gender equality and liberation emerged from a long history of activism within the milieu of ethnic Mexican politics in Los Angeles over the course of the twentieth century. When this politics shifted to a more militant Chicano ethos, activists such as Aceves who had been involved prior to its advent continued to participate in both grassroots and institutional political organizations, bridging the shift between older and younger political generations highlighted in the majority of the Chicano movement literature. That is, the women discussed in this study did not follow a pattern of generational divide. Aceves and her contemporaries, including Francisca Flores and Grace Montañez Davis, changed with the times. They may not have asserted militancy in the same vein as others, but they remained committed to the cause of social justice for Mexican Americans, especially as it pertained to women, and became Chicana feminists.[6] For these women, Chicana feminism meant that they embraced the ideals of the movimiento but believed that social, political, and economic liberation should apply to both genders.[7] This Chicana liberation also included abandoning strict gender roles and expectations, old and new. That is, at its core, Chicana feminism articulated an unapologetic belief in the worth and power of Chicanas as individuals, intellectuals, and political actors.

The political and professional experiences of the women involved in the Chicano movement counter stereotypical images of the urban Chicano insurgent as a young high school or college student with a newfound sense of self and purpose and reveal the cross-generational relationships that bridged activism under a new Chicano umbrella. Women such as Aceves did not clash with a more "radical" and "younger" generation, as much previous scholarship about the Chicano movement argues. While the generational framework of the Chicano movement has provided useful means to think about the ways in which common experiences among groups of activists became the foundation for their view of politics, this paradigm has also homogenized Chicano movement activists and those that came before. Additionally, the generational model, or the notion of a distinct break between the politics of previous Mexican American generations, generalizes a radical Chicano movement versus a more conservative Mexican American spirit of accommodation and assimilation. Yet Aceves and women like her, from the cohort that could be categorized as more conservative and older than Chicano militants, took part in forming one of the first women-only feminist organizations. Thus, the concept of bridging more accurately captures these dynamics because it allows that different tactics, organizations, ideologies, and demographic trends emerged while also emphasizing linkages that women developed to negotiate social and political cleavages. It also provides a metaphor that captures the reality that many individuals traveled back and forth between different organizations and movements throughout their lives, transporting ideas developed in one arena or chapter of activism to other activist pursuits along the way.

Sánchez's practice of bridging activism began while attending college. She entered as a regular student to continue her plan to teach athletics and history and eventually joined the United Mexican American Students, which then became El Movimiento Estudiantil Chicano de Aztlán (MEChA). She recalled, "I saw the discrepancy, the differences, and again, the discrimination against us as Latinas within our own [community]." As an athlete, Sánchez was surrounded by another group of women at CSU Long Beach who created a nurturing and supportive space. She recalled, "The women at Long Beach State really took an interest in me because I was Latina and outspoken. . . . So they really were my impetus to get involved in the [Chicano] movement. Because there was a women's movement as well, so there [were] the crossovers." At the time, Sánchez had connections with what she called the "feminist movement," or the mainstream women's movement, through athletics on campus. She remembered, "Even though I identified with feminist philosophy and objectives that they were fighting for, within our [Chicano] movement, I didn't see myself as separate." Indeed, as a student, Sánchez wanted to bridge the two movements, feminist and Chicano, but recalled, "We were not welcomed." She joined other politically active Chicanas in a women's study group informally connected to MEChA that formed as a response to the backlash against women attempting to take on leadership positions in the organization. This group subsequently became Hijas de Cuauhtémoc, started an eponymous newspaper specifically focused on Chicana issues, "and started getting involved with . . . the movement throughout the state." Sánchez later began to write for the Chicano newspaper *La Raza*, based in East Los Angeles. Eventually, after a brief hiatus from college, she returned to the Los Angeles area, finished her degree, and began to work for the Chicana Service Action Center in 1974.[8]

Aceves and Sánchez represent the diverse ways in which women claimed their own voices and space within larger political movements. Bridging activist spaces, generations, and sometimes divergent ideologies, they developed a political praxis that addressed a multiplicity of experiences under the same overarching goal of advancing Chicana liberation. Although ideologies that informed identity and political strategies may have shifted during the Chicano movement, structures in which women experienced second-class status in politics remained in place. Thus, rather than use cultural nationalism, generation, or class as an organizing theme, this book uses gender as a framework of analysis to explore how multiple and overlapping generations of ethnic Mexican women responded—in a variety of ways, both reactively and proactively—to their experiences in Mexican American and Chicano politics in Los Angeles, engendering multiple kinds of Chicana feminisms.

Prior to and as the Chicano movement unfolded, women engaged with ideologies that maintained their status as second to men and to male leaders. In the period after World War II, before the insurgency, women participating in Los Angeles politics in grassroots and more traditional organizations for the most part found themselves in women's auxiliaries or as the support staff. Historically, Mexicans in the United States, both male and female, had maintained traditions of political activism ranging from self-help mutual aid societies to Spanish-language newspapers. During the 1950s ethnic Mexicans challenged a variety of systemically racist practices, including immigration raids, police brutality, and political disenfranchisement in their efforts to protect and improve their communities. They also struggled with one of the most divisive of political ideologies: anti-communism. Due to the political activities and beliefs of many Mexican American activists, the forces of anti-communism, such as the House Un-American Activities Committee, the California Un-American Activities Committee, and the FBI, were very real threats to their personal liberties and their livelihoods.[9] Between the late 1950s and the early 1960s, women participated in these political activities to better their own lives and the lives of those in their communities in an era plagued with rampant and brutal discrimination against ethnic Mexicans.

As historians Vicki L. Ruiz, Mario T. García, and most recently Gabriela González have shown, some Mexican or pan-Latina/o political organizations of the past focused on women's issues. For example, El Congreso de Pueblos de Habla Española, founded in 1938, included a women's committee and issued a specific resolution on women at its second convention. The declaration highlighted the "double discrimination" faced by Mexican women in the United States and resolved that El Congreso would work toward Mexican women's equality in "social, economic, and civil liberties."[10] Women also participated in various political organizations in a range of capacities, and some formed their own separate groups. For example, in the border region during the same decade women formed benevolent associations such as Círculo Cultural "Isabel la Católica" (Cultural Circle "Isabel the Catholic"). As González asserts, "The Círculo was operated by women, for the benefit of women, a self-help ideology that recognized women's centrality to community uplift."[11] But within these types of organizations, they did not advocate to further their own political and social aims *as women*.[12] Women confronted societal mores about their political activities that deemed women's auxiliaries and benevolent associations as appropriate and a societal tradition that assumed men were the real public figures of any organization.

Similarly, women who participated in the movement confronted ideologies that brought to bear on a renewed cultural pride which functioned under the notion of the heterosexual and patriarchal family, the notion of a collective unity, or both. During the 1960s and 1970s, Mexican American politics underwent a shift that was in line with the national context of protests, social reforms, and identity reformations of the African American civil rights movement, New Left organizations such as Students for a Democratic Society and the Berkeley Free Speech Movement, the women's liberation movement, the Black power movement, the nascent antidraft and antiwar movement, and the growing labor movements spearheaded by Mexican American and Filipino American farm workers. Within this atmosphere and given the continued violence against people of color in the nation, Mexican Americans, including women, assumed a far more militant stance in regard to their economic, political, social, and educational conditions in the United States, spurring the Chicano movement.

Ultimately concerned with a quest for power and social reform based on a common Mexican American identity, Chicano movement activists called for self-determination and equal access to education as they celebrated a renewed cultural pride. They also sought to define a new identity for themselves and other Mexican Americans that took pride in their Mexican heritage, celebrated indigenous roots, and incorporated a political vision for social change. Due to years of debasing interactions with U.S. institutions, especially in education, many activists uncritically embraced Mexican traditions and cultural heritage, including an indigenous heritage based on Aztec (Mexica) culture. As Chicanos affirmed a past situated in an indigenous culture of the Americas, they followed a pattern that sociologists Floya Anthias and Nira Yuval-Davis identified in their review of the way nationalist ideologies are produced and reproduced. According to them, intellectuals from "oppressed collectivities" within a nation are "excluded from the hegemonic intelligentsia and from open access to the state apparatus." In their desire to affirm their own place and space within the nation that is oppressive, they thus "rediscover collective memories, transform popular oral traditions and languages into written ones, and portray a 'national golden age' in the far—mythical or historical—past, whose reconstitution becomes the basis for nationalist aspirations."[13]

As scholars Dionne Espinoza, María Cotera, and Maylei Blackwell write, "In the context of patriarchal relations governing many movement structures and labor relations, such collectivizing impulses often erased women's strategic, philosophical, and organizational contributions to movement activities."[14] Their work, and mine, builds on that of activists and scholars of the movement who have shown us that women contributed to the movement in significant ways as, for example, organizers, writers, and strategists, but recognized their own erasure. In 1980 Adelaida del Castillo, an activist and scholar during and after the movement, reflected that "student organizations lent themselves to a division of labor which dichotomized between obscure female and visible male activity" and that "women were crucial to the operation of the organization."[15] In addition, ethnic unity in the form of a movement based on the family unit also worked to ignore women's societal and familial contributions. In this ideological re-creation of the past and vision of the future of a Chicano nation, women played and were to perform important gendered roles that emphasized unity with the collective cause and anchored in various forms of motherhood. Sonia López, another movement activist and scholar, argued that in the movement, "Chicanas generally continued to fill the traditional roles assigned them within the Mexican culture and the American Anglo society. A woman's role has traditionally been defined in terms of her biological reproductive capacity, which is also the reproduction of the labor force, her role in the education and care of children and her role in the care of the sick and the elderly."[16] Any woman's departure from the constricted forms of gendered participation in the background meant that women were turning against the family of la raza. More recently, in ¡Chicana Power! Contested Histories of Feminism in the Chicano Movement, Maylei Blackwell has written, "The backlash against Chicana organizing was tied in part to how Chicano cultural nationalism was not just an ideology of cultural pride and unity but also a gendered construction that mediated how gender roles and expectations were played out in the political practices of the Chicano student movement."[17] The Chicano student movement as dominated by male leaders and organized around a familial imaginary did not seek to construct the same level of bridges back to women-centered goals.

As Blackwell has observed, Chicanas in the movement were not a homogenous entity, and their different visions and articulations of feminism in Los Angeles belied multiple and sometimes competing ideas about where they stood in the movement and where they and the movement needed to go.[18] Chicanas who sought a meaningful place in Mexican American politics during the 1960s and 1970s maneuvered between an overarching Chicano nationalist worldview and their already emerging feminist consciousness. Would they assert themselves as maintainers of culture and tradition as they fought for equal rights for Chicanos? Would they affirm and act on a belief in the equality of women to men in the movement? Would they proclaim a distinct vision of feminism that included race and class? Would they negate any association with feminism in disavowal of the women's liberation movement? In order to assert their importance both as Chicanas and as political activists in their own right, some women remained steadfast in their belief in cultural and ethnic unity, others believed that only same-sex and separate organizations could effect change for Mexican American women, and yet others linked women's issues with class issues and saw capitalism as the overall oppressor. Indeed, the role of women and feminism in the Chicano movement remained a contested issue well into the 1980s.

Even as ethnic Mexican women negotiated their positionality in a variety of ways, they exhibited some common core beliefs. First, like their male counterparts, they viewed themselves in ethnic and racial terms and took pride in this heritage, which sometimes included an acknowledgment of indigenous roots. This set them apart from Euro-American feminists of the period and provided commonality with Native American and African American women. Second, and again like their male counterparts, they believed that their class status influenced their lives. The majority of Mexican Americans during this period (and in the present day) were in the working class, in manual labor and the service sector. The majority of Mexican Americans also lived at or below the poverty line. Finally, regardless of the length of their experience in politics, Chicanas came to consciousness about feminist ideas and identities in response to the sexism and racism they experienced in society and within political organizations. Chicanas acknowledged that their experiences due to gender were different, but they acted on this knowledge in divergent ways that were in turn influenced by their individual lives and backgrounds. Like other women of color, Chicanas situated themselves within the panoply of feminist ideologies by firmly articulating that race, gender, and class were key factors in their experiences.[19] Despite their attempts to assert the importance of their place in the historical record, they have been overwhelmingly overlooked in the literature that chronicles mainstream U.S. feminist history.[20]

As the many monographs about Los Angeles's Chicano communities attest, the city is an important site for the study of ethnic Mexican experiences, specifically due to the growth of this population and its persistent political activism over the course of the twentieth century. Since 1900, Los Angeles has experienced a consistent increase in its ethnic Mexican population, concurrent with the general increase in Mexican migration to the nation. Between 1900 and 1930 the number of ethnic Mexicans in the United States rose more than tenfold through births and immigration, to reach approximately 1.4 million. In Los Angeles, this population grew threefold to reach 97,000 in 1930 and remained steady until 1940. The Great Depression and subsequent deportation of Mexicans caused a lull in immigration from Mexico to the United States, but World War II changed this dynamic. By 1950 the number of ethnic Mexicans in Los Angeles stood at 156,356 and it nearly doubled to 291,959 ten years later, encompassing 5 percent of the city's population. By 1980, around the end of the period covered by this book, the Mexican-origin population stood at just over 800,000.[21]

Despite its founding as a Spanish settlement in 1781 and the presence of Mexicans in Los Angeles since then, it was not until the mid-twentieth century that this group gained entry into state and local politics.[22] Prior to the 1949 election of Edward Roybal to the Los Angeles City Council, no Mexicans had been elected to that body since 1882. The local situation was similar to the statewide and national political reality. When the Chicano movement exploded on the scene in the late 1960s, Mexican Americans in California were nearly unrepresented in state and national politics. The Golden State had one Mexican American member of Congress, the same Edward Roybal, but no representation in the state legislature. Colorado had one Mexican American state representative, Arizona had four, and Texas had ten; the great exception was New Mexico, with thirty-three representatives in the state legislature.[23] In fact, when Roybal moved to Washington, Mexicans in Los Angeles lost their local representation. The exclusion of ethnic Mexicans from Los Angeles politics was the result of a variety of factors. For most of the century, Mexicans had little economic power and were concentrated in specific sections of the city. This residential segregation subjected Mexicans to gerrymandering of representational districts, while also fostering moments of political solidarity and power.[24]

Although Mexicans had been shut out of the electoral process in Los Angeles, they had a long history of political and labor activism in the city, which included the establishing of headquarters in the downtown area in the early twentieth century by the self-exiled Mexican anarchosyndicalist Magón brothers, the 1933 dressmakers' strike, the 1943 Sleepy Lagoon incident and trial (which set the zoot suit in historical memory), and the formation three years later of the Community Service Organization, which continued to be active throughout the following decade and still exists today. During the 1950s Mexican Americans continued to participate in politics via organizations such as the Civil Rights Congress and the Los Angeles Committee for the Protection of the Foreign Born. In the Vietnam era, Los Angeles witnessed some of the most important events of the Chicano movement as the site of the 1968 High School Blowouts and the 1970 Chicano Moratorium.

Los Angeles was also a lively center of Chicano and Chicana political expression, from the rich print culture that emerged in the 1960s and 1970s to the plethora of organizations that emerged. For example, although Francisca Flores and others founded the Comisión Femenil Mexicana Nacional (National Mexican Women's Commission, CFMN), one of the first Chicana feminist organizations, at a conference in Sacramento in 1970, the group set up shop in Los Angeles. The city was also home to the Brown Berets (a paramilitary organization), chapters of La Raza Unida Party (the Chicano third party), the Chicana Welfare Rights Organization, the Chicana Service Action Center, and many more. The vibrancy of Chicana and Chicano political expression in Los Angeles makes the city an ideal site for exploration of women's agency.

My own history is enmeshed in this book, not only because I was born and raised in Los Angeles and spent the formative years of my childhood among the bustle of the movement and its many activists, my parents among them, but also because I grew up in a large extended family that exposed me to the complexities of the lives of Mexican immigrant women, my grandmothers and mother included. Throughout my education, and especially in college, I experienced what historian Vicki L. Ruiz has described as "the two types of history—the one at home and the one at school." At home, I had grown up with grandmothers who would not have considered themselves feminists but whose day-to-day lives reflected a belief in their self-worth and their right to independent thought and action. My maternal grandmother, for example, divorced her abusive husband, my grandfather, less than ten years after arriving in Los Angeles. My paternal grandmother, a nurse and midwife in Mexico, was an intellectual in her own right, although family circumstances cut her formal education short at the age of thirteen. I had also grown up with women activists of the Chicano movement—powerful, passionate women who gave of themselves to make change in society. But until quite recently, neither of these groups were in the history books. Indeed, while in college I attempted to write about them for research assignments, but they were not in the sources. These moments led to the research for this project and to a deeper understanding of how the day-to-day practice of political ideology, gender, nationalism, class, and feminism influenced my own life and those of other Chicanas.[25]

In order to learn about the lives of these women I turned to oral history, a practice that I had been introduced to as an undergraduate. The book *Songs My Mother Sang to Me* by Patricia Preciado Martin, a collection of oral histories of Mexican American women in Arizona, was my foundation. I embarked on an oral history research project to interview my grandmothers about their experiences coming to the United States. With this project I saw the power of oral history and how it could be used as a tool for collecting the stories of those who did not always leave traditional sources such as letters, photographs, and diaries.[26] Oral history is therefore one of the foundations of *Chicana Liberation*, which draws from more than twenty-five interviews, both new and previously recorded, many of which I conducted myself. My family facilitated access to the majority of the interviewees, which allowed me to be seen as an "insider." Some of the people I interviewed had known me as a child. Those whom I did not know were connected to those previously interviewed.[27]

As in many studies of people of color in the United States, I could not solely rely on archives, government documents, or periodicals to tell this story. As Alessandro Portelli reminds us, "oral sources give us information about . . . social groups whose written history is either missing or distorted."[28] For example, there are two archival collections for the Comisión Femenil Mexicana Nacional, one at the University of California, Santa Barbara, and the other at the University of California, Los Angeles, both of which I utilized extensively. Yet neither of these contains the personal papers of Francisca Flores because they have been lost. Oral history interviews therefore provided what was not told or could not be told in the archives. Building on Maylei Blackwell's theory of "retrofitted memory," *Chicana Liberation* engages in the process of "re-membering" and exploring Chicana "strategies [that] include re-membering themselves in time and place" and "creat[ing] new terrains of memory in which to forge a vision of a history in which Chicanas and their communities have a central role in creating a better world."[29] While in some instances oral histories provided information that was unknown, in others, the interviews usefully corroborated what was already in the written sources. In many circumstances, various oral history narrators provided very similar accounts of events and even analyses of proceedings.

In addition to oral history, *Chicana Liberation* utilizes a wide array of materials to tell the story of ethnic Mexican women in Los Angeles politics. The book uses a variety of government documents and publications, more than twenty-eight periodicals of the period, manuscript collections, and ephemera. During the 1960s and 1970s, Chicano/a communities harnessed the power of the printed word in the form of periodicals to express the issues they viewed as important in their lives. This was not a new tradition, as ethnic and racial communities have historically produced their own publications. But this era's print culture, as well as those that emerged earlier, documented the conflicts and triumphs of these communities. In addition, Chicana-specific and Chicana-produced publications also surfaced during this era, serving as important fountains of women's expression. Combined, these sources allow a picture to form of not only women's experiences, but the context in which they became active in politics.

Chicana Liberation offers a roughly chronological narrative that focuses on historical moments in which ethnic Mexican women claimed space, voiced their concerns and demands, and leveraged their power through the practice of bridging activism. Engaging in a spectrum of feminist ideologies and practices, they utilized the significant political knowledge that they had gained in the time before the Chicano movement. The first chapter of the book traces the spectrum of Mexican American activism from the late 1950s through the 1960s, highlighting the diverse nature of women's political involvement and the heterogeneity of their approaches to the issues that were important to them. The chapter demonstrates the emerging consciousness of women as they worked in a variety of political endeavors ranging from the Community Service Organization to the Communist Party, eventually founding the League of Mexican American Women in 1963, one of the first women-only Latina political organizations in the nation, which sought both power and representation for women. Chapter 2 explores the early years (1970–1976) of one of the first Chicana feminist organizations in the nation, the Comisión Femenil Mexicana Nacional. Established in 1970 in a Chicana workshop organized by Francisca Flores and Simmie Romero Goldsmith, the Comisión Femenil was an outgrowth of the League of Mexican American Women, and as such included some of the same members. The Comisión Femenil provides an illuminating example of the ways in which a stand-alone women's organization brought together ethnic Mexican women with varying political experiences and ideologies. Focusing on both the challenges and successes of this newfound Chicana feminist sisterhood, the chapter highlights the ways in which the Comisión Femenil utilized governmental agencies to establish institutions they believed essential for Mexican American women to gain economic independence: job training and a childcare center. This set the groundwork for important bridges to be built between community activists and the formal political realm.

Chapter 3 explores the various ways in which Chicanas saw themselves and their place in the world, expanding the concept of bridging activism from the local to the international realm. Focusing on the experiences of Chicanas who traveled to the International Women's Year Conference in Mexico City in 1975, many of whom belonged to the Comisión Femenil, this chapter engages the international representation of Chicana feminism and issues of identity, ethnicity, and national belonging. For the women who attended, the conference inspired new levels of global consciousness about where they fit in the world as women of color in a "First World" nation and inspired new bridges across national borders.

The last chapter of the book demonstrates that Chicana feminisms did not progress in linear fashion, as Chicanas active in the movement in the 1970s directed their energies to different causes and issues on the basis of their own experiences, which at times brought competing ideologies into conflict. Chapter 4 brings into focus the struggle for reproductive justice in Los Angeles in the 1970s in order to explore the heterogenous Chicana feminist and nonfeminist experiences and ideologies that shaped the body politics of Chicana liberation activism. Chicanas' work for reproductive justice was challenging, considering nationalist ideology that privileged the family as the foundation of Chicano struggle. This chapter addresses how Mexican American women used bridging activist practices, in particular coalition building, print culture, and establishing institutions, to strategically bring this sensitive issue into a broader public discussion, which provided a template for campaigns dealing with other fraught topics.

This study concludes with a discussion of the current state of many of the institutions that Chicanas built during the 1960s and 1970s, highlighting how bridging activism provided a foundation of political linkages, networks, and knowledges to secure their permanence. This includes the ways in which Chicana activism served as a bridge to new spaces for Chicana studies in the academy. It also addresses the changing nature of the issues that Chicanas face in Los Angeles and the nation today.

1

Bridging Activism

Mexican American Women and Political Leadership from the Postwar Era to the Early Chicano Movement in Los Angeles

In 1913 Francisca Flores was born in Los Angeles. Not much is known about her early life except that she was raised in San Diego and at about the age of fifteen entered a San Diego tuberculosis sanatorium, remaining there until 1939. Although there appears to be no record of her educational experiences, it is clear that she did not have a college education and was self-taught. Previous narratives of Flores's life story relate that after she left the sanatorium she made her way to Los Angeles on her own to settle with family members, immersing herself in Mexican American politics and spending the war years engaged in that city's Mexican American political organizations such as the Sleepy Lagoon Defense Committee.[1] According to records from the Federal Bureau of Investigation and San Diego City Directories, however, Flores did not move to Los Angeles on leaving the sanatorium. Instead, she joined the Communist Party (CP) in San Diego, subsequently married a fellow party member, and moved to Los Angeles in 1945. She remained a CP member until approximately 1958, rising to leadership roles and even going underground in the early 1950s.[2]

The different versions of Flores's life story provide a prime example of the ways in which the history of Mexican American women is fraught with silences, tensions, and lore, which can lead to overly fragmented portraits of these women's lives and the decades-long intellectual and organizational arc of the movement for Chicana liberation. The story of Flores's migration to Los Angeles originated from a eulogy written by a family member that made no mention of Flores's Communist Party ties. This omission is not surprising given the ways in which CP membership was demonized during and after the Cold War.[3] It is also unknown whether Flores shared this aspect of her political life with family members. Yet the CP served an important role in facilitating Flores's entrée into politics, and the same was true for many of her contemporaries. While still active in party circles, Flores also pursued other ideological and organizational approaches to furthering her political goals, some of which intersected with or paralleled CP priorities and some of which headed in new directions.[4]

Flores's experiences before, during, and after her time in the CP were grounded in a strong desire to improve the lives of ethnic Mexicans in the United States. In these various political activities, Flores built relationships with other ethnic Mexican women who shared her vision. These women remained political sisters from the 1940s through the 1960s. During her time in the party, she also participated in the Asociación Nacional México-Americana (Mexican American National Association), taught courses on Mexican history at the California Labor School (a school founded by the CP), and worked for a very brief time for the renowned labor and political activist Luisa Moreno at the United Cannery, Agricultural, Packing, and Allied Workers of America. While she was still a member of the CP Flores joined with others to found the Community Service Organization (CSO) in 1947. After leaving the party, Flores, among many other activities, co-founded the League of Mexican American Women (LMAW) in 1958, participated in founding the Mexican American Political Association (MAPA) in 1960, co-founded the publication *Carta Editorial* (Editorial Letter) in 1963, established the periodical *Regeneración* (Regeneration) in 1970, and, in the same year, co-founded the Comisión Femenil Mexicana Nacional.[5]

Flores's story reflects the difficulty in chronicling Mexican American women's participation in politics in the years before the Chicano movement, highlighting the scarcity of documentation. This period is crucial, however, for understanding the deep and overlapping roots that anchor the political activism of Mexican American women and Chicanas from the 1940s to the late 1960s. This chapter, focusing on Los Angeles, recovers a part of this story, relying on government documents, oral history interviews, and periodicals of the era to explore the spectrum of such activism as well as the ways individuals traversed and shaped its evolution.

I argue that ethnic Mexican women such as Flores and her compatriots who engaged in politics did so with a fundamental understanding of their racialized, gendered, and classed positions within society, which informed their construction of the Chicana feminist praxis of bridging activism. As we will see, the activism practiced by women such as Flores and her political contemporaries such as Connie Pardo, Hope Mendoza Schechter, Ramona Morín, Dolores Sánchez, and others, was rooted in the specific issues facing ethnic Mexican communities in Los Angeles. That is, they approached the issues they deemed important within their communities from heterogeneous points of departure, not via one singular political organization or point of view. In this way, they moved from one organization to another over time, and participated in multiple organizations simultaneously, with common goals and actions. For example, Mexican American women participated in Communist Party–identified organizations that worked to intercede in deportation proceedings such as the Los Angeles Committee for the Protection of the Foreign Born and organizations that hoped to work within the structure of electoral politics to elect Mexican Americans to political office such as the Democratic Party and MAPA. In doing so, they brought new issues into official political discourse, creating a vision for Mexican American politics rooted in solidarity with those who had heretofore remained unrepresented. As their activism evolved, these women also came to analyze their experiences through the lens of gender and attempted to change the negative gender dynamics that they had experienced, both as Mexican women in society and as women working in movements. They developed the communications dimension of their activism by founding and contributing to myriad publications, voicing issues and concerns that affected their communities and those that affected them as women. Periodicals offered a platform for creating dialog between activists as well as for connecting organizations to a broader public they hoped to mobilize.[6]

Foregrounding these practices and the interconnections between them using the framework of bridging activism also captures something important about the chronology of the movement for Chicana liberation. As we will see, the women discussed in this chapter were already attuned to gender disparities in their lives and demonstrated a Mexican American feminist consciousness in these early years when they founded LMAW, in 1958. Thus, by the time the Chicano movement emerged in the mid-1960s, women in LMAW had already established themselves as important political activists in Los Angeles, and much future activism would be built on the work they had done and the social, ideological, and organizational bridges that had been built in these formative years.

Mexican American Women in Los Angeles Under Siege

Between 1945 and 1975 ethnic Mexicans lived, as one scholar puts it, "under siege" as Los Angeles power elites simultaneously ignored the needs of this community and blatantly discriminated against it.[7] For women, "under siege" also meant a gendered struggle for representation, recognition, and acknowledgment. As part of the larger ethnic Mexican community in Los Angeles, activist women such as Francisca Flores and her counterparts lived in a variety of areas of the city, but mainly on the East Side.[8] By the 1960s this area, established as a Mexican community in the postwar era, had the highest concentration of Mexicans in the city. This ethnic concentration on the East Side was the result of several economic and political factors. Historically, Mexicans had been barred from living in other areas of the city via restrictive covenants. When those were deemed illegal in California in the late 1940s, "real estate agents, developers, and lending institutions found ways to keep Mexicanos out of the Anglo neighborhoods," notes Ricardo Romo. East Los Angeles was also close to work sites and areas where businesses catered to the needs of ethnic Mexicans.[9]

As part of the Mexican population in California in the 1960s, these women lacked political representation. Mexican Americans in California were a nearly unrepresented group in state and local politics in the postwar years. In 1960, for example, Mexicans in the state totaled 1.43 million, or approximately 9 percent of the population; almost three hundred thousand, approximately 5 percent of the population, were in Los Angeles.[10] Yet the Golden State had just one Mexican American state representative, Edward R. Roybal, who served as a member of the Los Angeles City Council in the 1950s and in the U.S. House of Representatives from 1962 to 1992.[11] Roybal's campaign for the city council in the late 1940s galvanized the founding of the CSO, where ethnic Mexican women found a place for political involvement. At the local level, Julian Nava served on the Los Angeles School Board in the late 1960s. This lack of political representation resonated strongly with the women highlighted in this chapter.

Economically speaking, these women represent the variety of backgrounds that contributed to growing political and gender consciousness among Mexican Americans. Francisca Flores, for example, made her living as a clerical worker.[12] In this she was similar to most ethnic Mexicans in California in the late 1950s and early 1960s, who held low-wage and low-skill occupations and were categorized in the U.S. Census as "operative or kindred workers," "clerical and kindred workers," and "service workers, except private household." As a group, their annual income stood far below that of Euro-Americans and nonwhites. Nineteen percent of Spanish-surnamed families in California earned an annual income of less than $3,000 in 1960, and 85 percent earned less than $5,000, when the state average stood above $6,000.[13] In 1965 in East Los Angeles, Mexicans had a poverty rate of 25 percent.[14] In addition, 16 percent of Mexican American families received public assistance. This rate was at least double that of all families in the nation.[15] Some Mexican American women, however, such as Connie Pardo and Dolores Sánchez escaped these grim circumstances as professionals, as the spouses of professionals, and as small business owners. Pardo's husband was an attorney. Sánchez trained to be a registered nurse, but chose to put her efforts into the grocery business that she and her husband had purchased.[16]

In terms of their education, the women featured in this chapter also had a variety of experiences. In 1960, Spanish-surnamed women and men over the age of twenty-five finished high school at a rate approximately half that of white peers. The majority of the women profiled here completed high school (although it is unclear whether this was the case for Flores). In this way, these women stood apart from their counterparts because they did not fit the profile of Spanish-surnamed women, who, as a group, had a median length of schooling of 8.9 years, with 50 percent of this population having reached eighth grade, but not beyond. Moreover, only 3 percent of Spanish-surnamed women had a college education or more; one example is Grace Montañez Davis, who earned a master's degree.[17] Mexican American women in Los Angeles lived in a national context of educational disparities that had changed little by 1970; only 34 percent of this cohort over twenty-five years of age completed high school and only 2 percent went on to college. In addition, on average Mexican American women completed four fewer years of school than did white women.[18] Social programs that aimed to increase college attendance among Mexican Americans would not come to fruition until the mid-to-late 1960s.[19] Mexican Americans received less in wages, and the education gap between them and the larger population in the nation persisted. The women discussed in this chapter recognized these disparities between themselves and the dominant white population and actively worked to change these circumstances through political activism. Despite being under siege, they played critically important roles in the struggle to improve the economic, educational, and political lives of their communities before the advent of the Chicano movement.[20]

Mexican American Women and Los Angeles Politics

In 1950s and early 1960s Los Angeles, three organizations stood out in the political activities of Mexican American women: the Communist Party, the Community Service Organization, and the Mexican American Political Association. Although very different from each other, they established themselves as foundations of political activism during a time when Mexicans interested in politics had limited outlets. Ethnic Mexicans had affiliated with the CP since the turn of the twentieth century, and Chicana/o historians agree that this affiliation emerged via the connections between the party, labor organizing, and unions beginning in the late 1920s and early 1930s. In this era, Mario T. García notes, "In the fields and factories of the Southwest, the Communists recruited adherents and admirers because of their willingness to stand up for the rights of Mexican workers."[21] As George J. Sánchez writes concerning the 1930s, "No one pushed the theme of racial equality in this era more than American Communist Party organizers."[22] Douglas Monroy adds that in its alignment with the Congress of Industrial Organizations, the CP was "one of the few organizations that transcended white supremacy and sought to better the lives of Mexicans."[23] Attracted to the ideals of equality, especially due to the party's work with labor unions, Mexicans joined the party in an attempt to change their social and economic conditions in the United States, including those related to labor and immigration. In addition, as Enrique Buelna notes, Mexicans had a radical political tradition stemming from the Mexican Revolution and the transnational nature of the Partido Liberal Mexicano (Mexican Liberal Party), an anarchosyndicalist organization active from the early 1900s through the early 1920s.[24] As yet, however, there is very limited information about ethnic Mexican women in the CP.

The Communist Party USA underwent ups and downs in membership from its founding in 1919 through the late 1950s, when Francisca Flores, who had joined in 1939, eventually ceased being a member. Flores joined during its ascendancy as a political and cultural force in the United States. In 1930, CP membership stood at approximately seventy-five hundred, but by the end of the decade, according to historian Justin Akers Chacón, the party had grown more than elevenfold, not counting members of its auxiliary organization, the Young Communist League.[25] The rise in membership coincided with the party's Popular Front era during the New Deal, characterized by the party's engagement in broader political issues, moving beyond its focus on labor.[26] Party membership declined precipitously after 1939 but rose again dramatically by the mid-1940s to seventy-five thousand. And then membership dropped by approximately 20 percent. As historian Ellen Schrecker notes, "Though most of its cadres remained in the party until the mid-fifties, it had dwindled into a sect."[27]

Although scholars have been able to identify specific numbers for national membership, the case of California remains elusive, except for the 1930s, when CP membership stood at five thousand, with Mexican Americans making up about 20 percent of the total.[28] The nature of membership in the party and the political climate of the 1950s make information for this period difficult to obtain, especially for Mexican American women like Francisca Flores. In historian Jeffrey Garcilazo's words, "Anticommunism and anti-Mexican hysteria permeated the everyday lives of the Mexican Americans living in Los Angeles between 1950 and 1954. Combined with the anticommunist climate, the occurrence of mass raids on so-called 'wetbacks' had a chilling effect on virtually all people of Mexican background."[29] As Dorothy Healey, chair of the party in southern California from the late 1940s through the 1960s, recalled in her memoir, "The FBI did a much better job of keeping track of our members than we did."[30] During this period the CP itself did not keep many records due to the need to keep its members away from the eyes of the authorities as well as disorganization of the party itself.

We can only speculate about the motivations of women like Francisca Flores and others who joined the CP, but a desire for social justice for Mexicans in the United States appears to have influenced members. Two years after Flores joined, she married fellow party member La Verne Lym, chairman of the party in San Diego County. Perhaps we can learn from other ethnic Mexicans who joined the party in the same era. According to Enrique Buelna, Ralph Cuarón, a Los Angeles activist in the Congress of Industrial Organizations, joined the CP in 1942 "because of his belief in the potential of the common laborer to transform society and make it more democratic and egalitarian."[31] This rationale is consistent with the reasons given by other ethnic Mexicans and those of Latin American heritage who joined in earlier years. For example, in the late 1930s, labor activist Emma Tenayuca joined the party in San Antonio, Texas. As noted by historian Zaragoza Vargas, Tenayuca "belie[ved] that the workplace required radical revision to achieve equality" and joined the CP "because no one else but the communists expressed any interest in helping San Antonio's dispossessed Mexicans."[32]

After her marriage and during her membership in the San Diego branch of the party, Flores, who was also known as Frances Lym, managed the party's International Bookstore with her husband and actively participated in party meetings through the beginning of 1945, when she moved to Los Angeles. There is no record of why she made the move. In Los Angeles, Flores operated as a party liaison with Mexican American communities. To support herself, she took various jobs that were clerical in nature. For a very short time in early 1945 Flores worked with the noted labor and political activist Luisa Moreno at the Food, Tobacco, Agricultural, and Allied Workers (FTA) union (formerly the United Cannery, Agricultural, Packing, and Allied Workers of America) before moving on for a short time to the Progressive Bookstore, another project of the CP, among other jobs.[33]

Luisa Moreno is arguably one of the most important figures in the history of Latinas and of women in the United States. Born in Guatemala into a life of privilege, Moreno fled that life in her late teens and went to Mexico and then to New York, where she emerged as a powerful labor organizer in the garment industry by the late 1920s. As historian Vicki L. Ruiz writes, "Luisa Moreno remains the only transcontinental Latina union organizer. . . . She was the first Latina vice president of a major union." Moreover, Ruiz asserts that this major accomplishment was second to Moreno's role "as the driving force behind El Congreso de Pueblos de Habla Española (the Spanish-Speaking People's Congress), the first national Latino civil rights assembly."[34] It was during Moreno's time in the leadership of United Cannery, Agricultural, Packing and Allied Workers of America that Flores and she worked together, albeit briefly; there is no evidence of a concrete connection vis-à-vis the CP.[35] As Ruiz notes, Moreno remained a member of the CP for only five years, but her "commitment to Marxism never wavered."[36] By the time Flores moved to Los Angeles in 1945, the evidence suggests, her membership in the party opened the door for her employment with Moreno in the FTA. Although previous accounts of Flores's life posit that she had been active in the Sleepy Lagoon Defense Committee, it must have been when in San Diego, or not at all. By 1945 the Sleepy Lagoon Defense Committee had been "disbanded" when the committee's appeal efforts succeeded and the men they were defending were released from prison. It is conceivable that Flores was involved in El Congreso, but there is no conclusive evidence of this.[37]

During the nineteen years of her membership in the party, Flores worked to bring Mexican Americans into the fold by organizing clubs on the east side of Los Angeles such as the Zapata Section of the Cuauhtémoc Club, of which she became chair, and lobbying the party to take the plight of Mexican Americans seriously. Although she eventually rose to become a District Council delegate, Flores was part of the uneven relationship between the party and ethnic Mexicans. She had joined during the party's Popular Front era of the 1930s and 1940s. "When the party moderated its revolutionary stance and sought to join the mainstream, the activities of American Communists—both capital letter and lowercase—were often indistinguishable from those of the non-Communists with whom they worked," as Ellen Schrecker notes.[38] That is, during this era the CP joined forces with labor and other reform-minded activists. During the 1930s, at least, the party "served as the unofficial left wing of the New Deal, its cadres and rank and file supplying manpower and leadership for a wide array of social reform movements and progressive political groups."[39]

Although the party's position as an established U.S. entity declined in 1939 due to the nonagression agreement between Stalin and Hitler, this international context did not affect African American or Mexican American members domestically. By 1941 the CP in the United States returned to an antifascist position with the U.S. entrance into World War II, and the Popular Front reemerged. In the midst of these upheavals, the party grappled with its relationship with ethnic Mexicans. As a member since 1939, Francisca Flores would have been well aware of the party's attempts to address "the Mexican question," which changed over time. Historians agree that the position of the CP vis-à-vis Mexicans emerged concretely with the publication of "The Mexican Question in the Southwest" by Emma Tenayuca and Homer Brooks in *The Communist* in 1939. Tenayuca, a labor activist well known for her role in organizing the pecan shellers' strike in 1938, was the state chairperson of the CP in Texas, and her husband Brooks was the state secretary. In "The Mexican Question in the Southwest" they argued that Mexicans in the United States had dual histories as both a conquered people because of the Mexican land appropriated in 1848 by the United States after the U.S.-Mexico War, and in the twentieth century as immigrant laborers. As noted by Mario T. García, Tenayuca and Brooks posited that "Mexicans in the United States did not possess, according to Stalin's classical definition of a nation, either the economic or territorial base for a nation. On the contrary, Mexican Americans and Mexican nationals were inextricably tied to the larger American working class based on the economic and political integration of the Southwest with the rest of the nation plus an expanded Anglo population in the region."[40] The position of ethnic Mexicans as per Tenayuca and Brooks contrasted with the CP's position regarding African Americans as an "oppressed nation." Specifically, as historian Robin D. G. Kelley asserts, in 1928 the Communist International "insisted that blacks concentrated in the black belt counties of the Deep South constituted an oppressed nation," and therefore "had the right to self-determination: political power, control over the economy, and the right to secede from the United States."[41] According to Buelna, "Almost from its inception, the CP identified the struggle for Black equality as essential, if not crucial to the destruction of imperialism at home and abroad."[42] During the period of her involvement in the CP in Los Angeles, beginning in 1945, Flores experienced the contrasting perspectives of the party as she participated in various party conferences and in the Mexican American Commission of the party in Los Angeles, and contributed to documents such as the 1948 Resolution on Party Work Among the Mexican People.[43]

An article Flores wrote for *Jewish Life* in 1955 provides a clue about her motivations for joining the party. In "The Mexican Americans Organize," a special article for Cinco de Mayo, Flores, as Frances Lym, wrote,

> The intense chauvinism and discrimination against Mexican Americans have their historic origin in the practices and attitudes developed during the Mexican War of 1846–48. This was the expansionist war as a result of which Mexico was

robbed of about half her territory, which became the great Southwest of the United States. Since then Mexicans have been cruelly exploited economically and the objects of sharp discrimination.[44]

The context for Flores's article revealed a historical understanding of the place of Mexicans in the United States. She based her claims not on the recent history of immigration but on a century-old international relationship. Her analysis of U.S.-Mexico relations and the experiences of Mexican Americans most likely drew from her participation in Hermanas de la Revolución Mexicana (Sisters of the Mexican Revolution), a political discussion group at the tuberculosis sanatorium where she lived for over ten years, as well as her years of political education within the CP. Five years before the publication of this article Flores co-wrote a pamphlet called "Toward the Unity of the Mexican People in the United States" for the Asociación Nacional Mexico-Americana. With co-author Alfredo Montoya, president of the organization and organizer for the International Union of Mine, Mill and Smelter Workers (Mine Mill), Flores focused on the same principles of economic exploitation while also recognizing the importance of Mexican culture within the United States.[45] The thematic connections between these pieces shows how Flores's work as an active party member drew on and carried forward activist arguments she developed within Mexican American community organizations.

In 1958, however, Flores left the party. Her departure from the organization to which she had dedicated almost twenty years of her life was not necessarily unique, as others, including Mexican American members, also departed during this period. Mexican American members of the party, including Flores, had grown dissatisfied with the lack of priority the party gave to Mexican American issues. In addition, the CP in the United States was directly aligned with its parent organization in the Soviet Union. For most Mexican Americans in the CP, this relationship did not affect their everyday lives. Yet Flores's departure coincides with one of the most salient events in the history of the party, when in 1956, Nikita Khrushchev, the First Secretary of the Communist Party of the Soviet Union, gave a speech in which he revealed a panoply of atrocities committed by former Soviet leader Joseph Stalin. The revelations shook members of the U.S. Communist Party and eventually led to an exodus of members so that nationwide members numbered approximately three thousand and in Los Angeles fewer than five hundred by the end of the 1950s.[46] Though no longer a member, Flores retained ties with the party via events and fundraisers and eventually through her partnership as co-editor of the Los Angeles periodical *Carta Editorial* with Delfino Varela, who remained a party member. From her experiences with the party, Flores knew how to organize campaigns, how to give public talks, how to strategize for specific goals, and how to network. She would come to use these skills in her future endeavors with Mexican American women's politics.[47]

In addition to the CP, Mexican American women in Los Angeles were also active within the ranks of the CSO, making up approximately 30 percent of the original membership, and in fact were integral to its founding, establishment, and successes. Their participation in the CSO is yet another example of bridging activism. The organization was founded in 1947 in response to Edward Roybal's unsuccessful run for the Los Angeles City Council. With a grant from the Industrial Areas Foundation, the CSO gained stability and addressed community concerns such as improvement of the neighborhood, youth activities, and family health, but its most vital activities centered around voter registration and civil rights.[48] By 1960 the CSO, according to historian David Gutiérrez, "claimed to have assisted more than 40,000 Mexican nationals in obtaining American citizenship."[49] And by 1963, as historian Shana Bernstein writes, "the CSO had established thirty-four chapters across the Southwest, primarily in California, with over 10,000 paid members" and an equal number of men and women.[50] In addition, the group took an expansive approach to defining the Mexican American community, and included both immigrants and native-born.[51]

Women in the CSO, as in other organizations, "became the backbone" and worked to make the organization functional and viable by, for example, fundraising to provide the resources to keep the CSO operating, spearheading its signature voter registration campaigns, conducting citizenship classes for immigrants, and founding their own CSO chapters.[52] The organization grew through a recruitment strategy that consisted of meetings in private homes organized by women members who traveled across Los Angeles County to deliver personal invitations. Indeed, politics came from the home as "women used their roles in the home, family, and community to organize for social change" regarding issues such as "neighborhood improvement, education, and health," as historian Margaret Rose asserts. Women's activism made these issues part of "the mainstream of the CSO reform agenda."[53] By starting out in people's homes, these women were already practicing activism that bridged the traditional boundary between private and public concerns. The home served as a meeting place for a close-knit community that would address community concerns, and women who got their start organizing in domestic spaces could use this experience to branch outwards. By the 1960s women headed major CSO efforts such as its credit union and its buyers' club.[54] As such, women provided the structure and labor to keep the CSO successful. Regardless of these achievements, CSO women also recognized the gender disparities in the leadership of the organization itself, but at that time did not seek to change them.

Many CSO women came from families with some community service or activist background. For example, the CSO was Grace Montañez Davis's first community or political organization. Her entrance into politics was a complex affair. Her experiences in higher education and in community organizations eventually raised her consciousness about racial, ethnic, class, and gender disparities. Born in 1926, Montañez Davis earned a B.S. in chemistry from Immaculate Heart College in Los Angeles in 1948 and a master's degree in biochemistry from UCLA in 1955. At UCLA Montañez Davis experienced both ethnic and gender discrimination in her field of study. As a Mexican American and a woman she was twice a minority and doubly marginalized. She was the first Mexican American in the biochemistry department, in which there were very few women. She recalled that in her interview for entrance to the Biochemistry Department, the director told her, "Women do not belong in the laboratories, they belong in the kitchen, but this is a public institution and I cannot deny you attendance here." He added that "he never had a Mexican in his department before and if I had any problems in regards to that, he didn't want to hear about them."[55]

During her time there, Montañez Davis bonded with the many Jewish students in her program. Her friendship with them and her exposure to a broader world at UCLA opened up both political education and opportunities that correlated with the ideas of community service with which she had grown up; these ultimately led her to the CSO. In the process of becoming citizens, Montañez Davis's parents learned English in night school and her mother subsequently became a neighborhood go-to person, serving as an interpreter for her neighbors at their children's schools, at doctor's appointments, and in various other instances. Montañez Davis said of her mother, "She was always very socially alert about things. Whenever there was any kind of drive like an earthquake in Mexico or a fire, whatever, food, she always collected."[56] By the time Montañez Davis arrived at UCLA, she had a social awareness of the type of discrimination Mexicans in Los Angeles faced, having grown up in a predominantly Italian neighborhood of Lincoln Heights and having witnessed the treatment of Mexican American men who, like her brother, wore zoot suits.

At UCLA she befriended the undergraduate children of the Hollywood Ten, the group of motion picture screenwriters who during the 1950s House Un-American Activities Committee hearings refused to cooperate with authorities, and as a result, were barred from working in Hollywood.[57] Through these connections as well as her own curiosity about events publicized in the

Daily Bruin, the UCLA student newspaper, Montañez Davis eventually met Dorothy Healey, who headed the Los Angeles chapter of the CP, the musician and political activist Paul Robeson, the scholar W. E. B. DuBois, and many more. As she recalled, "it was an awakening."[58] During this same period, Montañez Davis got involved with the CSO via family connections. She began to volunteer for the organization after she attended a CSO citizenship graduation and saw that women were integral to making the group a success. For example, Elvina Carrillo led its citizenship classes, Maria Duran served on the CSO executive committee, and Henrietta Villaescusa established a chapter of the CSO in the Lincoln Heights area of Los Angeles.[59] When she entered politics in the 1950s, Montañez Davis was aware of the gender disparities within organizations. Recalling her experiences in the CSO and reflecting on an era when men assumed public leadership roles, she stated that although women were actively involved in the CSO and in fact were considered "equal, full voting members," unlike those in other organizations such as the League of United Latin American Citizens and the American GI Forum, Montañez Davis still felt that power was not equally shared. Although some women rose to leadership roles, she recalled, "We didn't . . . [in] the early beginnings, [ever have women] committee chairpersons or anything like that."[60] This early recognition of gender disparities influenced Montañez Davis's future political activities.

For Hope Mendoza Schechter, joining the CSO resulted from her union activism, another example of bridging activism in practice. After working for two years in the garment industry, Mendoza Schechter was recruited as an International Ladies' Garment Workers' Union (ILGWU) organizer and business agent. At the same time, she had her first experience with community organizing when she began working as a liaison for immigration issues with the field office of Congressman Chester "Chet" Holifield. Then, in 1947, she became a founding member of the Community Service Organization. As Edward Roybal remembered her, she was "a bright young woman who had gained both experience in labor relations and an understanding of human values in the picket lines of the International Ladies' Garment Workers Union. She and many other women became an integral part of CSO from its very beginning."[61]

Mendoza Schechter, like most women who were politically active in this period, organized simultaneously on a number of fronts, with an emphasis on the interlinked arenas of immigration and labor. Mendoza Schechter actively participated in Democratic Party politics in California and on the national level. Her time with in the Democratic Party seems to have begun officially with her volunteer work for Congressman Holifield, a Democrat who served fifteen terms in office beginning in 1942, representing the Nineteenth District, a district with a high proportion of Mexican Americans.[62] One of the few Congressmen to vote against the incarceration of Japanese Americans during World War II, he also opposed the House Committee on Un-American Activities. Holifield wrote a bill to establish the Cabinet Committee on Opportunities for Spanish Speaking People in the President's Office in 1969.[63] At the same time that Mendoza Schechter became a member of the Democratic State Central Committee in 1950, she was also on the executive board of the Central Labor Council's Committee on Political Education. Her term on the Central Labor Council ended in 1956. Within the Democratic Party, Mendoza Schechter served on the Credentials Committee and the Rules Committee at least until 1978. Within the Democratic Party, the union, and in the grassroots organizations she bridged, she identified specific roles that women were expected to fill and felt that, especially in the Democratic Party, women were the "drones." She said, "We're the ones that literally put the campaigns on, and they need us . . . we're the workers. We're the ones that really do the day in and day out manning of headquarters, volunteers, et cetera, and put on the campaign."[64]

Women such as Flores, Montañez Davis, and Mendoza Schechter remained active in politics through the 1960s, when the political practices of Mexican Americans in Los Angeles began to shift. In the face of heightened anticommunism, the prominence of the Communist Party went into decline. The CSO remained an important grassroots organization. Although it had been founded in the wake of an electoral campaign, it transitioned into a community-based organization. By the late 1950s and early 1960s, a new crop of organizations began to advocate for increasing representation of Mexican Americans in electoral politics, exemplified by the Mexican American Political Association.

While Mexican Americans continued as members of the CP, the influence of the party did not remain strong. For many in ethnic Mexican communities, other communities of color, and radical and left-leaning political activists, the 1940s and the 1950s had been periods of both great community activism and great fear. Mexicans in Los Angeles faced the aftermath of the Zoot Suit–Sailor Riots and the Sleepy Lagoon incident in the 1940s and, most notably, the consequences of Cold War legislation such as the Internal Security Act of 1950 and the Immigration and Nationality Act of 1952, also known as the McCarran-Walter Act. The Internal Security Act allowed for criminal prosecution of "anyone who had ever been even nominally affiliated with a Communist, Socialist, or other organization deemed subversive," as noted by David Gutiérrez. The McCarran-Walter Act allowed for the deportation of anyone who had entered the country after 1924 who fell into the category of "undesirable alien," were anarchists, or had any affiliation whatsoever with the CP.[65] In addition, ethnic Mexicans had experienced the trauma of Operation Wetback in 1954, when the border patrol and local police authorities in the Southwest deported between five hundred thousand and one million Mexicans, in many cases regardless of citizenship status. At the same time that organizations such as the CSO achieved success in local elections, activists of the 1940s and 1950s were visited and surveilled by the FBI and called before the House Un-American Activities Committee and its California counterpart, the Tenney Committee. In a climate where political beliefs could result in jail or deportation, Mexican Americans remained committed to securing their rights as American citizens and to pursuing other ideologies to achieve a just society.

Meanwhile, by 1960 the CSO, now more than a decade old, had expanded beyond voter registration campaigns. Women continued to work as important figures within its ranks, where they would remain prominent as it remained active in local issues in Los Angeles until 1995.[66] Yet there were also new organizations entering the scene. By the late 1950s Mexican Americans in Los Angeles and the Southwest began to organize politically in different ways, and in 1960 they formed MAPA to increase representation of Mexican Americans in public office via the Democratic Party. Historian Ernesto Chávez writes, "They channeled their energies into creating strong MAPA chapters in every California Assembly District inhabited by Mexican Americans."[67] Women such as Sánchez, Montañez Davis, and Flores bridged this new type of organizing.

Mexicans in Los Angeles continued to advocate for effective political representation and believed that those from their own communities would represent them best; women were integral members of these locally oriented organizations. That is, they believed that if they had representation in local, state and national arenas, the issues they faced as a group would be addressed and rectified. As historian Rodolfo Acuña reminds us, Mexicans in this era were concerned mostly with local issues, as they saw the effects of discriminatory practices at first hand. They focused on employment, neighborhood and community improvements, poverty, immigration, housing, education, and police brutality. For Mexican American women, however, the struggle also included representation for themselves as women within these male-dominated organizations and the larger community.[68] Although the majority of MAPA's founders were men, women were also integral to its founding and its development.

Dolores Sánchez was one such founding member. When asked about the reasons for her involvement, she recalled,

> I think I also had a more militant view of things after what happened with the House Un-American Activities Committee coming to town and the kind of pressure that people like Connie and Frank Muñoz, Delfino Varela and a lot of people that I knew had been put under. . . . So that made me a lot more militant than I had ever been. I was upset that we were spied upon. I was upset by the fact that we were called communists. And that our political activities were looked at as something dangerous.[69]

Sánchez saw her own political activity in relation to that of her peers. Although Delfino Varela had been and continued to be a member of the CP, neither Connie nor Frank Muñoz, also activists, had been members. Varela had indeed been called before the House Un-American Activities Committee hearings in southern California in 1959.[70] In Sánchez's view, she had been exercising her rights as an American citizen in pursuing her political activities along with her fellow political activists. She was offended that these activities were seen as dangerous and had been subject to surveillance by government authorities.

Notably, Sánchez's activism in MAPA was shaped by the activist practices of older women in her family. She recollected, "My mother, you might say, was a feminist. . . . She didn't call herself that."[71] This upbringing paved the way for her involvement in politics. Born in 1936 in Phoenix, Arizona, Sánchez was raised in Los Angeles by a family of strong, educated, and independent women. The majority of her family, including her parents, had finished high school. Her father, a navy veteran, had attended college and worked in aeronautical engineering. Her parents divorced when she was a young teenager, and her mother began to support the family with work in the garment industry, where she became an organizer for the ILGWU. As a youngster, Sánchez had accompanied her mother during events surrounding the City Council campaign of Edward Roybal in the late 1940s.[72] After graduating from high school Sánchez joined the workforce, eventually returning to school to earn her RN degree and become a nurse. She married, and with her first husband joined MAPA in 1959. For her, joining seemed "automatic." She recalled, "I can't say we made a decision. It was there, we heard about it and joined it." Through MAPA she became more engaged in politics, especially get-out-the-vote campaigns, and eventually became the treasurer of the group's operation in California's Fortieth Assembly District.[73]

Connie Pardo, a political contemporary of Sánchez, joined MAPA in tandem with her husband. Born in 1930 in the small northern California town of Dunsmuir, near Mt. Shasta, she moved with her Mexican immigrant parents to Los Angeles when she was still a toddler. Both of her parents had been involved in unions because her mother worked in laundries and her father in construction. Her parents divorced when she was a young girl, and her father sent her to Francis De Pauw, a Methodist boarding school in Hollywood, where she spent five years among many other Mexican-origin girls, including Lilia Aceves. She then returned to the Aliso Village housing projects in Los Angeles and began her own involvement in unions as part of the ILGWU. Although she did not graduate from high school, she eventually attended adult school to receive her high school diploma. When she married Frank Muñoz in the early 1950s, her political life blossomed. Muñoz received his law degree in 1957 from the University of Southern California, and the husband-and-wife team became a power couple in East Side politics. Pardo recalls, "I became interested in politics. I became interested in what was happening to our community, the Chicano community. I was a worker so I was active already in the unions and in labor issues."[74]

This political practice of traversing between issues and being part of various organizations was a common pattern among Mexican American women activists in Los Angeles during the decades following World War II. For example, Grace Montañez Davis, who had worked with the CSO in the 1950s, also began to work with MAPA, where she worked on electoral campaigns in addition to voter registration and get-out-the-vote campaigns. Unlike the CSO, which was a nonpartisan community-oriented organization, MAPA worked to endorse candidates for various public offices.[75]

Lilia Aceves was raised by her mother, a laundry worker, and attended Francis de Pauw. Her path to politics began with advocating for her children's education and then connecting with other political activities on the East Side of Los Angeles.[76] For Aceves, political activism had a snowball effect. She recalled that she became interested in community issues and remembered, "You find out [how] things are—that you have to get out there, and make a change. And you're young and idealistic."[77] She was first involved in her children's cooperative nursery school in the City Terrace area of Los Angeles, and from there became more deeply involved in other committees and issues, such as the Wabash Coordinating Council in City Terrace, the Los Angeles Human Relations Commission, and eventually MAPA.[78] Aceves had known Pardo since childhood, and in MAPA she met Montañez Davis and Flores, among others, creating important linkages within this activist generation.[79]

As the women profiled demonstrate, Mexican Americans in Los Angeles participated in political activities on multiple fronts, sometimes leaving one organization for another, and often participating in various organizations simultaneously. For many years the Communist Party provided key intellectual and organizational resources for Mexican American activists, including many of those who participated in the CSO, which made important inroads into achieving formal political representation for their community. With the rise of anticommunism and its associated challenges and dangers, Mexican American women did not retreat from activism. Instead, they contributed to building new routes to empowerment by widening the focus of existing organizations and building new ones such as MAPA. In doing so, they brought an intellectual and ideological insistence on self-representation as a key to community betterment that demanded increased representation for Mexican Americans in politics and for Chicanas in political organizations. Through the practice of bridging activism, they forged linkages between communist and other organizations, the domestic and the political realms, and the local, national, and transnational arenas. They created structures that would undergird the next chapter of the movement for Mexican American liberation. Central to this process, we will now see, was the tactic of writing for and publishing periodicals, which Mexican Americans, including women, used to communicate with one another and the broader reading public about myriad issues, ideas, and opinions, especially in regard to their experiences as women.

A Mexican American Woman's Voice: *Carta Editorial*

One of the few windows into the political world of ethnic Mexican women in Los Angeles during this era is the periodical *Carta Editorial*, edited by Francisca Flores and Delfino Varela, a fellow Communist Party member.[80] Flores's co-editorship of the periodical serves as yet another example of bridging activism. In her seven years in that post, she also participated in various political organizations including MAPA. Produced in Boyle Heights near the intersection of Soto Street and Brooklyn Avenue (now César E. Chávez Avenue), *Carta Editorial* was published twice a month from 1963 to 1967, then, when Flores became sole editor in January 1967, published monthly through 1969. The majority of its articles were penned by either Flores or Varela and included noteworthy news related to Mexican Americans in Los Angeles, with a heavy emphasis on politics. *Carta Editorial* served as a platform for the confident, to-the-point, and sometimes snarky views of its editors. Anna NietoGómez notes that "the purpose of the newsletter was to present a point of view absent in the mainstream press." In addition, the publication provided a space for a gendered critique of politics. Since the periodical did not usually include by-lines, it is not possible to precisely identify authorship for specific articles. Given Flores's activities prior to and during the run of *Carta Editorial*, however, there is a strong possibility that it was she who penned the articles offering gendered critiques of politics.[81]

For the editors of *Carta Editorial*, and ostensibly especially for Flores, the lack of political representation for Mexican Americans in Los Angeles and beyond was exacerbated by the fact that even less representation existed for Mexican American women. Throughout the run of *Carta Editorial*, this theme emerged frequently. In one of the first articles specifically about women, Flores (and Varela) analyzed the events surrounding a 1963 luncheon with special guest Vice President Lyndon B. Johnson organized by the Mexican American Education Conference Committee. The luncheon, an occasion for Mexican American leaders to meet with Johnson, was arranged because of Johnson's post as chair of the President's Committee on Equal Employment Opportunity.[82] The organizers of the meeting hoped to address a number of concerns with the vice president, chief among them labor and education for Mexican Americans. For *Carta Editorial*, however, an important issue arose due to the way in which seating arrangements showcased sexist attitudes among the organizers. Flores and Varela's article "Women and Dogs Not Allowed" caustically criticized the "MACHOS" who planned the luncheon because the all-male organizing committee refused to hear a motion at the planning meeting which would have "guarantee[d] that women would be considered for eating at the head table." As Anna NietoGómez points out, "The men were embarrassed when the women members, who were present at the meeting, explained to the 'brave bulls' that the vote to exclude women meant Lady Bird Johnson could not sit with her husband at the head table."[83] The editors concluded that "in some areas Mexicans and dogs are not allowed, although this way of thinking is rapidly being relegated to the trash can where it belongs . . . but not so where women are concerned."[84] In titling the editorial "No Women or Dogs Allowed," the editors called out the blatant sexism of the organizing committee for preventing women from sitting with Johnson and equated gender discrimination with the racist signs long seen on businesses that read "No Mexicans or Dogs Allowed." This early critique of sexism in *Carta Editorial* suggests that at least some Mexican Americans had begun to recognize gender and gender discrimination in the early 1960s.[85] While *Carta Editorial* criticized and chastised Mexican Americans and other city leaders regarding the treatment of women, the coverage of women themselves was uneven during its seven-year run. For the most part, the editors focused on local issues, occasionally branching out into national and international coverage.

Carta Editorial also focused on housing, one of the most salient issues for its readers, because of the lack of options and the poor conditions for Mexicans. For example, in the April 1964 article "The Statistics of Discrimination" *Carta Editorial* bemoaned the disconnect between the Mexican American community and political leaders, and those that they represented, stating, "They seldom encounter the brutal facts of discrimination in their own daily lives." Flores and Varela provided a summary of a report prepared by George W. Borrell for the California Assembly Subcommittee on Special Employment Problems "to provide some much needed perspective in several critical areas." With regard to housing specifically, Flores and Varela wrote that "Mexican Americans have 3 times the percentage of deterioration and 5 times the percentage of dilapidation as Anglo American homes."[86]

Moreover, the periodical railed against California's Proposition 14, on the ballot in 1964. For many, the initiative was a stark reminder that housing integration, even in Los Angeles, was still an issue to overcome. The Rumford Fair Housing Act, passed by the California legislature in 1963 to ban discriminatory practices based on race and other factors in renting and selling housing, was overturned in 1964 when California voters passed Proposition 14. As historian Daniel Hosang writes, "Proposition 14 nullified the Rumford Act, prohibiting the state from addressing patterns of racial discrimination and segregation in housing as entrenched as in any region in the nation."[87] For Mexican Americans, Proposition 14 served as a reminder of the discrimination they had faced in housing. In August 1964 Flores and Varela printed the comments of Sal Montenegro, a member of Realtors for Fair Housing, who provided first-hand accounts of such discrimination. According to his comments, Mexican Americans had been denied the purchase of homes in the Los Angeles suburbs of Monterey Park and West San Gabriel.[88]

The year after Proposition 14 passed, Flores and Varela returned to housing in another issue of *Carta Editorial* to highlight the fact that conditions for Mexican Americans seeking housing had not improved. Based on a report called the "Comparative Study of the Socio-Economic Situation of Mexican Americans, Negroes and Anglo-Caucasians in Los Angeles" by the California Commission on Human Relations, the article let readers know about the disparate quality of the housing available to their kind in Los Angeles. It highlighted the fact that "in relation to the Mexican-American community in the East Side—based on median rent paid of between $60 and $75 per month—only 6.7% of the Anglo population live in dilapidated and deteriorating housing whereas 31.5% of persons with Spanish-surnames pay this amount of rent and live in substandard houses."[89]

For Flores and Varela, immigration had an important place in Mexican American politics due to two main programs, Operation Wetback of 1954 and the Bracero Program of 1942–1964. Mexican American activists remembered Operation Wetback, a deportation campaign launched by the Immigration and Naturalization Service in which Mexicans in the United States were rounded up in raids and deported to Mexico.[90] The Bracero Program, a contract labor program negotiated between the United States and Mexico during World War II, had been quite controversial.[91] Some in the community severely critiqued the program because they believed that it undermined the labor power of ethnic Mexican workers in the United States. Others critiqued its exploitation of those same workers and lamented that they were perceived by employers as expendable. In 1963 Varela, in the pages of *Carta Editorial*, placed the Bracero Program within the larger context of Mexican labor and distinguished between Mexican immigrants and Mexican Americans. For the most part, however, Varela, speaking for himself and Flores, excoriated the program for its lack of effective administration and its exploitation of Mexican workers:

> We do not now nor have we ever meant an ounce of support for the bracero program.... We have seen paychecks of minus 18 cents for one week's work after the full week's room and board are deducted from the 2 or 3 days wages earned by the worker. We have helped to document the non-observance of contract provisions, and the shipping of braceros back to Mexico to avoid payment of medical and workmen's compensation claims. But we have said and we do say that simple termination of the program is too simple, and because it is too simple, it is not enough.[92]

The variety of issues addressed by *Carta Editorial* attest to the multiplicity of interests among Mexican American political actors, including women. Its coverage shows that Flores and women like her engaged with the changing political climate and viewed gender disparities and issues important to Mexican American women within the broad context of civil rights and political representation for all Mexican Americans. Yet their experiences of gender subordination in organizations such as the CP, the CSO, and MAPA provided a foundation for an emerging feminist consciousness that led to the establishment of the League of Mexican American Women, an organization that would build leaders from within.

The League of Mexican American Women

Given their experiences of marginalization in a variety of organizations, Mexican American women such as Flores recognized gendered patterns of unequal leadership that privileged their male counterparts and reinforced a status quo that proved frustrating in terms of both gender and politics. In 1958 Flores and fellow political activist Ramona Morín founded the League of Mexican American Women to provide avenues for women's leadership in politics during a period when opportunities had been closed off to them because of gender discrimination.[93] As NietoGómez notes, although the CSO counted women as "at least 50 percent of its membership," they held extremely few leadership roles.[94] The same would be true for MAPA until 1973. Flores and Morín had previously worked in various Mexican American organizations such as the American GI Forum, the CSO, and the Young Women's Christian Association, and they drew on the positive and negative aspects of these experiences to create this new organization, demonstrating bridging activism in motion as they created a women-centered and women-led organization that many members would encounter as a novel formation. In the tradition of MAPA, Flores and Morín formed LMAW with two main goals in mind. First, they wanted to increase the presence of Mexican American women in politics, especially political appointments to city, state, and national commissions. Second, they wanted to recognize the achievements and contributions of Mexican American women in politics.[95] As former LMAW member Dolores Sánchez remembered, "Yes, [gender] became an issue . . . the women in MAPA got kind of fed up—we became fed up with always doing the work, and never called on to give a speech. We were never given an award and so we formed an organization."[96]

Unlike previous organizations, LMAW explicitly placed Mexican American women in the forefront of political advocacy. Its goals did not differ much from MAPA's in terms of political representation for Mexican Americans, except that LMAW focused solely on women. This was evident in the organization's constitution, which stated: "In order to stimulate and promote the interest of the Mexican-American women in fields of social and legislative action, this organization is formed. It will also give special recognition to women for outstanding work in these fields" because "unfortunately, for many reasons the Mexican-American woman's work, contribution and/or activity has not been properly recognized."[97] The league aimed to unite Mexican American women of similar consciousness in an effort to facilitate dialogue among themselves and effect social change through its leadership training. It also sought to broaden the "socio-economic, political and cultural horizons" of Mexican American women with the ultimate goal of "undertaking responsibility and giving leadership to the community it serve[d]."[98]

The type of woman involved in LMAW tells us a great deal more about the lives of Mexican American women activists of the time. Ramona Morín began her political work in the 1950s. Born in 1919 in Kansas City, Missouri, she married Raul Morín and had six children. From 1952 through 1970, her political activities included various leadership positions in the California State Democratic Party, the American GI Forum, MAPA, the Ladies Aid

Society of the Belvedere Park Mexican Baptist Church, the Mayor's Latin American Advisory Council, the YWCA board of directors, and the board of directors of the Euclid Heights Foundation. In 1970 Morín worked as a social service assistant for the Los Angeles County Department of Human Resources Development and as a consultant on Mexican American problems for the Educational Staff Seminar at George Washington University. She also had experience working as a preschool teacher and a survey interviewer. Although she did not attain a bachelor's degree, Morín attended East Los Angeles College, Pasadena City College, and Chapman College and had taken extension courses at UCLA.[99]

Active in Los Angeles from 1963 through 1970, with a membership averaging twenty, LMAW campaigned for consumer education in East Los Angeles, supported Mexican American women running for political office and recognized women for their political achievements. The league also participated with the Consumer Action Council of Los Angeles in writing a proposal to establish a comprehensive consumer protection project.[100] For LMAW, consumer education was an issue of racial and economic justice, because disparate pricing strategies by grocers in the barrio affected the family budget and the economy of those who lived in these areas.[101] In 1968, for example, members of LMAW, in conjunction with Teamsters Local 848, the Housewives Economic Protection, and someone representing the federal government, began to document prices at various East Los Angeles supermarkets, as well as the general cleanliness and quality of the food.[102] In one case, this ad hoc group found that prices in East Los Angeles were from 6 percent to 8 percent higher than in markets in West Los Angeles's white suburbs. In addition, the group observed that most of the East Side stores had unclean conditions and often sold spoiled food.[103] In April 1969 the NAACP's Legal Defense and Education Fund joined the effort for consumer protection in East Los Angeles and provided the financial support for a consumer fraud project that continued the work LMAW had started to change the business practices of merchants.[104] Through this project members of LMAW, along with other members of the Mexican American community in East Los Angeles, disseminated information, met with grocery store management, and started a boycott leading to the successful clean-up of a local store.[105]

The league's proposal for a consumer protection project argued that Mexican Americans had been left out of discussions about race relations, which more often than not were framed as exclusively Black and white. The proposal contextualized this exclusion in two ways. First, it argued that Mexicans were "indigenous to the land" and therefore should have more rights accorded them. Second, it argued that Mexicans had been excluded from consumer education and protection, especially since these programs focused on African Americans in the aftermath of civil disorders in various large cities in the 1960s. After these uprisings, the proposal argued, government agencies investigated the business practices of inner-city merchants but had not extended these inquiries to the predominantly ethnic Mexican neighborhoods. The Consumer Action Council pointed to similar circumstances facing Mexican and Mexican American neighborhoods in Los Angeles, citing a 1967 report by the economist Frederick Sturdivant. Titled "Business and Mexican-American Relations in East Los Angeles," the report found ample evidence of unfair business practices in Mexican American neighborhoods.[106] While the Consumer Action Council's report called for a "comprehensive consumer protection project" with an annual budget of $244,900, LMAW proposed a "Consumer Opportunity Center" that would "counsel housewives on problems of consumer exploitation," hire a bilingual woman to "analyze merchandising," and "encourage democratic disciplinary community action against exploitative situations," which could include legal action.[107]

In addition to the consumer education campaign, LMAW sought public positions for its constituency and recognized their achievements at sponsored dinners. Between 1960 and 1969 the league held a yearly banquet to "acknowledge the value and significance of women's contributions to the movement." In 1969 LMAW supported Soledad García for the position of principal of Roosevelt High School and supported Irene Tovar in her bid for a seat on the Junior College Board by holding fundraisers on her behalf.[108] Bridging their connections and membership in organizations such as the East Los Angeles Belvedere Democratic Club, Flores and Morín strategically used their positions in other organizations to send out invitations for their awards banquet. In honoring women every year and endorsing women candidates for both employment and electoral positions, LMAW "gained recognition as a women's political organization."[109]

For most of its members, involvement in LMAW was their first woman-centered political activity. Their entrance into politics began with the Mexican American community more generally but was complicated by pervasive gender norms that kept them from leadership and kept their issues in the margins. They joined LMAW in response to these unequal gender relations within male-controlled organizations and received training and a sense of empowerment. As Dolores Sánchez recalled,

> Well, one of the things that it [LMAW] did, I think, was allow us to learn to work together. I don't think that as women we had ever really worked just [as] women together. And you begin to kind of learn to organize within ourselves

and for ourselves and to be able to go into an organization and demand a say on what went on more so than we had ever done. And I think it was a shock to the males who didn't ever experience that and it was kind of a shock to us too, to find out we can, we could really get a say into how things were done.[110]

Although LMAW's numbers were small, its existence was important. During the eleven years of its existence it established a precedent for Mexican American women in politics. Through the efforts of Flores and Morín, LMAW became the first Mexican American women's political organization focused on developing and recognizing women's leadership. Given its members' simultaneous participation in multiple political organizations, LMAW served as a crucial bridging hub for fostering social, intellectual, and political connections between Mexican American women activists working on varying issues across the wider political landscape. The league also provided a space for their empowerment, as members came to recognize their potential for leadership and political power at the same time Mexican Americans across the Southwest began to engage in a new kind of activist politics and identity formation: Chicanismo.

The Emergence of the Chicano Movement

Flores and the members of LMAW certainly witnessed and experienced the changes occurring within their Los Angeles community as the Chicano movement emerged. Although undoubtedly influenced by the rise in social protest actions in the United States and throughout the world, the Chicano movement arose in response to a unique set of social, geographic, and economic experiences for ethnic Mexicans in the United States, experiences that members of LMAW knew at first hand.[111] For those active in the Chicano movement, four issues were most salient, and they coincided with the issues that Flores and Varela had documented in *Carta Editorial* and that LMAW and other organizations such as MAPA and the CSO had addressed as well: the stagnant economic status of Mexican Americans, racial discrimination, lack of political power, and educational inequalities.

Although the men and women who were part of the movement responded to these problems in a variety of ways, their actions were unified in a shared language, rhetoric, and ideology called Chicanismo. The ideology of Chicanismo was manifested in a discourse that represented a political worldview and the notion of common experiences as a Spanish-speaking, working-class, and indigenous people of the land who faced class and racial oppression in the imperial United States. In addition, Chicanismo was an ethnic identity based on the idea of a common homeland called Aztlán, around which people articulated goals of self-determination and collectivism. As an imagined indigenous homeland, Aztlán presupposed a direct connection to the Aztec (Mexica) peoples, while disregarding the indigenous peoples of the Southwest of the United States. The imagined representative of Chicanismo was typically male-identified, and the patriarchal nuclear family loomed large as the representative metaphor for community.

This "new" ideology of Chicanismo, as it has been represented in historical memory, would have sounded quite familiar to women such as Aceves, Flores, and Montañez Davis, to name a few, for they had been on the front lines of fighting for Mexican political representation and economic advancement for Mexican Americans, and against class and racial oppression for decades. Flores was also familiar with the notion of collectivism, owing to her co-writing many articles for *Carta Editorial* without by-lines, and with male dominance, given her membership in the Communist Party. Indeed, by the time Chicanismo arose, these women had already begun to fight for their own representation as Mexican American women. Flores and her LMAW sisters practiced their politics alongside and as part of the emergence of the movimiento, while also pushing a woman-centered agenda. In 1966 *Carta Editorial* reported on LMAW's Sixth Annual Awards Banquet, which honored Dolores Huerta and Lilia Aceves, selected "because they symbolize the active Mexican-American feminists who, six years ago, banded together to assess the female contribution to the community."[112]

In the late 1960s younger generations of Mexican Americans began to take stock of their place in U.S. society, aided by seasoned activists but also enacting a new militancy and new sense of entitlement as the nation's citizens. Although referred to as a single entity, the Chicano movement was in fact a variety of social, political, and cultural actions waged primarily in the southwestern United States. In 1967 Mexican American students, both in high school and in college, began to organize themselves in California and Texas into organizations such as the United Mexican American Students. They were inspired greatly by four different political developments, all of which have been heralded as the cornerstones of the Chicano movement: the United Farm Workers Union in California, headed by Cesar Chávez and Dolores Huerta, founded in 1962; La Alianza Federal de Mercedes (The Federal Alliance of Land Grants), founded in 1963 by Reies López Tijerina in New Mexico; the Crusade for Justice, established in 1966 by Rodolfo "Corky" Gonzales in Denver; and the Mexican American Youth Organization, founded in 1967 and headed by José Angel Gutiérrez in Texas.[113] The activists involved in all these organizations saw direct action strategies such as boycotts, picket lines, school walkouts, marches, and demonstrations as the prime vehicles for social change. They also established community newspapers to voice their complaints and to report on conditions in their neighborhoods.

In *Carta Editorial*, for instance, Flores commented on the East Los Angeles high school walkouts of March 1968. In "The Children Shall Lead Them" Flores supported the actions of the students, writing, "The young people showed the way when they boycotted their classes to demand a better education and the elimination of existing symbols of oppression and discrimination." In a rebuke to previous attempts to change educational conditions for Mexican American youth, she added, "Their action, it is agreed by all, will do more to expose the sorry conditions of the schools and the poor education Mexican-American students have been receiving than all of the efforts put forth in the last ten years by the Mexican-American educators who have been planning and holding conferences on these problems."[114]

This chapter has shown the deep and overlapping roots of the political activities of ethnic Mexican women in Los Angeles, women who knew who they were in gendered, raced, and classed terms. At this point, these women did not venture into questions of sexuality, which was to come later. As they became active in organizations designed to better their communities such as the CP, the CSO, and MAPA, they traversed the different streams of political activism of the time, creating critical linkages with multiple organizations and issues and picking up new frameworks, strategies, and skills that would inform their work for years to come. They took on political leadership in organizing CSO chapters and credit unions, for example, or organizing citizenship classes. Like Francisca Flores, they may have participated in journalism, in electoral politics, and more radical CP politics, but they also came to manifest a gender consciousness rooted in their lived experience as ethnic Mexican women. This new gender consciousness found expression in the pages of *Carta Editorial* as well as in the League of Mexican American Women. The latter may have been a small Los Angeles organization, but the ideology that undergirded its founding, that women should be recognized for their political activism and should be supported in their electoral endeavors, paved the way for future organizations that more clearly espoused a feminist ideology. The following chapter explores how the organization that developed from of the League of Mexican American Women, the Comisión Femenil Mexicana Nacional, also co-founded by Francisca Flores and many of the women profiled heretofore, continued the practice of bridging activism within the complicated terrain of the emerging Chicano movement.

2

Forging a Chicana Feminist Praxis

THE COMISIÓN FEMENIL MEXICANA NACIONAL, 1970–1976

Within ten years after the founding of the League of Mexican American Women, Francisca Flores seized an opportunity to build a national Chicana organization. The league had successfully united a small group of Los Angeles Mexican American women with an interest in improving their communities and fighting for their own political representation and power. Flores's experience as a member of the Communist Party and the Mexican American Political Association, as editor of the periodical *Carta Editorial*, and as co-founder of LMAW, to name a few, led her to believe that a national organization for ethnic Mexican women would be the most effective vehicle for enacting substantive political and economic change for women such as herself.[1] The opportunity for such an organization arose in 1970, when Flores and the women of LMAW, including seasoned political activists such as Simmie Romero Goldsmith and Josephine Valdez Banda, were invited to organize a women's workshop for the first Mexican American National Issues Conference in Sacramento, California. In order to recruit women to the workshop, Flores and Romero Goldsmith mailed flyers to a carefully selected list culled from their decades of political activism and placed individual phone calls to women in Los Angeles such as Lilia Aceves, Connie Pardo, Dolores Sánchez, and Grace Montañez Davis. Aceves recalled Flores's words from the phone call she received: "You know that Manuel Banda is having an issues conference in Sacramento. He's asked me to have a woman's workshop. If I have a woman's workshop, will you attend?" Aceves and many others readily agreed. Through these efforts, which utilized existing activist connections to ensure the presence of women's voices and gender analysis at a statewide conference on national issues, Flores and Romero Goldsmith succeeded in recruiting approximately forty women to the meeting in Sacramento. There, in October 1970, these women founded the Comisión Femenil Mexicana (CFM, Mexican Women's Commission), the first national Chicana feminist organization in the nation. In 1973 leaders of the organization would establish the Comisión Femenil Mexicana Nacional as the umbrella organization for all chapters.[2]

This chapter places the CFMN within the context of Chicano and women's movement politics and illustrates the ways in which the organization attempted to implement a Chicana feminist praxis during its first five years. The CFMN's praxis was rooted in the historical context of ethnic Mexican experiences in the United States, specifically those of local communities in Los Angeles. Informed by decades of ethnic Mexican activism, the CFMN emerged within the milieu of the Chicano movement as a space for Chicana self-determination and self-sufficiency that subverted cultural nationalist ideals about gender and set itself apart from the movement's rhetoric, most notably by not incorporating the term *Chicana* in its name. Women formed the CFMN in order to leverage power for themselves within movements they characterized as exclusionary. The founding members of the group included seasoned activists with decades of political experience as well as emerging voices in the Chicano movement. The organization's platform was consequently premised on four main goals: building leadership, disseminating information, problem-solving for Chicanas/Mexicanas, and networking with other women's organizations and movements. The most immediate concerns for the group, however, were the economic status of Mexican American women and building a sense of Chicana sisterhood. These goals were informed by members' experiential knowledge of conditions in their communities and the specific challenges faced by women; they drew together various ideological approaches to analyzing and addressing social issues. In doing so, the CFMN's goals bridged the priorities of its intergenerational group of founders to advocate for changes that would benefit Mexican American women broadly while also attempting to mobilize this demographic as a more powerful political constituency.

Although the CFMN expected unity among members as Mexican American women, along much the same lines that Chicano nationalists expected ethnic unity, this solidarity did not occur organically. Members of the organization sought to create a woman-friendly environment that would become conducive to enacting Chicana feminist goals by emphasizing mentoring among members of the organization itself, the women who worked in CFMN-sponsored community centers, and the women whom those centers served.[3] As they learned, solidarity and sisterhood required the hard work of transcending class, educational, and political and ideological differences that were not easily bridged. Struggles within the organization and its projects, in other words, tested the limits of bridging activism as Chicana feminist praxis. The difficulties that this women's organization faced were not unique to Chicanas, and the CFMN's experience is reminiscent of that of other feminist social movement organizations. For example, the Combahee River Collective, a black socialist feminist organization based in Boston from 1973 to 1975, experienced very similar tensions stemming from educational disparities within the group. Concerning the collective, Winifred Breines writes, "While their class origins were not so different, their education and inclinations created differences, perceived in class terms, among them."[4] The women of the CFMN did not foresee the challenges they would face in putting their Chicana feminist ideals into practice. They believed that their goals of economic self-determination for women would trump the differences of class as they founded and maintained organization chapters, the Chicana Service Action Center, and the Centro de Niños, a childcare center. In reality, matters were more complicated, yet by the mid-1980s the CFMN claimed twenty chapters and approximately three hundred members nationwide, with thirty members in the Los Angeles chapter. Though this was seemingly a small number of women given the wide range of their activities and their accomplishments, the fact that the CFMN could claim a membership that consisted of a representative sample of the Chicana population in California, coupled with the success of its community programs, made it stand out as one of the most important Chicana organizations of the twentieth century. By building on the bridging activism of women and men in the previous generation, including early women-centered organizations and groups, and focusing on the long-term sustainability of social service organizations as well as having a voice in the arena of policy making, the CFMN became a viable and powerful organization, emblematic of a growing Chicana movement.[5]

Founding the Comisión Femenil Mexicana Nacional

Flores and the women who heeded her call established the CFMN as a necessary space to leverage power in the Chicano movement and in society in general.[6] The women who attended the 1970 founding workshop of the CFM wanted to address issues specific to Chicanas that they saw in their own communities and within the Chicano movement. These included stereotypes about Chicanas and higher education, the need to acknowledge Mexican American women as important political figures, and negative attitudes about Chicanas in leadership roles. Most important, as Anna NietoGómez points out, the women "agreed that it was unlikely that they would achieve equal status in male-dominated organizations. They concluded that although they did not want to become separatists, they reluctantly agreed there was no other choice but to form their own women's organization."⁷ The founding resolution for the organization emphasized the lack of recognition for women's leadership and insisted on women's capabilities, experience, and willing participation in politics, with respect to the Chicano movement. The document explained the need for the organization: "THEREFORE, in order to terminate the exclusion of female leadership in the Chicano/Mexican movement and the community, be it RESOLVED that a Chicana/Mexican Women's Commission be established at this conference which will represent women, in all areas that Mexicans prevail." The founders resolved that the new organization would concentrate on the following goals: (1) "organizing women to assume leadership positions within the Chicano movement and in community life"; (2) serving as a vehicle to circulate news and information about the "work and achievement of Mexican/Chicana women"; (3) promoting programs "which specifically lend themselves to help, assist, and promote solutions to female type problems and problems concerning the Mexican family"; and (4) establishing "relationships with other women's organizations and movements." Notably, the text ignored any reference to the women's movement of the period, and this silence underscores the disconnect that the founders of the organization felt with the movement.⁸

The women who attended this founding meeting represented a variety of organizations, age groups, geographic regions, educational backgrounds, and levels of political influence and power, but they were linked in their commitment to address the issues that they as ethnic Mexican women faced. Those from Los Angeles represented many organizations including LMAW, MAPA, and the more radical and younger Movimiento Estudiantil Chicano de Aztlán (Chicano Student Movement of Aztlán, or MEChA, a college student organization). They elided simple categorization as a homogenous group of Chicanas, with factors such as educational background differing significantly among them. Francisca Flores was a member of both LMAW and MAPA. Because she spent her teenage years in a tuberculosis sanatorium, it is unclear how much formal education she received, but she did not attend college. Connie Muñoz and Lilia Aceves had high school educations, and both were also involved with LMAW and MAPA. Frances Bojorquez, representing MEChA, became the student body president at California State University, Los Angeles, in 1971.⁹ Among those from outside California were Polly Baca and Graciela Olivares. At the time, Baca, who had earned a degree in political science, was the assistant to the chair of the Democratic National Committee, and later, in 1974, was elected to the Colorado House of Representatives.[10] Olivares, the first Latina to earn a Juris Doctor from the University of Notre Dame, worked for the Arizona Office of Economic Opportunity at the time.[11] In sum, the diversity of age, socioeconomic status, political experience, and education among these women influenced the organization that the CFMN would become.

When they resolved to launch the Comisión Femenil Mexicana Nacional, the women consciously chose a name that identified their ethnic heritage but remained conservative in nomenclature. The Spanish name belied a subtle Chicano nationalist influence but did not include the term *Chicana*, placing the organization outside the realm of Chicano movement rhetoric. The name is almost a direct take on the federal Commission on the Status of Women and the Department of Labor's Women's Commission. These factors point to the group's interest in working with and moving into established political networks and reflected the institutional direction that the organization would take. The name also had a larger significance. This relatively conservative name may have been able to attract women who supported the cause but might not have joined if the name sounded more militant.[12]

Despite the veneer of this conservative and governmental-sounding name, the conference resolutions make clear that the women acknowledged the roots of the systemic socioeconomic disenfranchisement that ethnic Mexican women faced in the United States. Lilia Aceves recalled that the rationale for the name was historical. She said, "This used to be Mexico. And it's not only Mexicana because of Mexican women. It's not only named Comisión Mexicana Nacional because we're Mexicans. It's named that way because of ... the history of the Southwest."[13] Aceves acknowledged the common Chicano movement claim about United States imperialism when she recalled that California was once part of Mexico. And she broadened the scope by linking the organization's name to the history of the Southwest, not only Los Angeles or California. In defining the context for CFMN, Aceves also placed the origin of the organization within the ideological framework of the Chicano movement.

The CFMN emerged during the beginnings of a Chicana feminist moment and alongside a spectrum of Chicano movement organizations such as the Chicano Moratorium Committee and La Raza Unida Party. The women of Flores's generation projected a firm understanding of themselves as Mexican American political actors. Flores's activities especially reflect this confidence. In the same year that Flores and Romero Goldsmith launched the CFMN, Flores began to edit and publish *Regeneración*, which became one of the most influential Chicano movement publications. Although Flores had ceased editing and publishing *Carta Editorial*, it did not completely die since it maintained a presence as a regular column in *Regeneración*. Flores positioned *Regeneración* within the framework of Chicano movement discourse by using terms such as "La Raza" and "La Causa" in her editorials and articles, but it was not a staunchly Chicano publication. In fact, in the editorial of the first issue Flores explained that *Regeneración* writers would be from the "Mexican movement."[14] With Flores spearheading the workshop, the women at the Mexican American National Issues Conference were not invested in creating a new Chicana identity. They were interested in creating a new vehicle through which they would positively change the lives of all Mexican American women via material and political empowerment.

The organization also had deep roots in ethnic Mexican activism of the World War II era and immediate postwar period. The CFMN was akin to the majority of ethnic Mexican organizations. Conferences, whether national or regional, served as logical grounds for the formation of political organizations and as launching pads for new programs. Other organizations founded at conferences include the League of United Latin American Citizens (1929), El Congreso del Pueblo de Habla Español (1938), the Asociación Nacional Mexico-Americana (1949), and MAPA (1959). During the same period in which the CFMN was established, national Chicano conferences served as sites for the founding of MEChA in 1969 and La Raza Unida Party in 1970.[15] Despite women being active participants in establishing all these organizations, the CFMN remains the first separate women's organization founded by women, for women, at a national mixed-gender meeting.

Although women's workshops and auxiliaries had existed over the course of ethnic Mexican political activism in the twentieth century, holding a women's workshop at a Chicano movement conference was a new phenomenon. Indeed, at that time, forming a separate women's organization was anathema to the way many defined the ideas of Chicano unity, collectivism, and tradition.[16] This can be seen by comparing the outcomes of the women's workshop at the Mexican American National Issues Conference and the resulting establishment of the CFMN to the outcomes of women's workshops at other conferences occurring at about the same time.

In 1969, at the Chicano Youth Liberation Conference in Denver, Colorado, organized by the Crusade for Justice, an important movimiento community organization, the organizers had not planned a workshop specifically for women. The conference had attracted more than fifteen hundred attendees of all genders from across the nation who attended workshops ranging in topics from the arts to political prisoners to religion. After criticizing the lack of gender awareness, by which they meant attention to women's empowerment, fifty to seventy of the women in attendance organized a women's workshop and discussed their roles in the movement. They decided that their main goal was equality within the movement and that they did not want to form separate women-only organizations.[17] When the conference participants convened to hear reports from all the workshops, the spokeswoman for the Chicana workshop rose and declared, "It was the consensus of the group that the Chicana woman does not want to be liberated."[18]

When women at the Chicano Youth Liberation Conference made this statement, it was the first time gender as an issue potentially requiring attention surfaced in such a public forum in the fledgling movement. Maylei Blackwell notes, "This statement illustrates the contested and contestatory nature of Chicana feminism and the difficulty of articulating a new kind of Chicana political subject within the confines of an emergent, masculinist nationalism."[19] Issues of gender, which also emerged in the newspapers of the movement in the same year, stood between two poles. Within the Chicano movement women had been expected to choose ethnic and racial unity over gender-specific issues. Their other option was the Euro-American women's liberation movement, commonly referred to as second-wave feminism. Many Chicanas saw the mainstream feminist movement as normatively white, elitist, individualistic, and imbricated in colonialism with respect to nonwhite groups. Characterizations of this movement's members as man-hating lesbians also found traction.[20]

To Chicanas, Euro-American feminism did not address issues of race and class in their political ideologies and their critiques of sexism. Although the socioeconomic status of Chicanas stood below that of Chicanos, as a group Chicanos stood below whites. Accordingly, most Chicanas who experienced socioeconomic disadvantage on a daily basis during this period believed that the only way for the Chicano movement to succeed in its goals was for men and women to work together, not antagonistically and separately, as they saw Euro-American women do. Elizabeth Martínez, a Chicana activist from New Mexico, wrote in the influential newspaper *El Grito del Norte*, "For the Chicana, the three types of oppression [race, class, and gender] cannot be separated. They are all part of the same system, they are three faces of the same enemy."[21] Yet of these three faces, many women prioritized focusing on race and class as the best way to mobilize collective action toward ending the forms of discrimination and oppression they encountered. Moreover, Chicanas who saw Euro-American feminists decry the traditional family as oppressive to women often felt that this was not where they wanted their movement to head. Although Chicanas would soon analyze their own family situations and critique the roles of women more systematically in their activism, during this period the family was "a source of unity and our major defense against the oppressor."[22] For all these reasons, Chicanas at the Denver Youth Conference did not want to create a separate movement apart from Chicano men. What they did not realize when they made this calculation, however, was that a separate Mexican American women's organization, LMAW, had already existed for nine years in Los Angeles.

Issues of sexism and gender politics within the burgeoning Chicano movement also played a part in the disavowal of liberation by the Denver women's workshop. During the early years of the Chicano movement, cultural nationalist ideology placed men and women activists into defined "traditional" roles. Men became the movement's visible and public leaders while most women "provided their invisible labor by being the cooks, secretaries, and janitors," as noted by Sonia López.[23] Historically, however, many women had proved their merits as ideologues, newspaper journalists and editors, organizers, artists, and poets. Nevertheless, when Chicanas called attention to the inequality in gender roles or raised the question of women's rights or issues, they were accused of dividing the movement, of becoming man haters like Euro-American feminists, and of being influenced (or even colonized) by Euro-American feminist ideology. Thus, by disassociating themselves from white women, Chicanas could claim legitimacy within the movement with regard to the issues of gender equity in the leadership of organizations, women's roles, and reproductive rights. In this way, they affirmed the general Chicano view, which deemphasized the necessity of prioritizing women's liberation while still maintaining a firm belief that their male counterparts needed to change their attitudes about Chicanas in the movement. As Enriqueta Longeaux y Vásquez, a Chicana from New Mexico, wrote, "I understood why the statement had been made and I realized that going along with the feelings of the men at the convention was perhaps the best thing to do at the time."[24] What Longeaux y Vásquez understood was that "when direct confrontation on women's issues was not tactically possible and not politically strategic, many demands were negotiated below the surface of public movement spaces," in the assessment of Maylei Blackwell.[25] In other words, women utilized "hidden insurgencies" to cooperate with the men at the conference that would develop over time into a more forceful demand for Chicana rights.

The rapidity with which gender issues and the discourses of liberation moved to the forefront of activism over the next few years is illustrated by the second Chicano Youth Liberation Conference, held in 1970. When reporting back to the general conference, the women's workshop, this time planned before the start of the conference, called for "women to struggle for the liberation of La Raza and for 'self-determination' of the women." The resolution itself stated, "The Chicana women resolve not to separate but to strengthen Aztlán, the family of la Raza!"[26] These statements carried significant meaning. As Dionne Espinoza asserts, the statements "touched upon the possibilities of women's communities as well as more egalitarian family structures" but also "reasserted the priority for Chicanas to remain within the fold of the movement's familia rather than to create an autonomous feminist movement."[27] Liberation of La Raza as a whole was the end goal. Maylei Blackwell notes that the "family was seen as the foundational unit of revolutionary culture," which was "rigidly framed around the patriarchal, heterosexual family (also known as heteropatriarchy) as the organizing principle."[28] Chicano/a unity, therefore, was premised on the notion of a normatively heterosexual family bound by a cultural quest for social justice. As Chicana feminism arose, it sought to incorporate these family-oriented ideals, along with ideas of self-determination for Chicanas, within the Chicano movement, not apart from it. For women who had just begun to analyze their gendered place in society, a separate women's organization like the CFMN would not fit in to this paradigm.[29]

The founding resolution of the CFMN shows a notable departure from the family-based activism, or what some scholars have called "political familism," that had heretofore characterized the Chicano movement.[30] Beginning with the premise that Chicanas have a right to self-determination, the resolution articulates a feminist perspective with deep historical roots in ethnic Mexican women's socioeconomic, political, and racialized experiences in the United States. A shared consciousness of the gendered dimensions of power, including those in relation to race and class, had begun to emerge within Chicano movement circles between 1966 and 1970, with such groups as Las Hijas de Cuauhtémoc, the women's workshops at the Denver Youth Liberation Conferences in 1969 and 1970, and periodicals such as *El Grito del Norte* in New Mexico. As the first national women-only organization in the Chicano movement outside the confines of a university campus, the CFMN played an important role in shaping and articulating the sensibilities of Chicana feminist activists. It moved away from "feminism-in-nationalism," historian Emma Pérez's categorization of women's activism in both the Yucatán Feminist Congress and the Partido Liberal Mexicano during the Mexican Revolution, a category often used to describe Chicana activism during the Chicano movement. That is, in "feminism-in-nationalism," women activists create "their own spaces interstitially, within nationalisms, nationalisms that often miss women's subtle interventions."[31] As Dionne Espinoza notes in her work on the women of the Brown Berets, a Los Angeles Chicano movement organization, "such an articulation speaks from a place where women remain (perhaps strategically) within the terms offered to them."[32] Women who resolved to form the Comisión Femenil Mexicana Nacional indeed created their own space amid a movement that grappled with a new identity, a "third space," as articulated by Pérez. But they went beyond creating spaces; the CFMN claimed autonomy and a voice for itself and its members, unhindered by a rigid patriarchal nationalism yet also utilizing nationalism as a bridging strategy when necessary.[33]

At the Mexican American National Issues Conference in 1970, the participants in the women's workshop merged the topics that Flores had originally proposed into four main resolutions, representing broad goals that addressed issues of the invisibility of Mexican American women on local, state, and national levels, as well as childcare and reproductive rights, which Flores viewed as economic issues. They demanded that "proportionate and representative appointments of the Mexican-American women be made to the Commission on the Status of Women at the State and Federal levels." They declared that they would form networks, or bridges, with other women's organizations, that they supported "free and legalized abortions for all women who want or need them," and that "every Chicano community [should] promote and set up 24-hour day care facilities to service our people." Putting their own spin on ideologies of the heterosexual family as the unit of social change prominent in the Chicano movement, the women declared that the childcare centers should "reflect the concept of La Raza as the united family. With the basis being brotherhood, La Raza. Men and women, young and old, must assume the responsibility for the love, care, education, and orientation of all the children of azlan [sic]."[34] Although all the decrees addressed issues specifically related to women, the two regarding abortion and childcare resonated with demands usually referred to as women's issues by Chicano movement advocates and society at large. The women at the workshop couched their demands for choice and childcare in rhetoric familiar to the Chicano movement, equating the right to abortion with "self-determination" and demanding childcare centers that would instill ethnic pride.

After the 1970 conference, the CFMN established its base of operations in Los Angeles, building on and linking with the work already begun by LMAW. The CFMN was organized on two levels, with local chapters and a national office. Localities developed their own guidelines about how their chapter would be run, with oversight from a larger governing body, which also sponsored projects. Activist practices aimed at bridging different communities, generations, and ideologies were inherent in the organizing of CFMN chapters. For example, in 1971 Frances Bojorquez, a member of MEChA, established the first chapter of the CFMN at California State University, Los Angeles. During the same period, the members of the CFMN's governing body held meetings at the International Institute in Boyle Heights to discuss their vision for Chicanas in the community. Using networks established over years of political activism, the energy that had emerged from the Chicano movement, and a belief in their Chicana sisterhood, they began to work toward the goals of establishing job training and childcare centers, since these were two initiatives that were essential for women in their communities to determine their own economic futures.

Women of the CFMN

The women who comprised the CFMN's Los Angeles base represented a transgenerational group who came to the organization with prior political experience, an interest in women's issues in general, and a desire for social justice that was informed by their families of origin, organized labor, community organizing, or the Chicano movement. Francisca Flores drew women of her generation—those born in the United States before-World War II such as Connie Pardo (Muñoz), Lilia Aceves, Dolores Sánchez, and Grace Montañez Davis—into women's politics through networks already established in the Mexican American community of Los Angeles. They joined others who had been active in Mexican American politics, such as Josephine Valdez Banda and Simmie Romero Goldsmith. Women like Gracia Molina de Pick, who had feminist experiences in Mexico before settling in the United States, also participated. Others including Anna NietoGómez, Corinne Sánchez, and Frances Bojorquez joined the CFMN because of their involvement in the Chicano movement, which they had joined by way of student activism. By the 1970s most had been involved in other political struggles and organizations. From the 1970s onward, the CFMN and later the Chicana Service Action Center became the major outlets through which they sought to change society.

The members of the CFMN also represented a cross-section of women of Mexican origin in terms of age, education, and socioeconomic status. The majority had been born in the United States and were bilingual in Spanish and English. They were born between the 1910s and the 1950s, which meant a forty-year span between their ages. Representative of the ethnic Mexican population in Los Angeles and the country at that time, most were born into working-class families and lived in predominantly ethnic Mexican neighborhoods. With education their socioeconomic class changed over time, placing them in the middle class, but their activism would continue to be informed by their origins in the barrio.

Higher education, coupled with political education, propelled the organization to function in a somewhat bureaucratic manner. Although a few members were, like Francisca Flores, self-educated, most of the women had graduated from high school, with educational experiences ranging from Catholic school and public school to a Methodist missionary boarding school in Los Angeles. Data about the educational attainment of Mexican American women for this period are difficult to attain given that the U.S. Census did not disaggregate for gender under specific countries of origin. In 1970 a total of 24.2 percent of all Mexicans in the nation over the age of twenty-five had a high school diploma or more. If Mexican American women constituted half of this total, then approximately 12.1 percent of their number earned a high school diploma at the time. By 1980 high school graduation rates for Mexicans jumped 13.4 percent so that at most, 18.8 percent of Mexican American women over the age of twenty-five attained a high school diploma. Members of CFMN, both older and younger, had some junior college education. Some, such as Montañez Davis, Nava, and NietoGómez, earned graduate degrees. Toward the end of the 1970s, at least three attended law school: Sánchez, Pardo, and Aceves, the latter two when they were fifty years old. Thus, the women in the CFMN were in a select group of the population for which they were advocating. For example, in 1970 only 2.5 percent of the Mexican-origin population over the age of twenty-five in the nation had attained a college degree. By 1980 the number had only risen to 4.9 percent. Therefore, at most, 1.25 percent of Mexican-origin women had college degrees in 1970, and at most, 2.5 percent had attained such degrees by 1980.[35] Educational experiences exposed the women of CFMN to more business-oriented methods of conducting their meetings and executing their projects, which influenced the CFMN to have both a civic focus with an emphasis on political recognition and a community focus geared toward services for women. Education mattered in practical terms as well, since these goals often required grant writing and project administration skills to get off the ground.

The CFMN attracted members who came from families with strong community identification and with previous exposure to politics, especially by parents who had been involved in community, political, or labor union affairs, and these experiences influenced the community orientation that the organization would take in its programming.[36] Yolanda Nava's and Sandra Serrano Sewell's experiences manifest these varied types of exposure. Nava, born in 1944, graduated from Marshall High School in 1962 and went on to community college, eventually graduating from the UCLA with a B.A. and an M.A. in history. She experienced civic activism practiced by Latin American social elites in Los Angeles and different types of philanthropy because of her father, who was a writer-reporter for *La Opinión*, the city's major Spanish-language newspaper. When, at the age of eight, her parents divorced, Nava's mother struggled to make ends meet on a seamstress's wages, showing Nava a different kind of life than she had experienced with her father. Nava therefore had a broad knowledge of civic activism and a sensitivity to working-class struggles, both of which she brought to the CFMN—she was the first proponent of a childcare center as a main project for the organization.[37]

Born in 1948 in Lorain, Ohio, Sandra Serrano Sewell graduated from high school there in 1966 and although her parents, both high school graduates, emphasized the importance of education, they did not consider education past high school for their daughter. In 1967 Serrano Sewell left the Buckeye State on her own and without her parents' permission to live with relatives in Altadena, California. Her parents were members of the Progressive Party of the late 1960s and strong union supporters. They had many friends and acquaintances who had been visited by the Federal Bureau of Investigation owing to their membership in the Communist Party, which left a strong impression on Serrano Sewell. She recalled that in her hometown, "the FBI posted names of people that were potential communists on the utility poles," her father's name included. Indeed, Sewell's father, a veteran, lost his position as a union steward at the steel mill where he worked.[38] Of the parents of CFMN's early members, Serrano Sewell's were by far some of the most formally politically active, but typical in that they came out of organized labor and were sympathetic to trade unions.

Of the women who became core members of the CFMN, most had a strong female influence on their lives, most often their mothers, but also grandmothers and aunts who emphasized the importance of political activism. These influences ignited a consciousness about women's struggles. Besides Yolanda Nava, other members had single mothers. Lilia Aceves was reared by her mother, a laundry worker. After Dolores Sánchez's parents divorced, her mother worked in the garment industry to support the family.

The tradition of Mexican Americans in trade unions and of mothers who worked outside the home both played a major part in the socialization of many of the women who became involved in the organization. Connie Pardo's parents had experience working as domestics, in laundries, and in construction, and were involved in union activities.[39] Corinne Sánchez and Anna NietoGómez, born in San Bernardino in 1946 and 1947, respectively, similarly were exposed to union activity via their parents' work in the railroads in that city. NietoGómez's mother worked as a clerk for the Santa Fe Railroad, and her father worked as a quality control inspector at Norton Air Force Base. NietoGómez's mother was a member of the Railroad Workers Association and the AFL-CIO. Sánchez's father was employed by the railroad and was a union man while her mother worked in housekeeping at country clubs.[40]

NietoGómez and Sánchez also represent a significant younger cohort of members who came from a background in Chicano movement politics. Both had attended California State College, Long Beach, where they had been active members of MEChA. In a 1996 interview NietoGómez recalled that in MEChA,

> [men] would harass you . . . make fun of your idea and have you defend it to the max. Your ideas had to be more well-informed than anybody else's. They would come and sexually harass you and say comments about your dress or your body or start flirting with you. Or diminish your thoughts, your ideas, your contributions.[41]

After these kinds of sexist experiences in MEChA, Sánchez, NietoGómez, and other women students formed one of the first Chicana student organizations, Las Hijas de Cuauhtémoc, at Long Beach State.[42] After graduation, NietoGómez and Sánchez joined the staff of the Chicana Service Action Center in 1974. At the time, NietoGómez was an assistant professor in the Chicano Studies Program at California State University, Northridge, and during her summers she worked at CSAC writing grants.[43] By way of CSAC, both NietoGómez and Sánchez joined the Los Angeles chapter of the CFMN.

The Mexican American women who became members of the CFMN via patterns of bridging activism discussed above believed that feminism had to be tied to their communities, and this belief influenced the kinds of bridging activism they then pursued going forward. They came to this conclusion on the basis of their personal experiences, which for some included years of political activism prior to the 1960s. Most of the core members of the CFMN shared certain characteristics. They were born in the United States, many of them to parents who were also native born. Most were influenced both by the union activity of their parents and reared by strong women. Aided by women of an older generation, younger activists learned political strategy. Above all else, they empowered themselves by doing for themselves and other Chicanas what neither the larger Chicano movement nor the women's liberation movement provided. In doing so, they worked together to create a powerful social, cultural, and institutional force that advanced the cause of Chicana liberation within Los Angeles and beyond.

The Chicana Service Action Center

The establishment of the Chicana Service Action Center stands as a key achievement of the CFMN's feminist praxis because the center represented the fundamental ideals of Flores's vision as it had been developed in her decades of bridging activism: women-centered, community-based, grounded in economics, and using the "system" to make it work. It was a job training and employment center specifically for Chicanas and Latinas in the community, born through networking, strategizing, timing, and the effective use of federal institutions. In 1972 Flores, along with one hundred other Latinas and Chicanas from across the country, attended the Consultation for Spanish-Speaking Women (CSSW) in Phoenix, Arizona, sponsored by the Women's Bureau of the U.S. Department of Labor.[44] Established in 1920, this was the Women's Bureau's first meeting with Spanish-speaking women, and for the first time ethnic Mexican women became part of a national conversation with access to government institutions.

The Women's Bureau envisioned the meeting as a networking opportunity for Latina leaders and as a way to disseminate information regarding state and federal sex discrimination laws.[45] Women at the meeting, however, did not take kindly to an agenda solely determined by the Women's Bureau and halted the proceedings to meet on their own. One observer commented, "It is not surprising that the Department of Labor is still running around planning and putting on programs without planning or participation of those involved." The Spanish-surnamed women met in state delegations and returned to the meeting with specific resolutions for the Women's Bureau ranging from funding another conference specifically for Spanish-speaking women and an additional conference for women of color, broadening employment opportunities for women to include bilingualism as an asset, and providing funding for programs specifically targeted for Latinas/Chicanas.[46]

As with the Mexican American National Issues Conference, where women established the CFMN, Flores and her counterparts saw the CSSW as a prime opportunity to launch their next project. When they arrived in Phoenix, Flores already had a proposal for a job training center drafted. Amid the change in program that occurred at the CSSW, Flores and other CFMN members met with Edward Aguirre, regional director of the Department of Labor, a connection made by Montañez Davis, who at the time worked for the Los Angeles office of the department as a field representative specializing in manpower development. Aguirre expressed support for the women's imperative as long as they provided him with a proposal.[47] Unbeknownst to Aguirre, Flores had prepared well and "open[ed] her purse and presented him with the proposal!"[48] With a subsequent grant of $50,000 from the Department of Labor, Flores and the other women established the Chicana Service Action Center, with Lilia Aceves as its first director.[49]

After receiving its startup funds in 1972, CSAC began its course as a full-fledged job training and employment center for Mexican American women in the Los Angeles area. The CFMN established the CSAC in the Boyle Heights area, and between August 1972 and February 1973 it served more than two hundred women.[50] From 1973 through 1977 the Department of Labor, the Comprehensive Employment and Training Act, the governor of California's discretionary funds, and a Los Angeles city grant provided financial support. Francisca Flores, founder of both the organization and the center, worked as executive director of CSAC until 1982.[51]

When these women launched the Chicana Service Action Center, they hoped to teach the women who would utilize the center to use "the system" to their advantage. They also hoped to build leadership among the women they served to help resolve the social and economic problems faced by others like them. The center's work also elucidates the skill of Flores and her generation of women in leveraging power and obtaining federal funds to meet their goals. The center fulfilled the CFMN's dream to achieve Chicana sisterhood that would materialize into fully functioning institutions.

Developing the Comisión Femenil

By 1973 the CFMN was already a formidable organization able to harness crucial networks and government funds, as the success of CSAC illustrates. Operating as both a Chicana political organization and a community service foundation, the CFMN had made remarkable headway in demonstrating how a women-led organization could successfully bridge, in theory and practice, the Chicano movement's focus on collective action for Mexican American advancement and feminist visions of empowerment for women. That year the CFMN broadened its political and organizational efforts; it testified on behalf of Mexican American women before the California Commission on the Status of Women (CCSW), organized a membership conference, and founded a child care center.

Testifying before the CCSW in February 1973 proved to be a turning point for the organization and its members, especially Lilia Aceves, Josefina (Jo) Banda, Gloria Molina, and Yolanda Nava. In late 1972 and early 1973, during the height of advocacy for the California legislature to ratify the Equal Rights Amendment, the state women's commission planned a series of hearings in Sacramento, San Francisco, and Los Angeles. When Flores learned that hearings would take place in Los Angeles, she mobilized Aceves, Banda, Molina, and Nava to conduct research on a variety of topics in order to testify. Nava, for example, would testify on the employment situation of Chicanas in the state.[52] The hearings served as a space for a variety of women from across the state to voice issues important to them in relation to state policies and laws, ranging from discrimination in employment, domestic violence, childcare, and divorce statutes.[53] Of particular importance to women of color who spoke at the hearings was their lack of representation on the state commission itself.

For most of the women whom Flores recruited to testify, it was their first exposure to the world of state politics. In addition to her specific topic at the hearings, Molina took up the cause of representation, or lack thereof. This was the first time Molina, future state assemblywoman and Los Angeles County Supervisor, had spoken in such a venue. At the hearing, she demanded that Mexican American women be represented on the commission. Present at the hearing were Richard Alatorre, a member of the California State Assembly, and Phil Montes, western regional director for the U.S. Civil Rights Commission. The members of the CFMN at the hearing approached Alatorre and Montes regarding the question of representation. Working together, the women presented a list of potential candidates for appointment, including a republican, Carolyn Orona. Orona, who described herself as passionate about women's equal rights but "not a militant," had a degree in occupational therapy but had moved to a career in human resources.[54] As a result of the CFMN members' and other women's testimony at the hearings, and through the influence of the CCSW, Governor Ronald Reagan appointed Orona to the commission, the first Chicana ever appointed as a fully vested member.[55] She later became a member of the CFMN. Nava recalled it as a

> real pivotal point ... and we developed confidence because here we said we should have a woman on that commission—a Chicana woman on that commission—and within a matter of weeks we got one. So we really were feeling our hopes, and after that, there was no stopping us because all you had to do was have a strategy and plan and do the work and you achieve. So by putting us in those situations where we could speak out, that was Francisca's way of developing leadership.[56]

This experience demonstrated the potential success of the CFMN and the importance of utilizing established political networks and cultivating relationships with state entities and male politicians to secure financial and political support in the future. Going forward, those pursuing Chicana liberation would be able to more easily pursue this path of bridging activism, utilizing connections to the political establishment created during the 1970s to leverage representation and resources.

Coming off the phenomenal success of the testimony before the CCSW, the CFMN held its first national and membership conference in Goleta, California, in May 1973. A public media event, a membership drive, and a constitutional convention, the gathering endeavored to attract women who could serve the organization in terms of leadership as well as recruit a variety of women who could provide important input on political and economic issues. It offered panels on alcohol and drug abuse, childcare, education, employment and strikes, immigration and deportation, media, welfare legislation, and family planning. In order to attract a wide variety of women, the conference organizers invited Los Angeles assemblyman Richard Alatorre and Mexican American actress Carmen Zapata to deliver the keynote addresses. Although only 136 women pre-registered for the conference, approximately 800 attended. Of the pre-registered women, almost half hailed from the Los Angeles area, and about one quarter came from San Diego. The pre-registered women from the Los Angeles area worked predominantly in education or community and social services, or were students. The rest of the women were either unemployed, were "housewives," worked as professionals in other fields, or did not specify their occupation.[57]

For many women, the conference touched their lives in profound ways. Above all, it influenced their identification as Chicanas. Sandra Serrano Sewell's experience provides an example of this life-changing impact. In 1973 Serrano Sewell, a twenty-five-year old married homemaker from Pasadena with two small children, heard about the CFMN's founding conference from her husband, who had read about the meeting in a newspaper article. Although Serrano Sewell had participated in Democratic Party politics and the Peace and Freedom Party since 1969, she was hesitant to attend the CFMN conference because of negative experiences with women's groups in the past. In a 2011 interview she recollected that in order to pay the registration fees for the conference, her husband sold his blood, "and that's how I got the money for the registration and went . . . and just was totally blown away and was totally excited." It was the first time Serrano Sewell had been in the company of so many Mexican American women of different walks of life. She reflected, "It was just such a wonderful group of women that it was so exciting, and I thought, 'Oh, my God, this is, like the best thing on Earth.'"[58] Serrano Sewell became president of the organization from 1977 to 1979 and director of the Centro de Niños.

The conference had a similarly transformative impact on Gloria de la Torre-Wycoff; indeed, she recalled that event as the point at which she became a Chicana feminist. Until 1972 she had been active in various political campaigns and antiwar efforts, but the CFMN meeting was her first women's conference. De la Torre-Wycoff noted

> The different speakers were so strong in their commitment to their Chicanisma and for all. For our community and for our families. And that's where I think

the core was for me, is that yes, you're there as an independent woman, as a Chicana, as a feminist in this political ambience. But you're also fighting for the rights of other women, and other workers, which means families. And I think that was probably, you know, one of the pivotal things for me.[59]

De la Torre-Wycoff's articulation of her feminism emphasizes the importance of a community- and family-oriented philosophy, which at the time contrasted sharply with the perceived individualist nature of the white middle-class-dominated women's liberation movement. Her words echo the ideas of the Chicano movement about the importance of the family as the unit of social change. But she placed equal importance on the significance of "Chicanisma," the sensibility of being Chicana, and for her, the empowerment of women. De la Torre-Wycoff, known at the time as Gloria Moreno-Wycoff, would go on to serve as president of the CFMN from 1980 to 1981.

Challenges to Sisterhood

Whereas the conference was a positive experience for many of the attendees, for others, inclusion within the fold of the conference, and hence, the CFMN, became a point of contention and revealed the conflict amid intended ethnic, racial, and gender unity. Divergence between women was not a new phenomenon at a Chicana conference. Two years earlier, at the first national Chicana conference, the Conferencia de Mujeres por La Raza, held at the YWCA in Houston, Texas, the women split into two opposing factions, and each group presented and then disseminated its own list of resolutions.[60] Almost six hundred women representing more than twenty-three states and entities such as "student organizations, unions, the Raza Unida Party, the land grant movement, and community organizers, among others," attended sessions such as "Sex and the Chicana—Noun and Verb," "Marriage: Chicana Style," and "The Feminist Movement: Do We Have a Place In It?" The split and walkout reflected the heterogenous nature of Chicana feminisms. Maylei Blackwell asserts that the conference "is a rich site from which to understand the political fault lines of early Chicana feminism. Many of the conflicts at the conference were the result of differences within regional political cultures, gendered movement discourses, and organizational tactics, which ultimately disrupted the emergence of a national Chicana movement during the 1970s."[61] The ideological divide between the two camps was evident in the resolutions that each put forth. The group that remained at the YWCA affirmed the following resolutions: support of birth control and family planning, the establishment of community day-care facilities open twenty-four hours a day, a communications campaign against experimentation with birth control drugs on Chicanas in San Antonio, Texas, and a call for drastic changes to the Catholic Church and its relation to Chicano communities. They also declared that their problems as Chicanas differed from those of other women and that they experienced discrimination from men within the movement.[62] Those put forth by the group that walked out addressed issues that were not specific to Chicanas concerning the Vietnam War, *El Plan de Aztlán*, Chicano media, and Chicanos in the Midwest, in addition to asserting that "men, women, and children—la familia—[should] work together with mutual respect in all efforts related to el movimiento" and that more needed to be done for Chicanas in penal institutions.[63] Much has been written about the conference that relies on the binary categorization of "feminists" (those who stayed) versus "loyalists" (those who left) by Chicana feminist and scholar Anna NietoGómez. But as Blackwell notes, the conference defies simple categorization. Indeed, "the split shaped the political terrain for years to come, exacerbating political divisions to such an extent that it disrupted the sense of a collective identity and political agenda. Some activists in women's groups continued to work together, other organizations fell apart."[64] The conference stands as one of the most important moments and spaces in which Chicanas engaged in consciousness-raising to articulate a common set of concerns. Published in movement periodicals across the Southwest, the resolutions from La Conferencia de Mujeres por La Raza declared and affirmed Chicana beliefs and experiences as active participants and leaders in the Chicano movement, validated and addressed the importance of gender-specific issues, and called for a shift in the ideology about women's roles in the home and family.[65] In this context, the 1973 CFMN conference stands out as a renewed attempt to bridge women's differences and form a collective national Chicana feminist organization.

The CFMN conference took place two years after the Houston conference. In essence, it was a constitutional convention that "formally established the Comisión Femenil, adopted a constitution, and elected officers." It was also the first national conference hosted by a Chicana feminist organization. It attracted as many as eight hundred women from a broad spectrum of experiences, from stay-at-home mothers to students to union activists who sought an organization that would represent their interests as Chicanas. The women reaffirmed the goals of the original resolution to establish the CFM: leadership development in the Chicano movement and society at large, publicization of Chicana accomplishments, attention to women's issues, and establishment of networks with other women's organizations.[66] The attendees achieved the goals of establishing a constitution and electing national officers, but bridging grassroots organizing with bureaucratic institution building proved difficult.⁶⁷ Two issues specifically hampered the spirit of sisterhood envisioned by the organizers: voting on resolutions and the bureaucratic nature of Robert's Rules of Order. First, CFMN members, who wore orange nametags, could vote on resolutions, but nonmembers, who wore white nametags, could not. Second the use of Robert's Rules of Order may have further alienated guests not familiar with these procedures. Women familiar with the rules and who had orange nametags viewed the others as inexperienced, while guests with white nametags saw the members as bourgeois.⁶⁸ Differences in educational level between those with formal educations and those without undergirded the conflict.⁶⁹

The conflicts at the meeting influenced its outcomes and raised questions about the future endeavors of the organization. Whereas previous Chicana conference resolutions had been published in a variety of movement newspapers, the periodical record is quite silent on the outcomes of the CFMN's first national conference. In addition, the archival record is silent about the conference itself. The participants proposed approximately thirty resolutions to be voted on by the voting body, but it appears that voting on resolutions did not take place. In a document titled "Responsibilities of the Comision Femenil Mexicana Nacional, Inc.," the author wrote that there were "no convention reports, minutes or financial report for the 1973 convention."⁷⁰ Post-conference evaluations from participants expressed frustration at a lack of clarity in the mission of the group. In August, three months after the conference, the executive committee of the national organization agreed to send all resolutions to the membership for their vote on the top priorities. On receiving members' responses, the leadership group would take on one to two issues per year.⁷¹ It is unclear whether the group followed through. The silence in the aftermath of the national conference could have signaled disillusionment that such a promising conference resulted in the spotlighting, and potential entrenchment of, differences between women. It also could have signaled the difficulties of building an organization from the ground up through voluntary labor. Regardless of these challenges, the 1973 conference established the national arm of the organization, which would serve as the umbrella organization for all local chapters.

The CFMN's idealism continued to be tested in the years after the conference, especially regarding the Chicana Service Action Center. Although CSAC continued to grow and to receive government funding, the center serves as an example of how the emerging bureaucratic and hierarchical models of the CFMN and CSAC collided with the vision of a collective and harmonious leadership and a more grassroots style.⁷² The CFMN's board of directors oversaw CSAC's operations, although the center operated with its own leaders and staff. In late 1974 Flores, who spent most of her time working at CSAC, vocalized a growing antagonism between the center's staff and the board of directors of the CFMN. She questioned the leadership of the board and called for a general meeting "so that the membership can have input on how their organization is being served."[73] The staff of CSAC saw itself as on equal terms with the board, but due to the bureaucratization of the CFMN, which had resulted from the responsibility of administering grants, a hierarchical structure had begun to emerge between the two organizations, with the CFMN board at the helm.

The goals of maintaining a broad sisterhood conflicted with this emerging bureaucracy. Lack of communication and conflicts over who was responsible for CSAC came to a head between July 1974 and January 1975. During this time the CFMN did not have a fully functioning board of directors; this situation meant that CSAC did not have CFMN oversight during a critical time because the center was in the process of incorporating. Taking matters into her own hands, Flores initiated the process herself and the center incorporated with the State of California at the end of 1974, unbeknownst to the few members of the CFMN board. Lack of communication also led to growing enmity between the organizations. Further compounding this enmity, the CFMN board asserted that as the parent body of CSAC, it maintained responsibility for signing new Comprehensive Employment and Training Act contracts with the City and County of Los Angeles. When the center's staff disagreed with this interpretation, the board requested an audit of CSAC's entire history. The board also implemented a training program for the members of the center's new board of directors and drafted an official agreement between the two entities outlining their affiliation.[74] Although it was attempting to clarify the leadership roles for both organizations by implementing board training and defining the relation between the two bodies, Flores and CSAC staff saw these demands as unmerited attacks on their leadership and criticized the CFMN leadership for overstepping its boundaries in the midst of a leadership vacuum within its own structure. Though formally an entity of the CFMN, the center had operated on a quasi-independent basis since its establishment, with its own executive director and staff. The conflict pitted two groups of women against each other who had seen each other as equals with the same vision.

The issue at stake for CSAC became autonomy—the authority to negotiate and sign contracts with institutions and government agencies on its own, especially because its staff had put in the hard work of making the center a success. In January 1975 directors of CSAC and the CFMN agreed to transfer city and county contracts under the Comprehensive Employment and Training Act directly to CSAC, eliminating the CFMN as liaison. But later that month, Connie Muñoz (nee Pardo), chair of the center, called an open meeting of the center, its executive board, and members of the Comisión board to address the relationship between CSAC and the CFMN. At this meeting, where approximately twenty people were in attendance, CSAC staff members voiced their belief that the Comisión was still attempting to control the center's direction. By this time the CFMN board had hired an attorney, Ilbert Phillips, who later wrote that at the meeting, "Hostility crackled in the air."[75]

At this meeting, Yolanda Nava, president of the CFMN, attempted to slow down the process of the transfer of contracts so that both organizations could be fully informed of the process itself. In the view of CSAC's board of directors, however, Nava was reneging on the agreement made on January 27 to transfer the contracts. In the ensuing debate, the center's board expressed little confidence in the bureaucracy of the CFMN. In their opinion, the Comisión had no standing to make any of these demands, especially that of an audit, because the organization itself had encountered difficulties maintaining its nonprofit corporate status due to an administrative oversight.[76]

After a closed-door meeting between the CSAC board of directors and members of the CFMN board, the open meeting resumed. According to Phillips, "People were screaming and hollering at each other. Yolanda [Nava] was attempting to tell the Comisión story, but very few wanted to hear it. The staff was threatening to strike and destroy the program."[77] In the end, the situation was somewhat resolved by a letter of transfer signed by Nava and Muñoz. They also signed a letter of intent to agree, which stated that in February 1975 CSAC would "expedite for the Center the transfer of all rights, obligations and audited liabilities from Comisión to Center." In addition, the CSAC board of directors agreed to an audit of the program.[78]

As of March 1975 CSAC had not yet made any transfer of "rights, obligations and audited liabilities." Phillips sent Muñoz a letter stating that the CFMN would "institute whatever legal procedures [were] necessary to enjoin Center Inc. from encroaching upon the property rights of the Comisión and unlawfully running [the] Comisión's program."[79] Phillips also sent a letter to Steven Porter, the assistant director of the Manpower Training Division, which disbursed the funds for CSAC, requesting that the city stop sending the center any funds.[80]

The conflict between CSAC and the CFMN reveals that although both groups may have truly wanted to provide a job training and employment center for Mexican American women, a bureaucratic structure that placed the two entities at odds with one another hindered this process. Indeed, sisterhood broke down precisely because of assumptions, miscommunications, and a power struggle. As CSAC saw it, the CFMN attempted to micromanage how the center ran its program, and its staffers believed that the Comisión's members had proved that they could not oversee their own organization because their bureaucratic mismanagement cost them their nonprofit status. On the other hand, the CFMN's members believed that they were responsible and liable for the actions of CSAC, which required the Comisión's oversight. Each group viewed the other as irresponsible, but it appears that the CFMN's leaders began to see themselves as more knowledgeable than those who ran CSAC, which led to a fracture in the sisterhood envisioned by the organization's leaders. The center formally split from the CFMN in 1975, an example of the difficulties of feminist praxis within a previously aligned group of women.

El Centro de Niños

A similar breakdown of sisterhood also emerged with the Centro de Niños, the childcare center established by the CFMN in 1973. The conflict at Centro de Niños provides yet another example of the challenges that the CFMN faced in administering its projects. The board of directors was trying to run a childcare center to fulfill one of the main goals of the CFMN and the CSAC: to provide women with quality childcare so that they could work outside the home and attain economic autonomy. Yet the women they employed, who may have needed childcare themselves, struggled with the organization about issues such as pay and union recognition. From its founding, the center confronted financial and leadership issues. As early as 1974, its finances were in disarray and its workers' salaries were cut. Sometimes, workers were not paid at all. Under these conditions, the employees of the childcare center, some drawing on their or their families' previous labor movement experience, attempted to join the California Federation of Teachers (CFT).

This desire to organize created a deep rift between the center and the CFMN. The board of directors believed it was working in the best interest of the center. Those who worked there believed their working conditions called for unionization. The Centro de Niños employees began their unionization in February 1976, but according to Raoul Teilhet of the CFT, they had been "faced with a series of union busting tactics." Referring to the center's board of directors, which was made up of members of the CFMN, center staff had reported to the CFT that they had "been humiliated, intimidated, fired, suspended without pay and in other ways disciplined, while their grievances have not been processed."[81] In addition, they had not always received their paychecks as scheduled. According to Rose Ungar, an organizer with the CFT, an attempt to drop off flyers announcing a union meeting in July 1976 highlighted tensions when the center's administrator did not allow her to leave the flyers.[82]

Although three groups were involved in this dispute, the staff of the Centro de Niños viewed CFMN entities as one unit. Employees of the center felt that their complaints about working conditions had gone unheard by the CFMN writ large. The center's board of directors requested that the CFT's representative, Rose Ungar, be replaced because they believed that Ungar had created the tensions by means of "disruptions and misinformation and has tremendous problems in interpreting the information we relay to her."[83] In addition, the CFMN's executive board decried any charges of being anti-union. In the words of CFMN president Gloria Molina, "The executive committee [of the Centro de Niños] voted against the holding of an election since they felt collective bargaining would financially ruin the center. CFMN Inc[.] rejected the recommendation and voted for an election."[84] Molina responded to criticism by saying, "Perhaps we inherited a traditional structure. But we're not a group of Chicanas that's out to oppress people. We wouldn't treat our employees like that."[85]

By August the center's workers had officially become members of the Early Childhood Federation, California Federation of Teachers, Local 1475 (AFL-CIO). The difference between both boards' responses to the union drive reflected the difficulties of bridging the employee-employer dynamic. The hierarchical structure gave both entities oversight of the center in the eyes of its employees. As one employee stated, "In fact, their whole attitude is out of touch with working people."[86] Although the CFMN certainly used its knowledge of government channels for financial backing and provided desperately needed childcare services to Mexican American communities through the Centro de Niños, the bureaucracy necessary to establish the CFMN as a sustainable organization created a rift with the very women it hoped to serve. In the long run, however, the Centro de Niños resolved these issues, survived, and is still in existence today.

When women established the Comisión Femenil Mexicana in 1970 and the Comisión Femenil Mexicana Nacional in 1973, they did so with the specific goals of empowering ethnic Mexican women in Los Angeles and nationwide, both politically and economically. Informed by the years of political activity and experience of Francisca Flores, Lilia Aceves, and others, as well as the experiences of women in the newly emerged Chicano movement, the Comisión Femenil sought to put the ideals of political and economic self-determination into practice. In a reformist tradition of utilizing the existing political and economic system to support their goals, they succeeded in establishing social service institutions for Mexican American and Latina women. By establishing a childcare center and job training and employment centers, in addition to political lobbying, the CFMN attempted to change the social and economic conditions that, they believed, kept Mexican American and Latina women in low-paying jobs with no hope for quality childcare.

Although women in the CFMN used these political experiences to garner the finances and political support to fulfill their visions, the bureaucracy involved in managing CSAC and the Centro de Niños caused conflicts in the CFMN. In the case of CSAC, the complicated processes of city grants, incorporation, and managing finances erupted in a battle that pitted the national CFMN organization against the center's staff. In the case of the Centro de Niños, the staff's desire to unionize again placed the managing body of the CFMN in conflict with their own staff. Both of these events fragmented the imagined Chicana sisterhood that forged the CFMN in the first place.

The events of the first half of the 1970s certainly tested the sisterhood that the Comisión Femenil had imagined at its founding, yet the organization stands as an important moment of Chicana sisterhood in practice. After its first national conference in 1973, the organization continued to hold an annual event to both recruit members nationwide and to discuss the salient issues facing Chicanas and Latinas. The organization served as a crucial training ground for Chicanas in politics. In 1982 Gloria Molina, who served as CFMN president from 1975 through 1977, was elected to the California State Assembly, the first Chicana to attain that office. Leticia Quezada, CFMN president from 1981 to 1982, was elected to the Los Angeles Unified School Board in 1987. As scholars Sonia R. García and Marisela Márquez conclude, the Comisión Femenil's goal of Chicana representation in elected office "solidified the Comisión's place in history by creating a 'scaffolding effect,' whereby Chicanas elected to public office both represented Chicanas in the political arena and provided assistance to other Chicanas seeking public office."[87] In 1975 members of the organization, along with other Chicanas from across the nation, took their organizing to the international level by attending the first International Women's Year Conference in Mexico City. How they traversed an international feminist landscape both politically and personally, and the ways in which their activities became part of the broader pattern of bridging activism they forged in their quest for Chicana liberation, is the subject of Chapter 3.

3
"We Would Go There and Be Part of a Great Audience"

CALIFORNIA CHICANAS AND INTERNATIONAL
WOMEN'S YEAR, MEXICO CITY, 1975

In the early months of 1975 Celia Herrera Rodríguez, a re-entry student at California State University, Sacramento, regularly attended Communist Party meetings held in northern California. At one of the meetings she heard about and was intrigued by the forthcoming International Women's Year Conference, to be held in Mexico City that June. With few financial resources, but determined to attend, she called Frances Romero, a friend who was active with El Teatro Campesino, and asked if she would also like to attend. The two women gathered their welfare and financial aid monies (Herrera Rodríguez was the mother of two young children, and both women were students) and hitchhiked from Fresno to the United States–Mexico border. From there, they walked to the bus station in Tijuana, Baja California, and took a bus destined for Mexico City. When they arrived two days later, the women, with four dollars left to their names, found their way to the house of Herrera Rodríguez's mother-in-law. In order to eat, Herrera Rodríguez, an artist, sold her sketches at the conference. In fact, this is how the women managed to make enough money for their trip back to California.

Although it was challenging and expensive to get there, Herrera Rodríguez wanted to attend the conference precisely because it was in Mexico. As a child she had traveled frequently to her family's hometown there, and as a young adult had visited the pyramids and other landmarks. Nonetheless, she recalled, "Well, . . . I really felt that I knew nothing about Mexico and that yet it was home. There was something there that . . . had a spiritual feeling to it . . . and I wanted to go." Her desire to know more, specifically via the International Women's Year Conference, was both cultural and political. Herrera Rodríguez wanted to experience Mexico on her own terms, through the political ideologies that she had come to embrace. She also sought connection with other women. She recalled that what drove her was "the idea of meeting women from all over. That was my only expectation. That I would be able to hear them and see them and talk to them and experience their issues."[1]

Herrera Rodríguez and Romero joined thousands of women and men, official government representatives and unofficial participants, when they descended on Mexico City in June 1975 for twelve days for the first United Nations–sponsored International Women's Year Conference and Tribune. The IWY activities, which included the official conference, with thirteen hundred official government representatives, and a tribune with approximately five thousand independent participants and representatives of nongovernmental organizations (NGOs), represented the culmination of more than thirty years of work by women organizing internationally and within the United Nations. Although women had called for an international conference in the era immediately after World War I, and later at the first session of the U.N. Commission on the Status of Women (CSW) in 1946, it was not until 1972 that the U.N. General Assembly approved an international women's year.[2] Then, in December 1974, the General Assembly approved the IWY program itself, including the inaugural conference.[3] At world conferences held before the IWY such as the 1974 Population Conference in Bucharest and the 1974 Food Conference in Rome, NGOs had participated in separate U.N.-sponsored venues and in the conference itself. Given this recent history, as a result of NGOs' lobbying for participation and because conference planners knew that many non-official participants would travel to Mexico City, officials planned a separate public meeting called the tribune, organized by and in cooperation with several NGOs affiliated with the United Nations.[4]

Among the thousands of women who attended the IWY tribune were between two hundred and three hundred Mexican American women from across the United States, representing another phase in the ongoing development of Chicana feminist consciousness and the bridging activism that continued to propel the Chicana liberation movement forward and in new directions.[5] The Chicanas from Los Angeles and other parts of California who attended the conference did so as part of organizations in which they participated. For Herrera Rodríguez, the connection had been Communist Party meetings. For Anna NietoGómez, it was her participation in the Comisión Femenil in Los Angeles, as it was for many of the women profiled in this chapter. By connecting their local struggles for recognition on regional, state, and national stages to the struggles of women worldwide, they hoped to be seen and heard on an international stage. They also wanted to make connections with Mexican feminists and learn from them. NietoGómez recalled,

"One of our goals was to meet women from the Mexican Women's Movement and see what was going on there. . . . What were their ideas?"[6]

Through an analysis of the expectations of Chicanas from California at the IWY tribune, the implications of their attendance, and the influence of the Mexico City conference on their future political activities, this chapter examines four interrelated developments that affected Chicana identity and political formation. First, by traveling to the conference without men, the participants enacted self-determination and women's leadership. Second, Chicanas attended an international women's meeting as representatives from an imagined Chicano nation. As such, they acted as public representatives of a movement typically defined by male figureheads and images of male-led families. Third, at the conference, which took place in a Third World setting where critiques of U.S. colonialism were strong, Chicanas reevaluated not only how they conceived of themselves as citizens of the United States but also as an oppressed minority group within the nation they called home.[7] Finally, attending the conference validated the struggle that Chicanas waged at home. These women came away from the tribune with a more global understanding of women's oppression and their own, at times, privileged place in world politics. This galvanized them to consider their own power and privilege as women of color in a First World empire, to look more deeply into the U.S. involvement in Latin America, and to continue their local and national activism on behalf of Chicanas while also illuminating new potential alliances and arenas of action that would transcend or bridge national borders. Their new consciousness coincided with transformations in the Chicano movement itself. In the early to mid-1970s Chicana/o activist ideology began to address transnational solidarity and identify with Mexicans in Mexico, and activists began to establish networks with other Latino/a and ethnic or racial groups.[8] Patterns of bridging activism oriented toward building connections with communities and organizations beyond the United States, as well as ideologies and political tactics associated with transnational movements against colonialism and racism, accelerated for Chicana activists in the wake of Mexico City.

The Historical Context of International Feminism

In 1945, after decades of organizing and lobbying by women active in international politics, the idea of women's equality with men became part of the U.N. charter, and a year later the U.N. Commission on the Status of Women was founded. Historian Leila Rupp argues that earlier activism dating from the late nineteenth century formed the first wave of the international women's movement. Highlighting the connections between these early histories of internationalism and the women who struggled for gender to be included in the U.N. charter and for the creation of the CSW, Rupp "links the pre-1945 international women's movement to what might otherwise seem the 'emergence' of such a movement in the 1970s."[9]

The International Women's Year Conference marked the second documented time Chicanas traveled en masse to an international women's conference but the first time such a conference specifically addressed women's issues worldwide. In April 1971 groups of Chicanas and other women of color attended the Indochinese Women's Conference in Vancouver, British Columbia, Canada. The conference, convened by the organizations Voice of Women and Women Strike for Peace, brought together women from across the spectrum of feminist movements in the United States to meet with six Indochinese women. "Organized against the backdrop of the US military intervention in Vietnam's civil war," Dionne Espinoza asserts, "the conference goal was to bring women together to learn about the US involvement in the war and its effects on the people of Vietnam, to discuss issues of peace and understanding, and ultimately, to unite and mobilize against the war and against imperialism."[10] At this conference, Chicana attendees confronted dynamics similar to those their counterparts would face at the IWY in Mexico City. That is, as they dialogued with each other, with the Indochinese women, and the other women of color from the United States, Chicanas interrogated the meaning of their identity in the United States in relation to a Third World perspective and engaged the idea of a "Third World womanism," a self-referent that could serve as "a term of coalition and solidarity to create their own agendas and grassroots solidarities."[11] When Chicanas traveled internationally to represent themselves and their interests, they bridged national, cultural, and racial borders that helped them refine their own identities and recognize that they could assert a "Chicana collective identity" and "a Third World collective identity," as well as "participat[e] in a shared understanding of Third World womanism."[12] San Diego Chicanas who attended the 1971 Indochinese Women's Conference returned home with a more solid understanding of themselves and their own struggles, a parallel with Chicanas who attended the 1975 IWY conference. They maintained the relationships established with other Chicanas at the conference and brought their experiences back to the issues they worked on at home. International experiences fortified the work they saw necessary in their own communities.

The 1975 U.N. conference, which launched the "Decade of Women," established the foundation for subsequent world conferences in 1980 and 1985 and provided a base for the formation of international feminist networks, especially via the establishment of the International Women's Tribune Center.[13] The 1975 U.N. conference also revealed the schism between First World and Third World women at the intersection of economics and women's issues. Indeed, a major fissure in an international consensus on feminism and women's rights appeared as those from the First World stressed equal rights while their counterparts from the Third World stressed the impact of economics and colonialism.[14]

Despite such conflicts, most scholars agree that by its initiation and support of women's conferences, the United Nations has been instrumental in fomenting international feminism. From the formation of the CSW in 1947 to the last U.N.-sponsored women's world conference in Beijing in 1995, the establishment of transnational networks represented a fundamental step in movements for equality worldwide.[15] In addition, the consciousness-raising effects on women at each world conference, including the one in Mexico City, inspired women participants to explore and understand the roots and ramifications of their social, economic, and cultural oppression.[16]

The Mexico City conference also held significance for Mexican women involved in feminist struggles. At the time, there were various streams of Mexican feminisms, with two main categorizations as noted by the historian Gisela Espinoza Damián. Women who were associated with what has been called "historical feminism" or "neofeminism" came out of the Mexican student movement of the 1960s.[17] These women called attention to issues of equal treatment and equal opportunity. Scholar Sylvia Marcos writes, "This movement demystified the patriarchal double moral in relation to sexuality, asking for access to abortion rights, and debunking feminine stereotypes by which a woman's identity was made exclusively dependent on having a husband and being a mother. Small consciousness-raising groups allowed new critical demands to be expressed and articulated."[18] The issues raised by historical feminists during this period differed from issues raised by women involved in "popular feminism," which emerged from both neighborhood associations and indigenous communities in the early 1980s.[19] Whereas historical feminists have focused on Mexican women as individuals who deserve equality, popular and indigenous feminisms that arose later included a class perspective. These latter movements "sought to overcome an economistic and dichotomous view of social classes to support a world inclusive of many worlds, within which indigenous feminism could develop."[20]

For Mexican feminists, the IWY conference in Mexico City provided legitimacy for their movements and organizations as well as space for them to interact with women from other nations, allowing for a dynamic interchange of ideas.[21] This was also the case for other feminists from Latin America.

Indeed, the IWY conference seems to have been a catalyst for additional meetings among Latin American women, called Encuentros, that occurred between 1981 and 1990.[22] In writing about such meetings, a collective of eight scholars wrote, "The Encuentros, like feminisms themselves, are arenas of solidarity and expansion but also of conflict and exclusion, negotiations, and renegotiations. These dynamics do not take shape in a vacuum but are always informed by the changing political and social contexts in which feminisms unfold."[23] Through events such as international women's conferences that were held beginning in the mid-1970s, Chicanas and women activists from other parts of the world built connections to one another that would create new transnational feminist organizations and exchanges.

The Road to Mexico City

Like Celia Herrera Rodríguez, Chicanas found out about the U.N. conference from networks established among women activists across California and the nation. For some, pure excitement, curiosity, and optimism about changing the world propelled them to participate in the first international women's conference. Artist Yolanda López, at the time a master's student in fine arts at the University of California, San Diego, and newsletter editor for the Chicano Federation in San Diego, remembered,

> I was . . . bright eyed and bushy-tailed. I thought there was going to be great stuff. We'd go there and meet Mexican women and meet other women and change the situation for women. We thought, at least I did, that we would go down there and be part of the great audience and actually begin to, you know, make policy for the U.N. regarding women.[24]

Most of the arriving Chicanas assumed that there would be one conference, which everyone would be able to attend in order to propose resolutions and changes to the World Plan of Action. They were shocked to find that they could not enter the official U.N. conference and could only attend the tribune. In fact, many of the Chicanas did not know that the tribune was not the official U.N. conference. As one Chicana attendee stated, "Most of the women who were there as observers or individuals were sort of in awe of the whole bigger question and the official UN stuff."[25]

Other women who were better informed about the processes of the IWY conference traveled to Mexico City because they did not believe the U.S. government would appoint people like themselves as official delegates. "I knew there was going to be a conference and I made up my mind—I was going to be a member," recalled Connie Pardo, who worked with the Chicana Service

Action Center and was also a member of the Comisión Femenil in Los Angeles. "We could only be members of the . . . non-governmental [meeting], because, you know, our government wasn't going to pick on somebody like me with my background. I had a left-wing background and no way was I going to be picked. . . . So we went."[26] Pardo's conclusion that she would not be seen as suitable to serve on the official U.S. delegation to the U.N. body spoke to her self-identified social, political, and economic position in the nation. At the time, Pardo lived what would be considered a middle-class life. Her husband, Frank Muñoz, was an attorney, and they had both been active in community issues since the 1950s. Yet in classifying herself as left-wing, in the sense of her prior union and community activism, she positioned herself in opposition to the national status quo and to conformist U.S. citizens, and therefore did not see herself as representative of nor as represented by the nation.

For Pardo and for many other Chicanas, that the conference would be held in Mexico City was compelling. Not only would they meet and connect with women from the world over, they would also have the opportunity to connect with Mexican feminists and to establish common ground in their respective, and in some respects, interconnected struggles. Sandra Serrano Sewell, at the time a homemaker and member of the Comisión Femenil, stated, "We thought, oh, yeah, we're Mexican Americans . . . we're going to find all these natural connections, you know. It was sort of like a romantic view that was quickly dispelled."[27] Other women such as Celia Herrera Rodríguez found the trip to Mexico liberating as an independent travel experience. For Herrera Rodríguez, the conference also provided a new international perspective. She recalled, "It was a thoroughly impressive time," where conversations with Latin American women provided inspiration to continue her education.

Mexico constituted part of Chicana cultural and spiritual roots. To be sure, many Chicanas would not have attended had the conference taken place in Europe, Asia, or any other distant place. Mexico City was geographically close, and most Chicanas who attended either spoke Spanish or at least had a rudimentary understanding of the language. They could therefore easily navigate the city once they arrived and did not need translators. Although many of them took issue with the masculinist aspects of Chicano nationalism, their experiences in the movement led them to idealize Mexico as a homeland. Dorinda Moreno of Concilio Mujeres, a San Francisco–based organization, avowed that "raza women should not be invisible, since this conference is going to be held in our motherland. This was the Mestiza's continent, from Alaska to the Patagonia, and she should be the most known."[28] Indeed, literary critic Sheila Contreras found that for activists of both sexes during this period, "the tie to Mexico [was] filial—one of kinship, blood ties, and a shared history of conquest and oppression. The idea of Mexico exude[d] comfort; it [felt] like *home*. When you [were] on *this* side that is."[29] Contreras identifies nostalgia for the Mexican homeland as a phenomenon occurring only within the borders of the United States. Yet on traveling to Mexico, many Chicanas and Chicanos, like those who attended the conference, realize that expectations of home or kinship do not always materialize.

The Chicanas who attended the Mexico City conference were relatively privileged; they included college and graduate students, businesswomen, political activists, artists, and writers. Their ages ranged from the late teens to the early sixties. They had the financial resources or the ability to obtain the funding for travel, and most were educated beyond high school and worked as professionals or aspired to such careers. If not formally educated, most brought years of experience in community work and organizing. It is not surprising that, although Chicanas from throughout the United States attended the IWY conference, the largest numbers of them came from California and Texas, where most Mexican American political activity occurred.

For the majority of the women attendees, their participation was intrinsic to their political activism in the Chicano movement and ethnic Mexican politics in Los Angeles as well as an international extension of this activism. Already politically engaged, the women attended in groups and as delegates of their respective organizations, including the Organización Chicana from the University of California, Los Angeles; the Comisión Femenil Mexicana Nacional; Poder Femenino; the Chicana Service Action Center; La Raza Unida Party; and the Chicano Federation in San Diego. From Texas, the most visible and largest group of women represented La Raza Unida Party.[30] Of the 200 to 300 women who attended from the United States, approximately 100 to 150 were California Chicanas.[31]

Attending the tribune required a certain dedication to activism and a commitment of time and resources. Many Chicana students obtained funding from their respective student body governments or used their financial aid or welfare funds. For example, the Organización Chicana of UCLA obtained funds from both the student government and the Chicano Studies Research Center to send a group of six women to the conference. In return, the women promised to document their experiences via slides, videotape, audiotape, and collection of pamphlets handed out at the conference.[32] Chicanas who were not students or who did not have this avenue of fundraising, like Celia Herrera Rodríguez and Frances Romero, saved their financial aid and welfare funds to attend. Staff and volunteers of the Chicana Service Action Center and members of the Comisión Femenil, many of whom were young professionals, financed their own travel.[33]

The IWY tribune took place at the Convention Hall of the National Medical Center of Mexico City, across town from the official IWY conference. Because this dual IWY conference was the first of its kind, many women, including the Chicanas profiled in this chapter, had no idea what to expect on arrival in the city. Although the official conference and the tribune occurred simultaneously, tribune participants had no prospect of attending or addressing the official meeting, where thirteen hundred delegates from 130 countries assembled to discuss a World Plan of Action, already drafted by the Secretariat of the United Nations.[34] The World Plan of Action, which was adopted by the national delegations, proposed guidelines for governments and nongovernmental groups to promote the goals of equality, development, and peace. In addition, the official meeting adopted the Declaration of Mexico, which is best known for equating Zionism with racism, although the United States, Israel, and Canada opposed it.[35] The tribune, organized by Mildred Persinger and Rosalind Harris, two women with long ties to NGOs and the United Nations, stood as an analogous forum that "enabled thousands of women activists and scholars from all regions of the world who were not official government-appointed delegates to witness and monitor firsthand government deliberations on international gender policy issues and to form multinational feminist networks."[36] Persinger and Harris, both from the United States, had been appointed by the U.N. CSW given their leadership and experience in established U.N. and NGO circles. Immediately prior to being appointed to head the tribune and continuing into the 1980s, Persinger had officially represented the World YWCA as an observer at the U.N. and on "various U.S. and UN NGO committees in New York."[37] Harris worked for the United States branch of International Social Service, a service agency for immigrants worldwide that was closely affiliated with the YWCA.[38] For the tribune, Persinger and Harris raised $225,000 from more than twelve sources including the Ford Foundation, John D. Rockefeller III, the Gulf Oil Corporation, the Government of Norway, and the Canadian International Development Agency.[39] A total of twenty-five hundred representatives of NGOs, along with an equal number of independent women, attended the tribune. Of the five thousand participants, one-third came from Latin America, one-third from North America, and one-third from Europe, with a total of eighty-two countries represented.[40]

Attendees at the IWY tribune included leaders of local and national women's organizations, legislators, judges, lawyers, female educators, members of professional associations, provocateurs (individuals hired by governments or groups to disrupt the gathering), and members of the media.[41] Women from the United States represented a range of groups including the League of Women Voters, the International Lesbian Caucus, Baha'i International, the American Association of University Women, Amnesty International, the YWCA, the World Population Society, trade unions, and the International Planned Parenthood Federation.[42] Chicanas represented approximately 5 percent, or 250 to 300, of the participants.[43]

Harris and Persinger planned a structured program of twenty-five tribune sessions organized in concert with the themes of the IWY such as the family, peace and disarmament, women in public life, women at work, education, law and the status of women, and health and nutrition. *Xilonen*, the tribune newspaper, reflected this format in its daily calendar. After a group of U.S. feminists took over a meeting at the U.S. Embassy on June 21, 1975, to complain about a too-rigid conference structure, the organizers added a lunchtime "global speak-out" and informal "rap sessions" to the daily agenda.[44] By the fifth day of the conference the sessions posted in *Xilonen* more than tripled, with presentations scheduled at least every half-hour from 9:00 a.m. to 9:30 p.m. Over the span of twelve days, women at the tribune could attend more than three hundred presentations.[45] Chicanas appeared on the agenda after the change in structure: On June 24 they led a session titled "Mujeres Chicanas del Partido Raza Unida" (Chicana Women of the Raza Unida Party), and on June 26, a session titled "National Chicana Coalition."[46]

Political Fault Lines

At both the official conference and the tribune, a central question emerged that paralleled the struggle Chicana feminists faced at home: What was to come first, national liberation and world economic justice, or women's rights? In the Chicano movement, women had faced the choice between fighting for the collective community or fighting for their liberation as women. For many women participating in both the tribune and the official conference, the battle lines were drawn between those who came from First World countries, who stressed women's rights, and those who came from Third World countries, who stressed national liberation and economic justice.[47] Although many Chicanas who attended the tribune stressed liberation for themselves at home as part and parcel of the liberation of Chicanos as a whole, at the meeting they found themselves aligning with Third World women, who stressed that women's equality could not come about without a change in the world economic order, or in other words, a redistribution of the world's wealth. This shift appears to contradict the positions that many of the Los Angeles Chicanas had asserted at home. Yet the international context of the tribune exposed Chicanas to a global politics that many had not necessarily engaged in. In this context they aligned with a position that prioritized political and economic issues. Back home, however, their position vis-à-vis Chicana liberation did not change.

At the tribune, the conflict between economic development and women's rights turned personal as women from the United States became targets for anti-American sentiments. For example, at one of the informal speak-outs, a woman from India, identifying herself as a resident of a developing nation, labeled American mainstream feminism as the "psychological liberation of Western women." She went on to say, "If you American ladies paid more attention to the imperialist economic policies of your government, women throughout the world would not have to worry about such unfashionable problems as starvation and homelessness."[48] This sentiment correlated with historian Jocelyn Olcott's conclusion that "US feminists sought to impose their particular conception of women's emancipation as just another example of cultural imperialism" at the tribune.[49]

Many U.S. women of color, including Chicanas, found themselves with no firm footing in this political arena because they were labeled Americans but were more closely aligned politically with Third World women, not mainstream U.S. feminism. Lilia Aceves, from Los Angeles, for example, was aware of other Chicanas and U.S. women at the conference but was drawn to presentations and conversations with women from Latin America. She recalled, "I was looking more into a class issue than a gender issue . . . [and] I would gravitate to the ones [presentations] that were coming from Central and South America. . . . These were the ones [presentations] I was interested in more."[50] For example, the delegation from the Raza Unida Party, with women hailing from California, Texas, Wisconsin, and Michigan, one of the few Chicana groups to hold a panel session at the tribune, brought a printed primer on the history and current socioeconomic and political situation of Chicanas. In a pamphlet titled "La Mujer Chicana" they described Chicanas (and Chicanos) as a colonized group within the United States as well as a group that suffered gender discrimination.[51] Chicanas of La Raza Unida Party wrote, "The history of the Chicana is the history of her people which began after the United States–Mexican War of 1846–1848. It was at this period in history when as a colonized people the Chicana and Chicanos began to evolve into a distinct and different people in the United States."[52] The primer was the basis for La Raza Unida Party's session at the tribune. It was important for the women in the delegation to show other tribune attendees that, similar to those who lived in colonized nations, Chicanos and Chicanas lived as second-class citizens in their own land as a legacy of colonization.[53]

The divisions at the tribune included conflicts within the contingent from the United States. Three separate disagreements surfaced. First, many women, especially women of color, did not feel that their country's official delegation adequately represented them. Second, these women of color felt that high-profile U.S. feminists at the tribune did not speak for them. Third, many felt that U.S. feminists were trying to monopolize the conference.

These fault lines materialized in Mexico City because of the nature of the conference. The IWY tribune served as a tangible representation of the world on a slightly more manageable level. For the fourteen days of the event, women from across the globe met each other in one central location. Face to face, they communicated their particular national issues, and the personal connections with one another made global issues more tangible. When women from different regions of the United States met in a centralized location, tensions that already existed between mainstream feminists and Chicanas rose to the surface. Indeed, many encounters between Chicanas and Euro-American feminists struck a familiar chord of disharmony. To Chicanas, mainstream feminists insisted on a gender-only agenda and positioned themselves as all-knowing on global and feminist issues. This type of contact occurred at two distinct levels: between Chicanas and the official U.S. delegation to the U.N. conference, and between Chicanas and mainstream Euro-American feminists at the tribune.

Chicanas' relations with the official U.S. delegation to the U.N. conference were tenuous, at best, since they felt that the delegation did not represent their views. The delegation had two chairpersons, Daniel Parker, head of the Agency for International Development, and Patricia Hutar, U.S. representative to the U.N. Economic and Social Council's Commission on the Status of Women and former vice chair of the Republican Party.[54] The rest of the delegation had been appointed by the U.S. State Department, and despite the fact that Gilda Bojorquez Gjurich, a Mexican American businesswoman from Los Angeles was part of the delegation and had been affiliated with various Mexican American organizations, including the Comisión Femenil, Chicanas at the conference remained adamant that the delegation did not represent them.[55] Yolanda López, a Chicana tribune attendee from San Diego, later wrote, "The U.S. delegation was in a sense a true representation of U.S. policy and our international posture—but in no way is it a true representation of American women."[56] Bea Vásquez Robinson, a Chicana from San Jose, California, wrote,

> The IWY Conference in Mexico City once again exemplified too few (and too white) making decisions for too many. Our country's delegation was a farce. Women were appointed with little or no regard given to their knowledge of and expertise in the problems facing the doubly oppressed women in this country.

Their backgrounds could in no way give them any insight into the concerns and issues of the minority or poor woman. They represented as usual the middle and upper-class white woman. Even the token minority was representative of that class.[57]

These critiques of the U.S. delegation as lacking "knowledge and expertise" about the situation of all women aligned Chicanas with others at the conference who called the legitimacy of their own government delegations into question.[58]

In this context, Chicanas began to organize on two fronts. First, in order to voice their discontent with the tribune and the official U.S. delegation, Chicanas joined with African American and Latin American women under the name Coalition of Unrepresented Women (CUW). The women in the group drafted a set of demands that protested the makeup of the U.S. delegation and voiced their frustration with the organization of the tribune. The CUW disrupted a press conference held by the official U.S. delegation on June 21, calling for the primacy of issues of race and class in regard to any feminist position. In this sense, many U.S. women of color concurred with the position of Third World women that economic equality needed to be addressed.[59]

The CUW demanded that minority women be "given immediate and equal representation in the United States delegation on the Presidential Advisory Commission on International Women's Year" and that the U.S. delegation "admit to and correct the political, economic, and social injustices that prevail in the United States." In order to be able to voice their political views, the CUW also wanted a time slot for a panel presentation where they could "expose and discuss the issues of racism, discrimination, economic exploitation, human rights and the oppression of women in the United States and throughout the world" and a conference room open at all times equipped with translation services and a public address system to discuss the same issues.[60]

The demands made by the CUW echoed sentiments in a call to action issued by the Mexican feminist organization Mujeres en Acción Solidaria (MAS) for a meeting at the tribune to discuss class, race, economic independence, and sexual repression. According to MAS, the tribune should have been discussing economics and its relation to women's daily experiences, which they saw as more important than any feminist ideologies. They thus called for a more profound discussion of the issues and needs of women worldwide that would result in "concrete and permanent action." They also supported "structural changes on an internal and international level to propagate an effective transformation of the woman's condition in all social groups."[61] Mainstream U.S. feminists at the conference, including members of NOW, however, saw this position as anti-feminist because they feared that emphasizing economics or race would ultimately make these issues take precedence over gender.[62]

These mainstream U.S. feminists characterized economic issues as a male paradigm. For example, Carole De Saram, president of the New York chapter of NOW and tribune participant, stated, "The true issues, the problems of women, are being forgotten here. Instead this conference is concentrating on political issues that represent the male mentality. The direction here is not coming from women, it's coming from men."[63] De Saram categorized political and economic issues as completely separate from the "problems of women." That is, no intersection existed between women's issues and economic or political issues. This view permeated press coverage of the meetings. Barbara Cady, a reporter for the *Los Angeles Times*, wrote, "Unfortunately, far too few women attending the United Nations International Women's Year Conference in Mexico City had come primarily as females.... In fact, their femaleness often seemed completely irrelevant to their intentions."[64]

As evident from these statements, a classic component of the women's movement in general played itself out at the tribune. De Saram, Cady, and others assumed that women could, in essence, check their race, ethnicity, class, nationality, and language at the door and assume positions as only "females." They could not understand why any woman would fail to concentrate solely on what they believed to be women's issues, and characterized all women who disagreed with their line of reasoning as male-identified. In this way, mainstream U.S. feminists engaged in what Angela Gilliam calls "sexualism," an ideology that focuses on sex and sexuality at the expense of economics and politics.[65] They positioned themselves as the true representatives of all women and criticized the others as anti-feminist, including U.S. women of color, or as puppets of men. While many female representatives of national governments at the official IWY conference did, indeed, participate as "spokesmen" for their governments and many times aired opinions that privileged economics at the expense of women's individual rights, such evidence has not been found for the tribune. Mainstream feminists could not understand that Chicana, African American, and Third World women did not have the privilege of a solely gendered perspective, given the salience of race and class in their lives.

The second level of organizing occurred solely within Chicana circles at the tribune. With concerns similar to those of the CUW, Chicanas met as a group under the name National Chicana Coalition. Bea Vásquez Robinson, from northern California, who organized the meeting, recalled, "It was very spontaneous," but also said, "I was really disgusted with the whole conference." At the meeting, approximately 250 to 300 Chicanas voiced their complaints about the tribune and the official U.S. delegation, and as a result, the National Chicana Coalition formed several groups to address these issues. At a meeting of the U.S. delegation at the tribune, Chicanas forced their way to the podium and articulated their complaints and demands. After this takeover, the National Chicana Coalition received an audience with the U.S. delegation.[66] As a result of this meeting and the actions of the Coalition of Unrepresented Women, some Chicanas believed they effected changes in the World Plan of Action. For example, Ada Peña, a Chicana from Texas, echoed the sentiments of many California Chicanas when she stated, "In some of the amendments to it, the Plan reflects our input, like when they mention involvement or discrimination referring to women of minority groups, blacks or women of an ethnic background."[67]

Class and race also came to the fore as women of color took issue with U.S. feminist superstars at the tribune such as Betty Friedan, who became the voice of American women for the media. Chicanas felt that mainstream feminists voiced the concerns of middle-class Euro-American women, a longstanding refrain. As Ada Peña put it, "Personally, I do not feel that Betty Friedan represents the women's movement in the United States. I feel she has made many inroads, but she has projected the middle-class white woman. Her presentation to the Tribune came as middle-class white women and made no mention of minorities."[68]

The inconsistent public statements that Friedan made at the tribune contributed to the critiques lodged by U.S. women of color, especially since she was one of the few women at the tribune to command the media's attention. An example of what may have angered Peña occurred at one of the many press conferences held by Friedan. At one point, Friedan stated that the women's movement had been the only social movement to survive from the 1960s to the 1970s and said, "But now, there is a new development of a separate Chicano feminist women's group and a black feminist group, and they are increasingly uniting in the old raw women's movement which is so very large now that you cannot possibly look at it in terms of one organization alone."[69] By characterizing Chicana and Black feminist organization as "new," her comments revealed a general ignorance about organizing by women of color in the United States in both historical and contemporary terms. Black women and Chicanas had founded a variety of separate women's groups by the late 1960s and early 1970s. Friedan's comments reveal that she saw Chicana and African American women's organizations as additions to the women's movement, sharing the same agenda, centering the mainstream women's liberation movement. Chicanas saw Friedan's misinformation as dangerous because she presented it as truth to an international audience. It was one thing to be ignored by the official delegation, a government-appointed one, but to be ignored by women who professed to be speaking for all American women reinforced the disillusionment Chicanas had already felt at home.

Chicanas and International Realizations

Through their participation at the tribune, Chicanas gained three main insights into international feminism. First, listening to and meeting women from all over the globe underscored the sense that women's oppression occurred everywhere. Second, they realized their relative nearsightedness in regard to their own struggles in the United States. Finally, meeting so many women actively engaged in bettering women's lives validated their own activism while inspiring future paths.

As Chicanas at the conference conversed with women from around the world, they began to think more globally about common issues, to feel a bond with those women on the basis of gender, and to transcend national and ethnic identity. For them, this bond differed from what they viewed as the limited universalist approach of mainstream U.S. feminists. For example, Yolanda López recalled that listening to women from Africa and South America "just totally imbued [her] with the idea that dealing with gender was the next frontier" in the "long road towards peace, justice, and equality."[70] While Chicanas came to believe that discrimination and oppression against women were universal phenomena, they held fast to the belief that race, class, and ethnicity had definite and tangible effects on how these phenomena affected the women of the world, including themselves. Connie Pardo recalled that the conference raised the consciousness of her fellow Chicana conference-goers, especially in terms of class issues around the world. For herself, Pardo recalled, "I felt stimulated. I felt uplifted. See, what I think of the feminist movement is this, is that a feminist, my kind of feminist, is an internationalist."[71]

For these Chicanas, idealized notions of forming transnational Mexican sisterhood varied depending on their existing transnational connections to Mexico and on their political priorities. Some Chicanas, such as NietoGómez and Serrano Sewell, had imagined connecting with women they viewed as their Mexican counterparts but had no personal or political connections in Mexico. Herrera Rodríguez, on the other hand, had a familial connection to Mexico through her mother-in-law, with whom she stayed while at the conference, though her mother-in-law was not politically active. Before the conference Pardo utilized her political connections in Mexico to arrange a meeting with Mexican feminists. As she recalled, "We ate with them and discussed a few issues. We didn't go deep into political issues. These women were not just concentrating on women's rights. They were concentrating [on] labor rights . . . their society, period. So we lost contact with them."[72] Corinne Sánchez recalled these meetings as well. "We had caucuses at night with them, [the women] from Mexico," she recounted, commenting that the issues that the Mexican women faced were "very similar to the Chicana situation. They were probably more radical than us . . . because they didn't have the conflict of 'who am I?'"[73]

For NietoGómez, meeting Mexican feminists at the conference brought even more issues to the fore. She believed that some Mexican women were not allowed to attend the conference and held an "underground conference." She was referring to the fact that many Mexican feminist groups had decided not to attend the IWY conference, publicized their position widely, and organized the Contracongreso a través del Frente de Mujeres contra el Año Internacional de la Mujer (Countercongress by the Women's Front Against International Women's Year).[74] It is unclear whether this boycott was followed by all Mexican feminist groups. For example, Mujeres en Acción Solidaria had called a meeting at the tribune to discuss North American liberal feminists who used a feminist language but were aligned with their own governments' geopolitical interests. This meeting of women of similar minds would take place at 1:00 p.m. on June 26, 1975, with the goal of crafting a resolution that would "reflect our analysis and our commitment for the transformation of all the structures that oppress us."[75] For many Mexican feminists, the IWY conference and tribune were affronts to the legacies of the Mexican Student Movement. As has been the case for other feminist movements, Olcott notes, Mexican feminisms "grew out of the struggles and frustrations of Mexico's 1968 movement," when activists had experienced state repression and violence. Indeed, to Mexican feminists, the Mexican government's decision to hold the UN conference at Tlatelolco Plaza indicated the government's attempt to cleanse "the site where their comrades had been massacred" just seven years earlier and create a new image for the nation.[76]

It does not appear that the California Chicanas who attended the IWY conference were aware of the complex issues surrounding the conference vis-à-vis Mexican feminist groups. For many of them, the conference offered new perspectives and realizations about women's oppression that challenged and broadened their ideological stance on what it meant to be a Chicana and showed how they were part of a larger struggle for social, economic, and political justice. At the conference, they came to see that they had to question their beliefs not only in regard to gender but also in regard to the Chicano movement itself. For example, general tribune panels were titled "Attitude Formation and Socialization Process," "Law and the Status of Women," "Population and Development: Women and Children," "Women at Work," and "The Family."[77] In a 2002 interview Corinne Sánchez remembered that the larger panels made her "realize the things [she] was experiencing, barriers, discrimination . . . were not barrio at all, they were universal."[78] Reflecting on the conversations and interactions she had with Latin American women at the tribune and how they affected her, Celia Herrera Rodríguez realized, "It was not just North America and that we as Chicanas were part of a huge, big history and big struggle and I think that was clear . . . we had our issues that resonated, that had place, that had purpose, that had a history. I think all that became manifested within that milieu of all of those women."[79]

In addition, Chicanas came to see that issues of gender in their own struggle could not be appendages but had to take center stage with racial, ethnic, and class concerns. Experiences in the Chicano movement had shown these women that gender had to be addressed, and the tribune gave them many visible examples of other women who were on the same path. This provided important new perspectives for these Chicanas, who, at the meetings, realized that they had been insular in their struggles as well as in their political outlook. For example, Chicanas were inspired by Domitila Barrios de Chungara, a Bolivian activist who rallied against her country's repressive government and had been jailed for her activities. Barrios de Chungara spoke of her experiences and thoughts about feminism, which linked the issue of women's oppression to economics and social justice. Equal rights for women was not the only goal, she claimed. She instead argued for a women's liberation that included "women being respected as human beings, who can solve problems and participate in everything . . . a liberation that means our opinion is respected at home and outside the home."[80] Barrios de Chungara's presentation, Yolanda López noted, "just totally imbued me with the idea that dealing with gender was the next frontier as far as how we were going to revolutionize, not only our society, but also our political agenda."[81] Lilia Aceves recalled that "there was just so much information." She "would get up early and go to the panels," where she met women from Chile and the Soviet Union at various workshops.[82] Since many of the struggles of women from other nations seemed more drastic than their own due to the repressive governments they faced, Chicanas gained a sense of hope in their country, one that at least practiced its democratic ideals to some extent. They therefore felt inspired that they might be able to work toward and achieve what they wanted at home.

The circumstances surrounding a presentation by Chilean women on June 26 strongly influenced Chicanas at the conference because of what they perceived to be a military presence. NietoGómez recalled, "A platoon of armed soldiers disrupted a panel discussion of women from Chile. First, they marched into the room and surrounded the audience and the panelists. Then they raised their rifles and pointed them at the audience as well as the panelists. Next, the leader said the meeting had ended and ordered everyone to leave immediately or be arrested. They did not give any explanations as to why they stopped the meeting."[83] There is no documentary evidence of this occurrence, yet NietoGómez recalled it vividly. Aceves and Pardo also recalled a military presence at specific sessions at the tribune. They did not specify what kinds of troops entered conference rooms, and it may be they called them "troops" because they carried rifles, which was not a common experience for Chicanas in the United States even if there had been widespread police brutality, for example.[84] For women like NietoGómez, this experience was important in two ways. First, she compared her experiences as a political activist in the United States to those of women in Latin America and the Middle East and concluded that living in the United States protected her from being apprehended by the military. In her estimation, her political activities, however antigovernment or antiestablishment, did not put her in danger of being arrested and incarcerated by federal authorities. Second, she concluded that women in countries like Chile and the state of Palestine manifested a particular degree of commitment because they put their lives on the line for their beliefs. She explained, "The Palestinian women did not have any rights as people. Though Chicanas faced discrimination, we were usually able to exercise our civil rights, even though police actions often ended our demonstrations."[85]

The perception of women's lack of rights in other countries made NietoGómez and the other Chicanas who attended the meetings recognize that they had to come to terms with their identities as U.S. citizens and the privileges that came with this status. Although police brutality, police and FBI infiltration, false arrests, and general harassment had plagued the Chicano movement, Mexican Americans, except those serving in Vietnam, had not faced the prospect of egregious torture or the possibility of military arrest for their antigovernment actions. Chicanas were aware of the repressive violence by law enforcement, local, state, and federal, against organizations such as the Black Panthers, for example, and the legacies of violence of the civil rights movement, but they made a clear distinction between these actions and what they thought could potentially happen to them. Therefore, while Chicanas may have expected to find natural connections and bonds with Third World women, they did not expect to appreciate the privilege of American citizenship. In this sense, Aceves, López, NietoGómez, and others engaged in "comparative measurement[s]" of state violence and repression that reinscribed the notion of American exceptionalism. Indeed, as historian Alan Gómez notes, "During the post-World War II period, political movements in Mexico and the United States were deeply impacted by government repression." Yet, according to mainstream ideology, political repression does not happen in the United States, especially in relation to other countries. This view does not take programs such as COINTELPRO into account. Consequently, "This political, historical, and psychological obfuscation has inoculated the public from considering state violence in the United States along the same register and analog as state violence in other parts of the world."[86] Political activists in the U.S. were not immune to this type of thinking.

American identity, however, also brought with it the unexpected experience of being affiliated with Euro-American feminists such as Betty Friedan, and with the United States government. At odds with Friedan's portrayal of American women, and adamant about educating others at the IWY Tribune about themselves as Chicanas, these women became de facto ambassadors for their people as a whole. In explaining their own identity, Chicanas gained affinity with other Third World women. Corinne Sánchez explained, "So our whole banner was, we're fighting oppression, we're fighting for self-determination and we call this Chicano. We are not Mexican Americans."[87] Although some Chicanas may not have felt themselves to be representatives of the United States, they became so when they provided an alternative view of the country to other women.

In other circumstances, however, being identified as Americans caused negative reactions and challenges from Third World women. Many of the women they met in Mexico City had foreign policy concerns, namely, the need for economic aid and what they viewed as the imperialist nature of the United States. For example, NietoGómez remembered, "The Palestinian women saw Chicanas as representatives of the United States and did not recognize us as a separate oppressed ethnic group.... Instead, they wanted to know what Chicanas were doing to influence the government to support the establishment of the state of Palestine."[88] For Chicanas, it proved ironic that they were held responsible for U.S. foreign policy decisions when they felt that they were struggling against very similar policies. As NietoGómez later recalled, Chicanas were "immersed in nationalism and what was going on in the Southwest," but many had not made connections to the broad reach of U.S. foreign policy in a global context. Most Mexican American women attending the meetings viewed U.S. foreign policy negatively, especially given the high percentage of Mexican American men who died in the Vietnam War and the violent repression exerted against antiwar protesters by law enforcement. Many of these women had been victims of, witnessed, or were aware of the brutal repression of Chicana/o activism against the war at the Chicano Moratorium in Los Angeles in 1970, when approximately thirty thousand Mexican Americans joined together in protest. For many, opposition to the war was about the domestic consequences of U.S. foreign policy in their communities. They were also angered by the reasons the United States went to war.

Although attendance at the tribune does not seem to have radically altered belief systems, it did reinforce Chicanas' views of the importance of gender in their own country and gave them a broader perspective on how their struggle fit into world politics. Connie Pardo, who was in her mid-forties when she attended the meetings, remembered, "It fit my sense of internationalism where women are concerned and it fit my sense of internationalism vis-à-vis the class struggle."[89] The tribune gave many women proof that they were not alone in their struggle. The Chicanas who attended the 1975 International Women's Year Conference returned to the United States emboldened by their new international perspective and determined to engage their own national political landscape.

The Road to Houston

As part of the Decade for Women, which began with the 1975 IWY and its Plan of Action, nations across the world began to develop their own plans. The Mexico City Plan of Action "call[ed] for intensified action to ensure the full integration of women in the total development effort" and the "involve[ment of] women widely in international co-operation and the strengthening of world peace on the basis of equal rights, opportunities, and responsibilities of women and men."[90] Each nation would "decide upon its own national strategy, and identify its own priorities within the present World Plan."[91] In the United States this would culminate in the 1977 National Women's Conference, held in Houston, Texas. According to Doreen J. Mattingly and Jessica L. Nare, the state and territorial meetings held in preparation for the first national meeting of women led to "the most diverse federal conference that had ever been held; over a third of delegates (35.5 percent) were racial or ethnic minorities and sixty delegates openly identified as lesbian."[92] This diversity did not come about through good will but because of intentional organizing by women of color, including Chicanas.

Chicanas, especially those from California, had felt disenfranchised at the 1975 meetings in Mexico City due to the separation between the official

U.N. conference and the tribune. As California Chicana activist Cecilia Burciaga recollected, "It was that sentiment of no voice and no consensus among American women that stimulated congresswomen like Bella Abzug to come home and begin to architect a plan for having the diverse population of women in this country meet, on a national basis, to decide our own issues and priorities."[93] In late 1975, during the presidential term of Richard Nixon, Congress passed Public Law 94–167, the result of a bill sponsored by Democratic congresswoman Bella Abzug, a Democrat from New York. The bill directed the National Commission on the Observance of International Women's Year to plan and convene a national women's conference with preparatory meetings in the states and authorized funding. In early 1977 Jimmy Carter took office as the nation's president, and thereafter, ordered an overhaul of the National Commission on Women. Acting on recommendations for the commission from Midge Costanza, the Presidential Assistant for Public Liaison, Carter approved the expansion of the commission to forty-two members, including thirteen women of color.[94]

Chicanas' experiences in Mexico City—both the affirmation and validation of women's experiences in a global context and the experiences of feeling excluded from the policies developed at the conference—were some of the factors that influenced these Los Angeles women's efforts to participate in the National Women's Conference in Houston, scheduled from November 18 through November 21, 1977, prior to which each state held its own preconference meetings. Each state established a coordinating committee, but according to activist Martha Cotera of Texas, there were no clear guidelines on the appointment process. In a draft of a statement titled "Chicanas Change Course of Texas IWY," Diana Camacho of Mujeres por la Causa wrote, "Chicanas have been monitoring IWY for years—since Mexico City, even. We were there, not officially but with our own money we made the trip. . . . We stayed on top of the nomination process [for the 1977 conference]. We wrote our congresspersons, called friends in Washington, held meetings, threatened and demanded representation, and we got *some*."[95] California's meeting, which sixty-five hundred women attended, was held from June 17 through June 19 in Los Angeles.[96] At this meeting the women elected their ninety-six delegates for Houston. Like their counterparts in Texas, they had lobbied and networked for representation. Indeed, "Gracia Molina-Pick, a former professor of Third World studies and a long-time Chicana activist, brought together women from the northern and southern parts of the State."[97] Molina-Pick, of San Diego, had also attended the IWY in Mexico City. Of these delegates, nineteen, or almost 20 percent, were of Spanish surname, and four were members of the Comisión Femenil.[98]

Moreover, California women decided who would lead the delegation. By this time, Chicanas had established networks built during years of bridging activism across the nation to "prioritize participation in our respective state IWY coordinating committees."[99] As Sandra Serrano Sewell of the Comisión Femenil recalled, the negotiations about leadership began to pit Latinas and African American against one another, but eventually, the California delegation reached a compromise: co-chairs of the delegation, California State Assemblywoman Maxine Waters and Los Angeles Deputy Mayor Grace Montañez Davis.[100] Given the experiences of Chicanas and African American women feeling unrepresented in Mexico City, this was an important outcome.

In late August 1977 the Comisión Femenil began its planning for travel and participation to assure that they would have the opportunity to fully participate in the conference. A meeting in October 1976 laid the groundwork for disseminating logistical information as well as addressing the goals for the Comisión Femenil's participation, including possible Chicana resolutions to propose or support in Houston.[101] Due to this careful planning, at the Houston conference the Comisión Femenil was one of four Latina organizations with official display booths in a total of 158 booths.[102] Staffed daily by Comisión members, the booth provided a brochure published by the organization that gave basic information about the group, established a central space for Latinas at the conference to leave message for one another, and provided a calendar of events specifically for them at the conference. In Mexico City, Chicanas from the Comisión Femenil had felt inadequately prepared to provide their political positionality to an international audience and felt unrepresented by the official and unofficial U.S. delegations. At the Houston conference the brochure, titled *La Mujer: International Women's Year 1977*, articulated the organization's vision of itself. Highlighting the historic nature of the conference and of Latina participation, the brochure placed the Comisión Femenil under the broad umbrella of feminism by writing that the organization supported "all women's issues" and the "National Plan of Action." The brochure also differentiated the Comisión Femenil as representing other interests, claiming that it would "insure the input of Hispanic women and their concerns" at the national event. Indeed, the brochure highlighted the three Latinas who sat on the national planning committee and the delegation vice chair Grace Montañez Davis, as a way to underscore the growing political power of its members. On one hand, the brochure made clear that the Comisión Femenil would stand up for Latina interests. On the other, it affirmed the Comisión's position as a feminist organization by articulating a notion of sisterhood. It stated, "During these four days, as the national focus is upon us, let us show the carinos [caring], support and lasting unity that we have for one another. Las Mujeres de California [the women of California]."[103]

Many retrospectives on the conference highlight the unity among women and point to the passage of the minority women's plank but elide the struggles on the road to its success. Cotera explained, "Sadly, our experiences in 1976–77, similar to the 1920s suffrage movement, revealed that white women leaders' passion for preserving the privilege of their race, class, and heterosexual preferences outweighed liberation for 'every woman.'"[104] The minority women's plank represented work by Latina, African American, Asian American, and Native American women in response to the lack of inclusion of any minority women's issues in the originally proposed planks that were circulated to each state prior to the national conference. It was also a response to a three-paragraph minority women's plank that also had been circulated before the conference. According to Lindsey Van Gelder, "Hammered out under deadline pressure from statements produced before or during the conference by four caucuses representing eight major minority groups, this dramatic resolution was the result of a drafting committee that was itself a major coalition, with representatives from each caucus who worked through much of Saturday night and Sunday morning."[105] According to historians Doreen J. Mattingly and Jessica L. Nare, the plank "was supported by a large majority and [was] received with thunderous applause. In the short term, at least, many women of color felt the revision of the Minority Women's Plank marked a decline in racism within the feminist movement."[106] As a testament to the Comisión Femenil's proactive stance and coalition building at the Houston conference, Sandra Serrano Sewell, the president of the national organization at the time, stood on stage on the last day with Ana Maria Perera of the National Association of Cuban Women and Celeste Benítez, senator from Puerto Rico and chair of the Puerto Rican delegation, to present the Hispanic women's plank as part of the minority women's plank to the entire gathering. The minority women's plank was the only resolution to be passed by the conference unanimously.[107]

Serrano Sewell recollected that the Comisión Femenil's position at the conference was "much more sophisticated ... by that time." As she recalled, the women in the Comisión Femenil "knew how to flex our weight, and knew how to intimidate, and knew how to articulate. And so our sophistication level had just grown so much that we were able to change ... the minority women's plank."[108] As the Comisión Femenil reported in its conference newsletter, "The unity demonstrated among all minority women was unprecedented. Even Bella Abzug, presiding officer of the conference, was inspired to comment that the unity among all the minority women was the most impressive ever at a feminist convention."[109] These actions cemented the growing political awareness and influence of the Comisión Femenil.[110] They also reflect how the Comisión was able to take the lessons of an international experience to guide efforts on a national level, reflecting a means of important bridging activism.

In an ongoing effort for more visibility for the organization, as well as for Chicanas in general, the Comisión Femenil continued to expand its linkages with global women's networks by attending other international conferences. In 1980 members attended the International Women's Conference in Copenhagen, this time as a nongovernmental organization affiliated with the United Nations, which allowed the organization to hold an official panel session and to set up an official booth to distribute information. Once again, the Comisión Femenil published a newsletter for the conference.[111] Serrano Sewell remembered,

> When you have a booth, and when you print information, and when you have things to hand out, and when you put together your fact sheets and when you do all those things you make other women aware of who you are. My belief is that when we were in Mexico City we were probably—other women thought we were just Mexicans. And so, you're just in a different ballgame.[112]

In this new arena, Chicanas envisioned liberation as a process that would need to unfold not only in their local communities and domestically, but also across the globe. This heightened international consciousness would have important impacts on the ways they continued to organize at home.

In 1975, when California Chicanas traveled to Mexico City for the first International Women's Year Conference, most arrived with a political ideology framed by cultural nationalism and a U.S.-specific awareness of racial, economic, political, and gendered oppression. Within the Chicano movement, they had attempted to reconcile cultural nationalism with feminism and had forged various methods of achieving this goal, such as working within existing organizations, founding periodicals, and establishing Chicana-specific organizations such as the Comisión Femenil Mexicana Nacional. In Mexico City, Chicanas began to understand the global nature of women's oppression and their own place in world politics. Their attendance at the U.N. meetings also confirmed the importance of their struggle at home. Their experiences revealed that they could think of themselves as part of a worldwide movement of women while they worked on issues at home.

The Mexico City conference laid the groundwork for the U.S. International Women's Year Conference in Houston in 1977. From their experiences in

Mexico City, Chicanas learned that they needed to lobby for and assure their own representation on official bodies planning for and participating in the conference. They utilized networks built through bridging activism in the Chicano movement and beyond to organize themselves. Women from the Comisión Femenil Mexicana Nacional in Los Angeles who had attended the IWY tribune were part of this effort among Chicanas from the Southwest. Chicanas organized strong platforms in the Hispanic Women's Caucus of the conference and built strong coalitions with other women of color.

By 1977 many of those who had attended the meetings in Mexico City worked to ensure their representation at the women's conference in Houston. Realizing the strength of coalition building, Chicanas worked with other U.S. women of color to pass the minority women's plank at the conference. In addition, the Comisión Femenil became an NGO with the United Nations and thus maintained a presence at the subsequent conference for International Women's Year in Copenhagen. Although they continued these international linkages, it is unclear that such activities led to sustained relationships with women and women's organizations in the international realm. Nevertheless, these global and local *encuentros* shaped the practice of Chicana feminism via the transnational exchange of ideas and experiences that helped Chicanas understand their struggle in the context of global struggles for justice and exposed the blind spots of U.S. feminism. Additionally, these encuentros cause us to attend to what Maylei Blackwell calls the "interpretive dilemmas" that emerge when studying influential events beset by political fault lines. Complex stories with a multitude of political actors evade simple categorization.[113] Chapter 4 returns to Los Angeles to explore how Chicanas utilized bridging activism to address Chicana body politics in the context of the Chicano movement.

4
"The Right to Govern Their Own Bodies"
CHICANA BODY POLITICS IN LOS ANGELES, 1969–1981

As an undergraduate student and activist in the 1960s, and before her involvement with the Comisión Femenil, Chicana feminist Anna NietoGómez worked as a counselor for the Educational Opportunity Program at Long Beach State College.[1] Reflecting on her experiences in the Chicano movement and as a counselor, she recalled that abortion and family planning were taboo subjects among students active in Chicano politics on campus and that, "it was not talked about, and if you talked about it you were a feminist and you would be talking against your man. And it was a loyalty issue. And the movement in L.A. was about la familia, keeping it together."[2] Indeed, discussions of reproductive rights in the era before *Roe v. Wade* would have been anomalous for young ethnic Mexican women. In addition, within the burgeoning Chicano movement, reproductive rights existed within the context of a cultural nationalism based on the notion that the Chicano family was both the foundation and the future of Chicano liberation. Women such as NietoGómez also observed the ways in which the pursuit of higher education provided newfound freedoms and independence for many young ethnic Mexican women, especially when they lived away from home in college housing. In a 1991 interview NietoGómez recalled that without the domestic responsibilities of home, young Chicana students could devote their time to their studies. They also enjoyed a new sexual liberation. For the young women she counseled, these new freedoms sometimes resulted in unwanted pregnancies, which, as NietoGómez witnessed, would often mean an end to higher education and shame from their families and communities. These circumstances led some women to put their health and lives at risk with self-induced abortions. NietoGómez concluded, "I realized for the women, [the] number one problem was they didn't have control over their bodies."[3]

NietoGómez's experience at Long Beach State College reflects the complicated arena of gendered body politics that Chicanas faced in the movimiento. Here, I use Nadia Brown's and Sarah Allen Gershon's definition of *body politics*, in which "the body itself is politically inscribed and is shaped by practices of containment and control" and is itself a site "where power is contested and negotiated."[4] In the movement, body politics arose in a context that placed the Chicano family, heterosexual and nuclear, one of its main foundations for liberation, with women's bodies at the center. That is, women in the movement embodied the future of Chicanos, in both reproduction and caretaking.[5] The movement was not "a monolithic entity," as Richard T. Rodríguez notes, but existed "as a social force emerging from distinct regions and multiple social justice trajectories." Nevertheless, the "family principle" was a touchstone that "figured prominently in various organizational practices and discursive strategies put forth by movement leaders."[6] This family principle "engendered constructions of idealized femininity largely by conflating a conservative cultural construct of 'tradition' with a particular version of family," writes Maylei Blackwell. Blackwell goes on to say that "this view of family was seen as the foundational unit of revolutionary culture" and as such "needed every man, woman, and child—in that order."[7] In this sense, because birth control, abortion, and the practice of forced sterilization curtailed the reproduction of the heterosexual Chicano family, many in the movement viewed these practices as being under the umbrella of genocide. This framework left no room for reproductive rights for individual women because the Chicano family served the collective Chicano community, and women's bodies served the movement sexually and as domestic labor. Consequently, Chicana feminists such as NietoGómez came to recognize that the belief that women should control their own bodies conflicted with the ideology that the family, its procreation, and its maintenance were foremost in achieving social justice for Chicanos. As the scholar Laura Elisa Pérez argues, Chicanas' struggle for the right to control their own bodies "with respect to the reshaping of both Aztlán and the United States—was disordering the content of patriarchal and Eurocentric notions of subject, family, community, and nation."[8]

I argue that Chicanas in the late 1960s and throughout the 1970s, whether they believed in ancient methods of birth control, rallied against forced sterilization, or established free clinics that provided reproductive counseling, consistently asserted that as women they had the right to make their own decisions about their bodies. The declaration of Chicana bodily autonomy served as a strong counternarrative to the ways in which cultural nationalist ideas rooted in the concept of the Chicano family positioned the Chicana body as a sex object, as a vessel for producing children for the movement, as a stalwart against a perceived master plan for ethnic extinction, and as a conduit for transmitting culture. Indeed, just as the movement was not monolithic, neither were the ways in which women in the movement thought about or acted on issues related to bodily autonomy. Both proactively and reactively Chicanas utilized the Chicano movement's goal of self-determination and applied it to themselves, specifically with regard to control over their bodies, grounded in their understanding of how gender, race, ethnicity, and class affected their lives. At this point in the conversation, they did not, generally speaking, conceive of the way in which sexuality was also an important factor.[9]

Chicanas developed their understandings of body politics within the national discourse about family planning and abortion rights in the 1960s and 1970s. Birth control had been legalized in 1965, there was a surge of activity vis-à-vis women's liberation, and the right to abortion had been affirmed by the Supreme Court in Roe v. Wade in 1973. These developments occurred against a backdrop of a national concern founded on racial anxieties about population growth and an increase in immigration to the country, specifically, immigration from Mexico. As sociologist Elena R. Gutiérrez notes, these issues converged to place Mexican-origin women in the spotlight. Not only should immigration from Mexico be curtailed, especially in California, but so should the reproductive capabilities of women of Mexican origin.[10] This idea, of course, built on a much longer history of popular and state actions that targeted Mexicans and Mexican American populations in the United States, from deportation to coercive sterilization campaigns.[11]

Women in the Chicano movement faced a complicated reality. Their desire to assert control over their bodies confronted new national and state priorities of family planning that targeted them. Indeed, some viewed this governmental push toward family planning as another mechanism of state control. They also did not feel connected to nor a part of the mainstream women's liberation movement, however, due to its narrow focus on gender, which did not account for how class and race impacted women's reproductive freedoms. Historian Estelle Freedman reminds us that "the feminist movements of the twentieth century increasingly embraced contraception and abortion as necessary for reproductive choice."[12] Chicanas and other ethnic Mexican women contended with forced sterilization, which was not a mainstream women's liberation issue. As scholar Jennifer Nelson writes, "In 1973, few mainstream feminists viewed ending sterilization abuse as an important demand in the fight for women's reproductive freedom. For most white women involved in women's liberation, reproductive freedom meant access to safe legal abortion and contraception."[13] Most white women had no knowledge of or experience with forced sterilization within their communities. In fact, many white feminist organizations lobbied for sterilization on demand.[14] Because of the activism of Chicanas and other women of color in the 1970s, "reproductive rights feminists came to maintain that the right to bear children was as important to reproductive freedom as the legal right to terminate a pregnancy."[15]

In Los Angeles, Chicanas published their views on body politics in various venues, engaged in serious discussions about reproductive rights and justice, established and ran a free clinic, and led the fight against the forced sterilization of ethnic Mexican women. In this chapter I use oral history interviews with key participants, archival sources, and editorials and articles from Chicano movement and other periodicals of the era to elucidate the ways in which ethnic Mexican women of the era took various and sometimes opposing positions on important women's issues of their time such as abortion. Yet even as we will see that disparate organizations such as the Brown Berets, the Committee to Free Los Tres, and the Comisión Femenil did not advocate for the same policies, their praxis was grounded in a firm belief in a woman's right to control and make decisions about her own body. Through their bridging activism in this arena, Chicanas brought a tradition of organizing to raise Mexican American women's collective status and rights to bear on contemporary theoretical and conversations about women's bodily self-determination while also making key contributions to the emerging conceptual framework of reproductive justice.[16]

Reproductive Rights and the Founding of the Comisión Femenil

We now return to the founding of the Comisión Femenil Mexicana at the 1970 Mexican American National Issues Conference, where participants regarded abortion rights and childcare as paramount issues on their agenda. Although the CFMN consistently asserted itself as a staunchly pro-choice and pro–reproductive rights organization since its founding, its public position did not mean that internal debates about these issues did not take place.[17] Examining the resolutions presented at this founding meeting provides insights into the process by which the Comisión Femenil developed its public pro-choice approach to body politics. More specifically, it highlights how Chicana activists strategized about bridging political and generational differences in order to advance a sophisticated pro-choice vision that would include abortion among a host of other reproductive rights for women.[18]

The Women's Workshop resolutions included women's right to self-determination, stressing Mexican American women's plight of "unwanted pregnancies," traditional relegation "to the home," and "the right to govern their own bodies." The resolution highlighted these issues as a preamble to the following: "That the Comision Femenil goes on record as supporting free and legalized abortions for all women who want or need them." They also resolved that the "Women's Workshop go on record as recommending that every Chicano community promote and set up 24-hour day care facilities in every Chicano community to service our people."[19]

These internal Women's Workshop resolutions were intended for presentation to and adoption by the Mexican American National Issues Conference as a body, including men and women who did not take part in the Women's Workshop. In this period, various groups had identified abortion as against the Chicano movement, anti-family, and anti-revolution. As such, the forceful and direct support of both abortion rights and childcare, although for a conference-specific audience, showed the importance of these issues for participants in the Women's Workshop. The Comisión Femenil resolution, however, mentioned neither childcare centers nor support of abortion. The statement that most closely addressed such issues in this resolution stated, "That the Comisión concern itself in promoting programs which specifically lend themselves to help, assist and promote solutions to female type problems and problems concerning the Mexican family."[20] Thus, the second resolution that the Comisión Femenil publicly declared in its founding document made no explicit mention of abortion rights.[21]

These resolutions tell simultaneous stories of internal conflict, organizational pragmatism, and political know-how. According to one anonymous participant's meeting notes from the Women's Workshop, most women who participated in the meeting saw abortion as their right as women. According to this observer, however, the issue engendered conflict between older and younger women who were present. She wrote, "It was clear that a lot of discussion needs to be held on such questions. Both from the point of view of the young women as well as for the benefit of older women that still hold closely ideas of the past."[22] This generational distinction may have been too simple, however. As Dolores Sánchez, a member of the CFMN, recalled, "Abortion was something—if it was practiced, it wasn't overt. It wasn't something that we were comfortable in discussing and it wasn't something that we allowed to come between us."[23] Francisca Flores, a contemporary of Sánchez and co-convener and co-organizer of the Women's Workshop, felt differently. The following year, she published "Comisión Femenil Mexicana" in the periodical that she edited, *Regeneración*, where she wrote that the Comisión was a place where women could come together to discuss abortion "without having to first discuss the emotional question or moral issue."²⁴ Flores posited that terminating a pregnancy was "a fact of life" and that women faced with this decision "do not first get into a discussion of moral issues . . . [its need] is present, urgent and the quicker they can address themselves to that issue the better."²⁵

Flores's public announcement that the Comisión Femenil accepted abortion as a fact of life was an important resolution to any internal debate that had arisen when the organization that she co-led was founded. The Comisión Femenil resolution, however, was an astute political move that melded the variety of opinions about abortion into a generalized statement that would still encompass that same spirit. As a bridging mechanism, the resolution is also an example of both the "Hallway Movidas" and "Home-Making Movidas" that Espinoza, Cotera, and Blackwell denote in *Chicana Movidas*. That is, by altering the Resolution to Establish Comisión Femenil Mexicana Nacional, Inc., with a call to "promot[e] programs" to "help, assist and promote solutions to female type problems and problems concerning the Mexican family," the women who drafted this resolution both practiced "hidden insurgencies within and at the margins of political and institutional spaces" and "[made] a space for Chicana feminism to live and develop."²⁶ That is, they utilized the space of the National Mexican American Issues Conference to "challenge the internalities of power and form new networks of resistance." By establishing their own Chicana organization, these women also "work[ed] within existing Chicano movement projects" and "create[d] separate and independent Chicana institutions."²⁷ This chapter now turns to how and why Chicanas maneuvered in different ways to address and challenge prevailing ideas about women and their place in the midst of Chicano nationalist ideology.

Body Politics Within the Movimiento

Within the movement, Chicanas faced a nationalist ideology founded on the nuclear and heterosexual family. One of the pivotal documents of the movement, El Plan Espiritual de Aztlán, written for the Chicano Youth Liberation Conference in Denver, Colorado, in 1969, declared that "cultural values of life, family, and home will serve as a powerful weapon to defeat the gringo dollar value system and encourage the process of love and brotherhood." As a symbol of the movement, El Plan de Aztlán indeed provided a unifying language and sensibility that rested on an Aztec indigenous heritage and the right to reclaim land, and as scholar Lee Bebout points out, "provided a means of imagining community and mediating the heterogeneity of the movement." Importantly, El Plan elided any acknowledgment of indigenous peoples in the land Chicanos were to reclaim. Indeed, Maylei Blackwell asserts that El Plan "enabled the transformation of a historically specific configuration of race, class, and gender into a seemingly timeless ideal through an interlocking definition of manhood, peoplehood, self-determination, and the reclamation of working-class ideals." Furthermore, "asserting 'machismo' then became a pathway to resist the gendered implications of white supremacy."[28] Moreover, as Rodríguez notes, El Plan de Aztlán explicitly espoused the idea of "la familia de la raza," wherein "la familia and la raza" were formulated "to complement and service one another."[29] When women critiqued these formulations of family, they confronted a cultural nationalism that categorized them as what Anne McClintock calls the "symbolic bearers of the nation" who were "denied any direct relation to national agency" because they were not seen as full citizens of this Chicano nation.[30]

In addition to calling for a separate women's organization such as the Comisión Femenil, women confronted and critiqued ideologies and practices that circumscribed their lives in service to the movement by means of the printed word, as discussed in previous chapters. This included letters to the editor. The 1970 and 1971 issues of the literary magazine *Con Safos*, published in East Los Angeles from 1968 to 1972, provide an example of the very distinct and conflicting views of women's roles in the movement.[31] In 1971 the editors of the magazine printed two letters to the editor, one from "A Chicana from Pittsburg" and one from Yolanda O. Rodriguez. Both letters sharply criticized Oscar Zeta Acosta's "Love Letter to the Girls of Aztlan," published in the 1970 issue. In his "Love Letter" Zeta Acosta, a well-known Chicano movement attorney, activist, and writer, professed an extremely narrow and sexist vision of love based on what the "girls of Aztlan" and their bodies could do for him and men like him. For Zeta Acosta, these "girls" served no other purpose than as sexual and domestic objects, useful only for sex with "muy macho guys of the movement" like himself and for the "making of our brown babies who shall bear our names and not yours," and as cooks, maids, and typists.[32]

Yolanda O. Rodriguez and "Una Chicana de Pittsburg" expressed their frustration with Zeta Acosta's clear misogyny and sexism. Rodriguez addressed her letter "Para 'Zeta' y para otros que piensan como el" (For 'Zeta' and for those that think like him), and wrote, "Your letter addressed to the girls of Aztlán is a good example of the Chicano mentality prevalent in the movement. From the contents of it I gather that you want Chicanas to join the movement for the sole purpose of helping you booze it up, smoking pot, having brown babies, and unbuckling brassieres."[33] She continued, "Is there no place for us Chicanas in your world other than in your bed or petate? Don't you believe that we are capable of contributing something constructive to the revolution you so fervently await?" "Una Chicana de Pittsburg" expressed similar sentiments, articulating her familiarity with the main tenets of Zeta Acosta's views. She wrote, "Your love letter sounds more like a proposition, and not a very good one at that. Again, you are bringing us down and burdening us with the responsibilities for your hang-ups. Man, you are so full of ca-ca it hurts me. Especially when I see you multiplied hundreds of times in the name of the revolution."[34] In their letters to *Con Safos*, "Una Chicana" and Rodriguez did not take the editors of the literary magazine, all men, to task for publishing Zeta Acosta's piece in the first place. Although they were identified as letters to the editor, both writers addressed their missives directly to Zeta Acosta.

Indeed, for Zeta Acosta, "girls of Aztlan" did not and should not think for themselves. Ideas about gender equality, or as he called them, "poems speeches and little bits of propaganda," could not come from the minds of Chicanas but had to be "copied from some white woman's notes." Any mention of gender equality was "an attack on [his] machismo . . . a relic of yesterdays' hangups." As a "muy macho guy of the movement," Zeta Acosta reminded brown women of their duties and obligations "lest we perish forever from this land." They were to "love feel feed laugh structure and lift us out of history's muck and mire of a despondent-dependency and it is for you and only for you that we struggle to maintain our identity in our language tradition culture and way of life which is brown chicano raza." In Zeta Acosta's conception, Chicanas were responsible for not only satisfying the sexual desires of Chicanos and bearing "brown babies" but also keeping and transmitting culture. Men did not share this responsibility.[35]

The letter from "Una Chicana" chastised Zeta Acosta for perpetuating stereotypical tropes about Chicanas. In fact, the author had solicited opinions from other Chicanas, whom she quoted in her letter. She wrote, "One young lady, nineteen years old, that I asked to react to your love letter wrote[,] 'Most of the Chicanas I know were brought up to keep their self-respect (virginity). So it seems to me it is part of our tradition. But now, even in our own Raza, girls are more loose with themselves. The decision, in my opinion, should be left up to the individual.'" "Una Chicana" also provided historical context when she brought Sor Juana de la Cruz into the conversation, stating that Sor Juana "lived years ago and the Mexican male chauvinism hasn't been liberalized much in all these years." Sor Juana Inés de la Cruz, a seventeenth-century Catholic nun and criolla born in colonial Mexico, is regarded by some as Latin America's first feminist. In the layout of "Una Chicana de Pittsburg's" letter, the editors of *Con Safos* placed an asterisk next to Sor Juana's name, and at the end of the letter they noted in parentheses, "Poems of Sor Juana Ines de la Cruz, translated by Srta. Bernice Rincón[,] are printed in another portion of this issue." The editors included one of Sor Juana's best-known poems, "Hombres necios" ("Foolish Men"), published in *Las Redondillas* in 1689 (also known as *A Philosophical Satire*). The poem pointed out the double standard regarding men's and women's behavior, especially regarding sexual relations.[36] Including this poem was certainly an acknowledgment that the editors read their correspondence carefully and attempted to provide a counterbalance to Zeta Acosta's views. But the editors soon dispelled any suggestion that they themselves found Zeta Acosta's views problematic.

In the next issue the editors published an excerpt of Zeta Acosta's *Autobiography of a Brown Buffalo* (as Zeta Acosta called himself) and indicated that the *Autobiography* would be serialized in their magazine. By continuing to provide Zeta Acosta with a platform, the editors conveyed tacit support of Zeta Acosta's views. In the 1972 issue they published "El Memo de Con Safos, Subject: Brown Buffalo," in which they compared the Brown Buffalo to the animals that "roamed the prairies long before the Europeans came across" and that were never "domesticated" or made "beast[s] of burden." The editors celebrated Zeta Acosta's wild nature and commended the "few concerned people [who] prevented the inevitable extinction by caring for him, protecting him and allowing him once again to roam free." Claiming him as one of their own, and with both lament and admiration, the editors announced, "So it is that our Brown Buffalo has been reborn."[37]

Although the influence of *Con Safos* in the Chicano movement is unclear, Oscar Zeta Acosta was a well-known figure; he was one of the few Chicano lawyers of the era who represented activists charged with various crimes. As scholar Ian Haney-Lopez writes, "Consumed by a hatred of the courts and committed to the Chicano struggle, Acosta became the lead attorney for the Chicano movement in Los Angeles."[38] His attitude toward women may not have been shared by all men in the movement, but his "Love Letter to the Girls of Aztlan" manifested the tolerance and enabling of sexist ideas as well as general anxieties about women. Those ideas provided the milieu in which Chicanas forged their own vision of their value and worth in the movement and in society.[39]

Chicanas Write Body Politics

As a group, Chicanas held positions about specific issues ranging from birth control to abortion that reflected a diversity of thought, yet still articulated a central belief in a Chicana's right to control her body. Chicanas connected this right to a broader vision in which women's abilities to control their own fertility provided a strategic framework for resisting, rather than allowing or being complicit in, genocidal state violence against their communities. Like "Una Chicana de Pittsburg" and Yolanda Rodriguez, Chicanas, including members of the Comisión Femenil, voiced their visions for a place and a future within the movement with respect to body politics in various periodicals and within the organizations they joined. In doing so, they expressed their views on many fronts, creating bridges that connected their various struggles.

For some Chicanas, bodily autonomy meant that "La Raza's future depend[ed] on the health of all Chicanas in order for them to be able to continue to bear healthy Chicanitos." The "Concerned Chicanas" who penned "Genocide on the Chicano Family" (published in the Brown Beret newspaper *La Causa* in March 1970) grounded their position in cultural nationalist tenets. Although they clearly believed in the idea of la familia de la raza as a revolutionary foundation, their position differed from that of men such as Zeta Acosta and the women who founded the Comisión Femenil. The authors articulated a deep mistrust of government family planning efforts, but did not envisage a world that regarded women as sex objects for men. They posited that all family planning programs, federal or state, were funded by a "racist white government to exterminate 'La Raza Chicana.'"[40] As mentioned above, they were not completely incorrect. In 1970 Congress passed the Family Planning Services and Research Act, the nation's first act to "provide[] federal funding for family planning services and research and support[] the formation of the office of Population Affairs within the Department of Health, Education and Welfare."[41] Prior to this federal legislation, California had implemented a Population Study Commission in 1966 "charged with reviewing the state's activities to increase 'freedom of choice' in family planning and to investigate discrimination in making these services available in public programming." California did not adopt the recommendations of the Population Study Commission, but the state continued to explore the perceived connection between overpopulation and family planning, and specifically the role of immigrants (especially those from Mexico) as the main drivers of the state's growing population.[42] When "Concerned Chicanas" wrote about the state's goal of exterminating "la raza Chicana," their alarm had merit. Historian Alexandra Minna Stern writes, "As early as the 1920s, California eugenicists such as Goethe, Jordan, and Holms asserted that Mexicans were irresponsible breeders who flooded over the border in 'hordes' and undeservingly sapped fiscal resources."[43] Indeed, these ideas were put into practice in various laws across the nation and in California, which hosted by far the nation's largest coercive sterilization program beginning in the early twentieth century. It was not until 1979 that California's sterilization law was repealed.[44] The authors of "Genocide on the Chicano Family" had made the racialized and gendered connections between the nation's and the state's interest in promoting family planning and their interest in controlling the population, specifically those not classified as white.

The "Concerned Chicanas" were also skeptical of the birth control pill, noting that it was "still in experimental stages," as well as all other forms of birth control at the time. They blamed the "white race" for creating the socioeconomic circumstances which circumscribed Chicanas' ability to choose to have children. The writers looked back to the "balance of nature" that had "always been understood by our people" as the way forward for Chicanas to reclaim their ancestral ways and the "love and respect we have for both life and nature."[45] Railing against government institutions, Concerned Chicanas articulated a common nationalist vision of women's physical place in the movement.

While these views of Chicanas as procreators for the movement placed the responsibility for child rearing in the hands of women, their emphasis on the right of Chicanas to have children regardless of socioeconomic status went beyond the typical conversations about choice. By stressing a Chicana right to have children unfettered by socioeconomic constraints, the authors came closer to the reproductive justice perspective that emerged in the 1990s. As Loretta Ross and Rickie Solinger write, "The definition of reproductive justice goes beyond the pro-choice/pro-life debate and has three primary principles: 1) the right *not* to have a child; 2) the right to *have* a child; and 3) the right to *parent* children in safe and healthy environments. In addition, reproductive justice demands sexual autonomy and gender freedom for every human being."[46] The authors who called themselves Concerned Chicanas certainly expressed their views in a cultural nationalist framework, but as women they articulated their desire for revolutionary babies in a way that called attention to the right of women to parent their children with all the resources for those children to thrive. In this way, the position of "Concerned Chicanas" reflected a general agreement with the participants in the Women's Workshop at the Mexican American National Issues Conference in 1970 when the latter discussed parenting and childcare. That is, "Concerned Chicanas" may have framed their position in cultural nationalist terms, but their agenda called for women's bodily autonomy overall.

"Concerned Chicanas" stood on one side of this spectrum of reproductive rights, while Sylvia Delgado, author of a 1971 two-part article on Chicanas, discussed their self-determination in day-to-day terms as she wrote about beauty, marriage, and abortion. Delgado's "Young Chicana Speaks Up on

Problems Faced by Young Girls," which summarized the contradictions and double standards of growing up a woman, was published in *Regeneración*. The article was part plea to Chicanos and part advice column for young Chicanas. In the same year that she published these articles, Delgado worked as a "birth control counselor at a clinic in East Los Angeles."[47] In a sympathetic tone she urged young Chicanas to make their own choices but to be aware of their consequences. She wrote, "You must choose your own morals. If you believe that sex before marriage is wrong, then fine, this is your feelings. But remember, they may not be shared by others. Others may feel you are wrong for thinking so." She also cautioned, "You've yourself to think about. He may pledge undying love for you but as soon as you mention you are late on your period you may never catch sight of him again."[48] Here, Delgado implied both the economic and social consequences of single motherhood, reminiscent of Anna NietoGómez's observations of Chicana college students at Long Beach State. But she left it in the hands of Chicanas to decide how they would proceed.

In part 2, "Chicana: The Forgotten Woman," Delgado critiqued the idea that Chicana bodily autonomy worked as a mechanism of cultural genocide. Emphasizing Chicana/o poverty, Delgado depicted scenarios in the life of a Chicana single mother and her struggles to feed and provide a foundation for her children. Delgado portrayed her protagonist as someone with no future prospects due to lack of education, cultural exposure, and expression, and as the last person to be considered in the Chicano struggle. Directing her language to men in the community, she wrote, "If one person is in slavery, then there is no such thing as liberation. The battle is half lost for you if you have forgotten about your women." Concerning birth control, abortion, and their relation to genocide, Delgado wrote, "We accuse genocide. La Raza's cry. So we turn to increasing the population. But what kind of padres are we, if we are going to see our sons raised in slavery, with cut-rate education, poverty, and to watch our children die? I say no to fools who say women are tools for copulation and birth."[49] In so writing, Delgado clearly rebuffed the ideas that birth control was genocide in action and that Chicanas served the movement solely as sex objects. The appearance of Delgado's articles in Francisca Flores's publication highlights the intentional bridging of Chicana work, ideology, and political activism. As editor of *Regeneración*, Flores had accepted Delgado's articles. In 1971 Flores was also an active member of the Comisión Femenil Mexicana Nacional. It is possible that Delgado, as someone who worked in healthcare, used her work experience to inform her writing; she also took her perspectives public. In these ways, Delgado and Flores bridged many fronts simultaneously to spread their message.

Providing a perspective similar to Delgado's, Anna NietoGómez, a founding member of the Hijas de Cuauhtémoc at California State University, Long Beach, who was later affiliated with the Chicana Service Action Center and the Comisión Femenil, among other groups and organizations, focused on issues of reproduction within the social context of Chicana experiences. In a 1974 article published in the "first journal of Chicana scholarship," *Encuentro Femenil*, NietoGómez contended that Chicana reproductive issues and rights had to be examined with attention to "doctor's racism, insensitivity to the Chicano culture[,] the lack of bilingual medical staff," and "inadequate health services." Only by considering the "dangerous combination of racism and sexism" could "health programs such as birth control and abortion clinics" fairly serve Chicanas' needs. In order to accomplish this, the programs had to be "community controlled." Community control was important in this context in light of what "Concerned Chicanas" had expressed years earlier. NietoGómez wrote, "When a Chicana talks about birth control and abortion she does so in the context of understanding the cultural genocidal acts of this country."[50] In this way, she asserted Chicanas' intelligence and understanding of these complex relationships. Institutions she interacted with would therefore need to share this consciousness, for instance, through their community locations and personnel, in order to allow her to be justly cared for by them. An academic journal, *Encuentro Femenil* was founded by members of Hijas de Cuauhtémoc at CSU Long Beach, among others. Blackwell writes that "the journal served as an important space for autonomous Chicana cultural production and the emergence of Chicana feminist scholarship that was deeply embedded in community-based Chicana organizing."[51]

As Chicanas articulated strong critiques of U.S. government policies and history in regard to women's bodily autonomy, especially that of women of color, they also critiqued other institutions such as the Catholic Church. In a 1971 article published in *Las Hijas de Cuauhtémoc*, a precursor to *Encuentro Femenil*, Sandra Ugarte reported on a regional Chicana conference in Los Angeles where participants resolved that "The Church has supported the necessity to keep the woman ignorant, barefoot, and pregnant by condemning legal abortions and birth control."[52] The critique was not limited to Los Angeles; Chicanas in other areas voiced similar concerns. For example, at the first national Chicana conference, held in Houston in 1971, the women passed the resolution "Sex and the Chicana," stating, "We should destroy the myth that religion and culture control our sexual lives" and "We recognize that we have been oppressed by religion and that the religious writing was done by men and interpreted by men."[53]

The linking of reproductive rights with self-determination was a powerful rhetorical tool and a belief system that guided many women's bridging activism during this era as they became more involved in issues related to reproductive rights. At the same Houston conference the women provided rationales for a resolution asking "that the National Chicana Conference go on record as supporting family planning and free and legal abortions for all women who want or need them." The rationales touched on the "social problems" of "unwanted babies" and stated that "the need for self-determination and the right to govern their own bodies is a necessity for the freedom of all people."[54] In 1972, highlighting the social structures that impinged on many Chicanas, *The Militant*, the national newspaper of the Socialist Workers Party, published a piece by Beverly Padilla, who wrote, "Control of one's own body and mind is *not* up to each individual woman at this stage of reality. All Chicanas are asking for is a choice whether or not to be a wife or mother, to be given a chance to choose their life roles."[55] Although ruptures existed between Chicanas and mainstream feminist ideologies and practices, Chicanas consistently asserted their right to bodily autonomy. Padilla wrote, "Many feel that the issue of 'right to abortion' and 'control of one's own body' is a white women's liberation hang-up. Like hell; it is not a white woman's hang-up exclusively. For years Chicanas, just as all women, have been bearing children that they didn't want. For years they have suffered and died from self-induced and illegal abortions."[56]

This small sample of articles penned by Chicanas during this period highlights the ways in which body politics intersected with religious beliefs, cultural nationalism, and reliance on traditional or indigenous healing methods. The authors of these articles approached the issue from a variety of perspectives, but they all shared a clear belief in the importance of Chicanas' autonomy over their bodies as an essential pillar of liberation for their communities.

Matters of body politics, including abortion and birth control, also had a particular meaning for Chicanas in relation to Euro-American mainstream feminism, and Chicanas strove to expand the issues in the discourse of "choice." For them, as for other women of color, "abortion was not the only, or even primary focus," writes Jennifer Nelson.[57] Chicanas believed that white feminists cared only about gender issues and actively ignored issues of class and race, including when it came to body politics. Despite the contentious relation between ideas of women's bodily autonomy, feminism, and the Chicano movement's foundation in patriarchal notions of family, Chicanas in the movement put their ideology into practice regarding these issues in movement organizations. In doing so, they set a Chicana feminist foundation for community and political action around issues of reproductive rights, which they continually connected through bridging activism to broader campaigns of community empowerment. This chapter now turns to moments in the movement when a Chicana praxis of bodily autonomy took place in the first free clinic in East Los Angeles, the struggle against forced sterilization, and finally an exploration of the complexities of organizational politics in the Comisión Femenil Mexicana Nacional.

The Brown Berets and El Barrio Free Clinic

In 1969 Gloria Arellanes, a member of the Chicano paramilitary organization the Brown Berets, became the director of the newly established El Barrio Free Clinic (EBFC) in East Los Angeles. The clinic offered birth control and other sexual health services, well baby visits, lab services, and psychological services, all provided by volunteer doctors, nurses, and psychologists.[58] It also provided abortion counseling (though not abortion services) based on the belief that women needed to be informed about as many alternatives as possible in order to make their own choices. Well before any Chicana conferences that drafted resolutions on Chicana rights to abortion or reproductive rights, the EBFC was putting support for bodily autonomy into practice.[59] Although the clinic was a project of the Brown Berets, Arellanes recalled, by default it was a Chicana-run operation since only women Brown Beret members volunteered.

Arellenes's experience with the Brown Berets and the Free Clinic are additional examples of bridging activism. As a member of one organization devoted to social change, Arellanes took on additional responsibilities at another, the clinic, that advanced a vision of social justice, one that offered unique services specifically for women. Arellanes, who was born in 1946 in East Los Angeles and grew up in El Monte, a suburb of Los Angeles, had become involved with the Chicano movement during her high school years. In the mid-1960s she attended the Mexican-American Youth Leadership Conference sponsored by the Los Angeles Commission on Human Relations and hosted at Camp Hess Kramer in Malibu, California, part of the Wilshire Boulevard Temple. The youth leadership conference "became the vehicle for igniting a new generation of Mexican-American reformers" through community building and dialogue among the high school leaders in attendance. One of the outgrowths of this leadership conference was Young Citizens for Community Action, a precursor to the Brown Berets.[60] After graduating from high school, Arellanes attended East Los Angeles College, where she eventually joined the Brown Berets along with a group of women friends, paving the way to the EBFC.

The Brown Berets emerged in 1968 as a new incarnation of an organization called Young Chicanos for Community Action (YCCA).[61] The group saw itself as protector of the Mexican American community in East Los Angeles, especially in regard to police brutality. For example, in March 1968, the Brown Berets participated in the East Los Angeles High School Walkouts both as participants and as security for Mexican American students boycotting their high schools to protest and call attention to the inferior education that they were receiving.

When the Brown Berets established the El Barrio Free Clinic they saw it as a way to provide healthcare services to their community, an additional way to serve.[62] As in other Chicano movement organizations, the Brown Berets practiced a gendered division of labor such that when the clinic was established, women such as Gloria Arellanes, a minister of the Brown Berets at the time, took on the responsibility of its administration and day-to-day activities.[63] It was unusual for a woman to hold a position of public leadership, as did Arellanes. Her leadership of the Free Clinic, an outgrowth of her status in the organization, however, was in line with this gendered division of labor. The Brown Berets saw reproductive and family healthcare as a women's issue, so the Free Clinic became a women's operation.

Her assignment as director of the Free Clinic, an implicitly gendered space, represents the complex interplay between women's public leadership in the Chicano movement and the limits and sometimes the dangers of their activism. Arellanes recalled that during her membership in the Brown Berets, at one point she had escaped rape by members of another Brown Beret chapter and had also known about sexual harassment and physical assault of women in the movement. In a 2011 interview, she reflected, "I was very blessed that I wasn't ever physically hit and I wasn't sexually harassed. But other women, they were harassed."[64] It is possible that spaces such as the clinic, because they were staffed by women, offered Chicanas in the movement a safer environment in which to operate. It is also possible that familiarity with experiences of sexual violence and harassment like those detailed by Arellanes impelled some women to want to direct their activism toward projects that bolstered women's health and bodily autonomy.

The clinic had been established through a collaborative effort between the Brown Berets and groups such as Psychologists for Social Action and the Fairfax Free Clinic. Funding support came from the Mexican-American Community Programs, and for a time, from the Catholic Church.[65] Not limited to reproductive healthcare, the clinic catered to all members of the community in East Los Angeles, treating gunshot wounds as well as providing immunizations for children. Although the clinic was short-lived, it served as a symbol of the possibilities of healthcare by and for ethnic Mexican communities. El Barrio Free Clinic also serves as an example of how women in the Chicano movement bridged their activism across various organizations, often simultaneously. It exemplifies how they utilized their political networks to found institutions to address conditions they saw in their communities. El Barrio Free Clinic also expanded the notion of reproductive rights in its efforts to incorporate some reproductive care for its patients. In the next section, we turn to the ways in which multiple organizations engaged in the struggle against forced sterilization in Los Angeles and the ways in which this effort moved the Comisión Femenil toward a reproductive justice agenda.

Forced Sterilization

During the late 1960s the Chicana Welfare Rights Organization, under the leadership of Alicia Escalante, encouraged the formation of a forum where women could openly discuss their issues. During meetings, several women revealed that they had been unknowingly sterilized after childbirth. These revelations, among others, led to the first lawsuit regarding the forced sterilization of ethnic Mexican women at the University of Southern California–Los Angeles County Medical Center, filed in early 1974. In these early years, the Bar Sinister Legal Collective, a Marxist legal defense organization in the Los Angeles area, contacted a leftist Chicano organization called the Committee to Free Los Tres (Committee to Free the Three) regarding a forced sterilization civil lawsuit, *Andrade v. Los Angeles County*, that Chicano lawyer Ricardo Cruz was preparing against this medical center.[66] Numerous Chicana activists would become involved in the events that transpired, which helped raise awareness of the genocidal nature of public health programs and contributed to the growth of a wider antisterilization campaign.

The Committee to Free Los Tres (CTFLT), which was active between 1972 and 1975, had probably been contacted by the Bar Sinister because both had similar ideologies and causes. The committee had been formed as a defense organization for Juan Fernández, Alberto Ortiz, and Rodolfo Sánchez, three young men from the Pico Gardens–Aliso Village housing projects in Boyle Heights who had been arrested and incarcerated after a confrontation with a drug dealer in the neighborhood who was later found to be an undercover federal agent. As the committee developed its defense strategy for Fernández, Ortiz, and Sánchez, the organization concluded that the case of Los Tres was one of political imprisonment. As a defense organization, the committee had adopted a Marxist ideology and had come to view the United States as an imperialist nation. On these ideological grounds, the CTFLT connected with other radical organizations in the Los Angeles area, including the Bar Sinister.⁶⁷

A case of sterilization without consent was quite different from political imprisonment, but as an organization that emerged as part of the Chicano movement, the CTFLT concluded that the sterilization case was but "another example of the violation of the rights of Latinos and working-class people by an imperialist nation."⁶⁸ *Andrade v. Los Angeles County*, filed in 1974 by Cruz, asked for $6 million in damages on behalf of five women who had been sterilized without their consent at USC-LACMC. In preparation for the case, CTFLT members Isabel Chávez Rodríguez and Patricia Córdova helped locate women to take part in the case and worked as bilingual interpreters for Cruz.⁶⁹ Participation in the research for this lawsuit led Chávez Rodríguez, Córdova, and the CTFLT to join the Committee to Stop Forced Sterilizations (CSFS), which was not a solely Chicana/o organization but rather a broad, cross-racial coalition of groups with an array of political orientations. The CTFLT's purpose in participating in the CSFS was twofold. It organized Latina women to participate in the cause and it attempted to develop "general principles of unity" for their "anti-imperialist attack" against the system that had perpetuated this bodily violence against so many women and communities.⁷⁰

In late 1974 an interracial coalition of community and political groups began to agitate against forced sterilization, including the Committee to Stop Forced Sterilizations, the Committee to Free Los Tres, the Solidarity Band, and the Bread and Roses Guerrilla Theatre of the Los Angeles Women's Union. In rallies and demonstrations, these groups identified the leading perpetrators of this practice as the United States government, the Ford Foundation, the Rockefeller Foundation, and Planned Parenthood. In December 1974 these groups staged a joint demonstration at the hospital and taped their demands, in English and Spanish, to the hospital doors. At that demonstration, CTFLT member Isabel Chávez was the first to speak. Comparing the sterilization of Mexican women to the spaying of dogs, Chávez, "called it by its real names: fascism and genocide."⁷¹ Although the forced sterilization of Mexican women at USC-LACMC might have been a call to arms for other Chicano movement organizations, only the CTFLT was present.

The demands taped to the hospital doors called for the hospital to follow national guidelines for sterilizations, to perform hysterectomies for patient health and not for "surgical practice," to screen and treat gonorrhea to prevent sterilization, to hire bilingual staff and provide bilingual consent forms, and to put an "end to medical experimentation on poor people." They also called for the hospital to "provide sterilization statistics regarding how many sterilizations were performed each year and on whom."⁷² But friction arose regarding the organization's next steps.⁷³

The hospital had invited the Committee to Stop Forced Sterilizations to a private meeting, but members of the CSFS were split on the question of whether to accept this invitation. Some members advocated for attending the meeting, if only to use that meeting as a starting point to plan a public meeting. Other members, including the CTFLT, the Revolutionary Union, and the Revolutionary Student Brigade, strongly opposed this tactic. As historian Virginia Espino notes, the members who supported a private meeting with the hospital seemed to lose sight of the purpose of their organization and "insisted that their response to the hospital should keep with the broader goal of the organization, which was to improve health care for the poor and mobilize hospital employees to demand better working conditions." Those who supported the meeting were eventually ousted from the CSFS, and the organization dissolved soon thereafter. It is unclear whether race, political ideology, or a combination thereof played the biggest role in the life and death of the CSFS. However, "those who were either purged or left the group voluntarily decided to leave the issue in the hands of the Chicano community, the group most impacted by the abuse."⁷⁴ According to Espino, the Committee to Free Los Tres joined with the CSFS as an exercise in coalition building, or what we might call an example of intentional bridging activism. Sterilization abuse opened the eyes of CTFLT members to gender issues within their own community, and they undertook specific studies to understand the issue in a gendered context, "but the issue itself led the organization to intellectualize the meaning of sterilization abuse for poor Mexican women and to place it into a context they were already familiar with: imperialism and its effects on the colonized."⁷⁵ Although much preparation took place for the lawsuit, *Andrade* did not go to court. The lawsuit did, however, bring the issue of forced sterilization into the light.⁷⁶

The fight against forced sterilization evolved throughout the 1970s. During the period when women first began to disclose their experiences at a growing rate, the issue remained little known among the public and those in the Chicano movement. As Espino notes, groups such as the Chicana Welfare Rights Organization and those in the Committee to Stop Forced Sterilization had very limited financial resources to seek redress for this wrong, but a new cohort of Mexican American professionals, including attorneys trained during the late 1960s and early 1970s, provided a new impetus to take up the cause. It then changed from an interracial grassroots coalition to a race-specific cause when Mexican American attorneys filed a new lawsuit against the hospital on behalf of women from their communities.

In 1975 two women became influential in bringing forced sterilization to the courts: Antonia Hernández, a graduate of the UCLA Law School, who at the time worked for the Center for Law and Justice in Los Angeles, and Gloria Molina, an active member of the Comisión Femenil Los Angeles and of the national office, who would later be elected a state assemblywoman, city councilwoman, and county supervisor. Espino argues that this shift in focus marked a significant change for the Comisión Femenil as a whole because of the transition from issues of employment to "the gender and race issues connected with forced sterilization that transcended class differences among Chicanas."[77]

In a broader context, when the issue of forced sterilization began to surface in the early to mid-1970s, many Chicano activists saw the violation as a racial or ethnic problem, not a gendered problem. Members of the Comisión Femenil, like many Chicanas who articulated feminist ideologies, faced tremendous challenges in arguing for reproductive freedoms in light of forced sterilization, abortion, and the nationalism of the Chicano movement, issues that placed the family at the center of the struggle; because Chicano activists saw genocide as a real threat, opposition to abortion and birth control was widespread, as sociologist Elena R. Gutiérrez argues.[78] Indeed, many activists in the movement believed that one of the ways to gain power was to have more children and saw "birth control as the tool of the 'white man' deliberately designed to kill off the community."[79] Both the Brown Berets and César Chávez of the United Farm Workers voiced an anti–birth control, pro-natalist position. But some Chicana activists saw sterilization abuse as both genocide and a crime against women, providing the intellectual force that connected these wrongs.

Lost in this debate, however, was the central premise held by many Chicana activists and writers that "women should have the right to choose whether or not to bear a child if they became pregnant" and more simply, the right to choose if and when to have children at all.[80] Although this ideal of Chicana bodily autonomy encompassed a wide array of practices, its applicability to sterilization was vexed by its association with abortion, which remained controversial within the movement as it was nationally. Yet as Chicana feminists participated in seeking to end and obtain redress for forced sterilization campaigns, they did indeed articulate a vision of "choice"—that is, the right of a woman to choose the outcome of her pregnancy—thus bridging the issue of sterilization with the issues of abortion and birth control, as scholars such as Gutiérrez posit. Returning to look at the Comisión Femenil, we can see how Chicana feminists were constructing, in part by engaging with sterilization, a theory of body politics that valorized women's choice as the foundation for an autonomy of gender and race in tandem. Forced sterilization and abortion rights were part of the same spectrum: the right of women to control their bodies.[81] This broader vision of choice points to a praxis in line with reproductive justice, as defined in the 1990s.[82] As the authors of *Undivided Rights: Women of Color Organizing for Reproductive Justice* write, "Reproductive justice is a theory, a practice, and a strategy that can provide a common language and broader unity in movements for women's health and rights. It defines the complicated, intersectional injuries endured and enables the re-envisioning of collective futures."[83] By existing as an autonomous Chicana feminist organization, the Comisión Femenil was able to navigate the reproductive rights terrain of the Chicano movement and reconfigure its topography and borders in ways that better reflected their activist vision.

Throughout the 1970s and in the early 1980s, the Comisión Femenil focused on public policy as it related to ethnic Mexican women and abortion. In 1975 the organization reiterated its pro-choice stance. The issue re-emerged in 1978, primarily because in 1976 Congress approved various amendments to the appropriations for the Department of Health, Education and Welfare, one of which, the Hyde Amendment, prohibited the use of Medicaid funds to pay for abortions unless the mother's life was in danger. Following the adoption of the Hyde Amendment, in 1978 the California legislature also passed a bill that prohibited state, or Medi-Cal, funds for abortion.[84] This threw into sharper relief the economic and racial justice angles of the abortion issue, thereby offering Chicana pro-choice advocates additional opportunities to pursue bridging activism with people and organizations that had previously conceptualized abortion as primarily a women's or gender issue.

Across the nation, women began to organize to keep federal and state abortion funding in place. At their 1978 annual conference the members of the Comisión Femenil Mexicana Nacional passed a resolution on reproductive freedom that stated,

> We believe that a woman who cannot afford private medical care should not be discriminated against and that the right enunciated by the Supreme Court should not be denied to the poor Hispana/Chicanas; and Therefore be it further resolved that CFMN is in favor of continued Medi-Cal funding of abortions.... Moreover, that this resolution be taken to the IWY Continuing Committee for inclusion in their recommendations to the President, United States Congress, and respective governmental agencies.[85]

Following their expression of support for Medi-Cal funding of abortions and after their involvement in the forced sterilization case *Madrigal v. Quilligan*, waged against USC-LACMC and decided in May 1978, Comisión

Femenil de Los Angeles members formed a Freedom of Choice task force, and the national group formed a Health Committee in 1979. The task force, with attorney Antonia Hernández as its advisor, served as a research arm, addressing the topics of abortion funding, Chicana medical rights, sterilization, and raising funds for the appeal of the *Madrigal* decision.[86] In 1979 the Health Committee, headed by Alice Cedillos, sought connections with national and state organizations. In that year Cedillos attended the Washington, DC, meeting of the Pro Choice Coalition in August and the NOW Minority Women's Conference; she also participated in the committee planning the national Abortion Rights Action Week in October.[87]

Continuing the tradition of Comisión Femenil's involvement in law and public policy, in August 1978, along with the Mexican American Legal Defense and Education Fund (MALDEF) and the American Civil Liberties Union (ACLU), it joined a lawsuit challenging the decision by California State Department of Health to stop funding abortions through Medi-Cal. In addition, the Comisión filed an amicus brief in the New York case *McCrae v. Califano*, which also challenged the ban on Medicaid funding of abortions.[88]

In 1981 the Comisión Femenil reiterated its public position in support of abortion itself. Many Comisión members had attended the National Hispanic Feminist Conference in 1980, at which the majority of the participants voted to support abortion rights. Later that year the president of the Comisión Femenil, Leticia Quezada, participated in a press conference with the ACLU and MALDEF regarding the legality of the state's prohibition of Medi-Cal funds for abortion. In the same period, the National Council of Jewish Women asked the Comisión Femenil to provide representatives to speak on abortion from a "Chicana/Latina perspective." "Because of the controversy surrounding the issue of abortion and the area of reproductive rights," minutes of the discussion stated, "it was recommended that the [Health] committee be co-chaired in order that all points of view be voiced. It was recommended that the committee present a statistical report on Chicanas and abortions, obtain input from women lobbyists in Sacramento and recruit from the Central area in order that rural women's concerns be voiced in Sacramento."[89] The Comisión Femenil consequently asked two members to write such a report. Hortensia Amaro, a PhD candidate in psychology at UCLA, and Maria Rodríguez, a staff attorney for the Chicana Rights Project of MALDEF, presented the Comisión Femenil with a thirty-page report in November 1981 titled "Latinas and Abortion: Legal and Social Issues."[90]

The report unequivocally recommended that the Comisión Femenil support abortion and oppose any measures, whether national, state, or local, that impinged on women's access to abortion. At the time, Amaro had studied attitudes about abortion among 250 Mexican American women in East Los Angeles as a part of her doctoral work, and she concluded that although it was commonly believed that Mexican women staunchly opposed abortion because of their Catholic beliefs, there existed a great diversity of attitudes toward abortion among these women. This conclusion challenged the idea that all Mexican American women were opposed to abortion under any circumstances. Indeed, she also found that at least 20 percent of the women in her study had obtained abortions. Because her subjects were overwhelmingly more "traditional" in that they were immigrants, were married, spoke Spanish, and had little education and low incomes, Amaro concluded that less traditional Chicanas likely had higher abortion rates.[91]

Outlining the legal history of abortion, the report also addressed the social and medical consequences of various state and national measures aimed at curtailing the practice. The analysis was clearly framed within the context of feminism. "The right of women to govern their own bodies," the authors stated, "is a basic theme underlying the concept of feminism."[92] Tracing the medical consequences of illegal abortion prior to 1973, they found that Latinas and African American women died from abortions ten times more often than Euro-American women, and that in some states, Mexican American women suffered a complication rate from illegal abortions that was 75 percent higher than for Euro-American women. Thus, the fundamental premise of the report was that any measures that impinged on women's access and right to abortion would have disproportionately detrimental effects on Chicanas.[93]

The report recommended that the Comisión Femenil "take a position that asserts abortion is an individual choice . . . we recommend that the Comisión Femenil Mexicana Nacional oppose any legislation that impedes a woman's ability to exert this choice."[94] The report also recommended that the Comisión Femenil oppose any statutes that attempted to pinpoint the beginning of human life and oppose parental consent statutes and any legislation that would restrict funding of abortions. Although the Comisión Femenil's board of directors had commissioned the report in order to take a more informed stance on abortion, it appears that the board did not readily accept the report's findings. In a 2003 interview Hortensia Amaro recollected, "I think that they had a hard time accepting what we were saying . . . that they themselves were afraid to come out with a position of saying the things that we said."[95]

The board of directors met the week following the receipt of the report and decided to distribute it to all chapter presidents, who were charged with facilitating a discussion among their members to ascertain their general opinion. But the board also asked the committee in charge of commissioning the report to broaden its purview beyond the issue of abortion and to be ready for the next meeting. The board sought to address "reproductive freedom," which would include "sterilization, provision of childcare services, right to access to public funding if [a] woman carries pregnancy to full term, access to information on sexuality, access to contraception and family planning services, the right to utilize folk medicine." In addition, it wanted the report to include a "discussion of the consequences of abortion and the consequences of carrying a pregnancy to full term." It is unclear why, but neither Amaro nor Rodríguez expanded the report. The minutes of the meeting stated, "The members were reluctant to take a position only on abortion because they believe it is only one issue among many other in the reproductive rights arena."[96]

Amaro may have been accurate in her conclusion, but the national discussion about abortion, coupled with the struggle against forced sterilization, had shifted the conversation toward a reproductive rights framework. As Jennifer Nelson writes, "By the late 1970s, many white feminists had expanded their definition of reproductive freedom beyond abortion rights. In response to arguments made by women of color that legal abortion was not synonymous with reproductive freedom, reproductive rights feminists came to maintain that the right to bear children was as important to reproductive freedom as the legal right to terminate a pregnancy."[97] It is logical that the board of directors wanted to expand the notion of reproductive rights beyond abortion, because the organization had been at the forefront of the class-action lawsuit filed by ten Mexican women who had been forcibly sterilized at University of Southern California–Los Angeles County Medical Center. Pragmatism and political experience came into play in the abortion debate. By allowing an issue such as abortion to fall under the guise of "female type problems and problems concerning the Mexican family," the CFMN began a tradition of harnessing broad support for goals specific to Chicanas. In the long run, this proved to be an essential skill as the women involved lobbied for grants to fund its childcare centers, job training centers, and various other programs.

When Gloria Arellanes became the director of the El Barrio Free Clinic in 1969, her position signaled the Chicana feminist belief that medical care and reproductive rights were essential to the goals of self-determination of the Chicano movement. Indeed, when the relationship with the Brown Berets began to create conflicts regarding labor and control of the clinic, Arellanes sought, albeit unsuccessfully, to separate the clinic from Brown Beret oversight.[98] With this particular action, Arellanes demonstrated the importance of Chicana autonomy, both in terms of healthcare and reproductive rights and in terms of Chicana leadership, contrary to the cultural nationalist ideals of the movimiento, which considered self-determination to be a collectivist ideal and which, in actuality, subrogated as secondary the issues that women specifically confronted. Arellanes and women like her who brought the issues of health and reproduction into the discourse of the Chicano movement did so as part of a wider array of movement organizations, both coed and all-female, advocating for Chicanos as a whole through advocacy work they did for Chicanas as women.

Women in the movement in Los Angeles and in other areas of the Southwest publicly articulated their concerns about the ways in which the body politics of the Chicano movement rendered women as useful for reproducing the race without fully considering the needs of women as fully fledged human beings. They also articulated their dissatisfaction with the mainstream women's liberation movement's views of reproductive rights, which posited a universal ideal of womanhood that ignored the questions of class and race that affected Chicanas. As such, Chicanas in Los Angeles sought to address reproductive rights such as family planning, abortion, and forced sterilization on their own terms in organizations such as the Comisión Femenil. Regardless of their positions on family planning and whether they believed in women's responsibility to bear children for the movement, Chicanas expressed a common belief that they should be in control of their own bodies. The disparate and sometimes surface-level contradictions in Chicana thought masked this commonality with regard to the importance of women's self-determination.

Epilogue

In 1971 Francisca Flores informed readers of *Regeneración*, the Chicano movement periodical that she founded and edited that "the issues of equality, freedom and self-determination of the Chicana—like the right of self-determination, equality and liberation of the Mexican community—*is not negotiable* . . . FREEDOM IS FOR EVERYONE."[1] It is fitting to conclude *Chicana Liberation* with Flores, as her life experiences represent the book's main theme: bridging activism. When Flores proclaimed that self-determination, a main tenet of the movimiento, applied to women, she did so as a fifty-eight-year-old woman who did not fit the stereotypical image of the Chicana activist as a college-aged student. In fact, by the time Flores became a key figure in the Chicano movement, she had been a member and leader in the Communist Party in Los Angeles and had gone on to co-found a variety of organizations ranging from the Mexican American Political Association, which focused on electoral politics, to one of the first Chicana feminist organizations in the nation, the Comisión Femenil Mexicana Nacional. Her dedication to improving her community took her from organization to organization over time; she also participated simultaneously in many. These factors exemplify what I have identified as the practice of bridging activism that ethnic Mexican women in Los Angeles engaged in from the postwar period through the era of social movements. Flores's activism began in her own community of San Diego and continued in Los Angeles as she moved through a variety of ideologies over the long period of her political involvement, during which she continuously advocated for women such as herself.

Utilizing the concept of bridging activism, this book has used a gendered analysis to center women's lived experiences across various generations and partisan leanings as they engaged in activism in groups ranging from the Communist Party to the Comisión Femenil. In Los Angeles, ethnic Mexican women addressed issues of gender inequality, access to education, and disparities in healthcare using a variety of strategies and participating in a range of organizations that were rooted in the politics of the pre-movement era, specifically in Los Angeles. Before the era of social movements they had gained invaluable experience in civic campaigns via the Communist Party, the Community Service Organization, the Mexican American Political Association, and other groups, including labor unions. Ethnic Mexican women had also already begun to advocate for themselves as women via the League of Mexican American Women. Los Angeles was a key site for activism, not only because of the sheer size of the ethnic Mexican population, which continued to grow through immigration, but also because the geography of the city and the spaces in which Mexicans historically resided created shared goals. These experiences were not lost as the Chicano movement emerged, especially in Los Angeles.

From the late 1960s through the late 1970s, Chicanas in Los Angeles and across the Southwest addressed and questioned their roles in the movement in much the same ways as women had before them. Some argued that a woman's place was behind her man while others authoritatively stated that they would walk behind no one. Regardless of where Chicanas stood on the topic, they encountered the specter of Chicanismo, which held unity, solidarity, and tradition as the ultimate strategies for attaining social justice. Due to negative reactions on the part of many activists, some Chicanas chose to form separate women's organizations whereas others continued to work within traditional movement organizations, and often they did so simultaneously, serving as bridges between these different types of bodies. These various responses laid the foundation for the variety of Chicana feminisms that emerged and for the continued existence of these different types of organizations, especially those that restricted membership solely to Chicanas and Latinas.

In 1970, when Comisión Femenil Mexicana emerged, its founders hoped to apply the movement's ideas about self-determination to their situation as women. As such, they established job training and employment centers, along with childcare centers based on the idea that women needed economic self-sufficiency in order to prosper. In addition to these pursuits, the Comisión claimed a place in politics on the local, state, national, and international levels. The Los Angles chapter of the Comisión Femenil was a key training ground for women to become elected officials representing ethnic Mexicans and others in city, county, and state government, and eventually in the national arena.

When Chicanas broadened their focus, those from Los Angeles, in particular, engaged with global issues. After traveling to Mexico City and participating in the first international women's conference, sponsored by the United Nations in 1975, the subjects of this study came to the realization that they were part of a larger struggle for equal rights. By so doing they bridged the local to the international and validated their battles at home. Accordingly, members of the Comisión Femenil who had attended the Mexico City conference used their experiences to organize and prepare for the 1977 U.S. International Women's Year Conference held in Houston. There, utilizing new and previously established networks, the Comisión Femenil worked with other women of color to pass the minority women's plank successfully.

One of the consistent issues that Chicanas addressed in the movement back home was body politics, specifically reproductive rights. When Chicana activists engaged in dialogue, strategy, and policy making regarding this issue in the 1960s and 1970s, they faced the limitation of the gendered ideology of cultural nationalism, but they maintained that women, Chicanas especially, had the right to control their own bodies. This belief was articulated across the ideological spectrum of movement activists. Some believed in achieving Chicano liberation by having babies in order to combat population control measures used against ethnic Mexicans, others fought for all women to obtain abortions as needed, and another group viewed the ability to control their own fertility in the face of forced sterilization as the paramount cause. Regardless of their focus, they grounded these beliefs in what they saw as the fundamental right of bodily autonomy.

By the late 1970s the Chicano/a activism that had erupted in marches, demonstrations, boycotts, and walkouts had slowed to a simmer of political discontent among Mexican Americans in the Southwest. Many movement organizations such as La Raza Unida Party had disbanded, and either others took their place, or their members moved on to other forms of activism, whether in labor unions, the electoral arena, or a continued role in grassroots politics. Yet organizations like the Comisión Femenil, led by women, continued their quest to establish institutions benefiting Latinas. Where many movement newspapers and magazines had ceased production, other publications and literary works began to emerge as forceful manifestations of the movement's intellectual history. Indeed, *Encuentro Femenil*, the first Chicana academic journal, was founded by women who had been active in organizations such as the Hijas de Cuauhtémoc, the Comisión Femenil, and the Chicana Service Action Center. Works published by scholar-activists such as Adelaida del Castillo's and Magdalena Mora's *Mexican Women in the United States: Struggles Past and Present*, Martha Cotera's *The Chicana*

Feminist, Diosa y Hembra: The History and Heritage of Chicanas in the United States, and *Profile on the Mexican-American Woman* are quintessential to the fields of Chicana and Chicano studies. This book, as with many others on Chicana activism, is a direct descendant of these women's contributions.

These volumes also served as precursors to the publication of *This Bridge Called My Back: Writings by Radical Women of Color* in 1981, which celebrated the writing of women of color while also validating the experiences of Chicanas in their own right, and proved groundbreaking. In its introduction, editors Gloria Anzaldúa and Cherríe Moraga, who identified as Chicana lesbians, wrote, "We named this anthology 'radical' for we were interested in the writing of women of color who want nothing short of a revolution in the hands of women." Moraga and Anzaldúa conceived of the anthology in 1979 after years of experiencing racism from Euro-American feminists and organizations. They also had experienced forms of sexism and homophobia in their involvement in Chicano militancy. "What began as a reaction to the racism of white feminists soon became a positive affirmation of the commitment of women of color to our own feminism," they wrote, which "emerges from the roots of both . . . our cultural oppression and heritage."[2] In the fourth edition of *This Bridge Called My Back*, Moraga reflects on the need for "political memory" and the importance of "our foremothers."[3] The volume introduced a broader vision of feminism that would eventually play an important role in academia, built on the work and efforts of Chicanas in the movement and of other women of color who had consistently been involved in the print community.

It is significant that *This Bridge Called My Back* also called attention to the experiences of Chicanx queer activists, many of whom remained in the shadows of movement histories. As the editors of the recently published anthology *Chicana Movidas: New Narratives of Activism in the Movement Era* write, "Indeed, many gays and lesbians were active in Chicano movement organizations, sometimes even in leadership positions, but these spaces were not always conducive to outward self-identification, forcing some activists to negotiate their identities with comrades inside movement spaces." Chicana lesbians emerged "as bridging figures to the next phase in the Chicana feminist movement."[4] This is an important area that remains under-researched.

Chicana feminism has remained rooted in the concept of self-determination for Chicanas and Latinas. For example, California Latinas for Reproductive Justice, founded in Los Angeles in 2004 and still active today, articulates this concept in its mission statement. It reads, in part, "We recognize that Latinas/xs' access to culturally and linguistically appropriate healthcare, a living wage job, quality education, freedom from discrimination and violence, among many other issues that affect Latinas'/xs' daily lives, have a profound effect on Latinas' reproductive and sexual health, as well as our right to self-determination in all aspects of our lives."⁵ California Latinas for Reproductive Justice is just one of the many organizations that have emerged to address this issue.

As the previous discussion has demonstrated, ethnic Mexican women's political outlook and their participation in this arena have not remained static. Women have changed with the times and adapted to new realities and landscapes over the course of their careers in the public sphere. In the present day, ethnic Mexican women, other Latinas, and women of color in general have made strides as political actors in a multiplicity of forms. In the 1960s and 1970s no ethnic Mexican women served as elected representatives in any city, regional, state, or national body. The efforts of Chicana feminists of the pre-movement era through the 1970s changed this fact. In a historic win, Gloria Molina, former member and president of the Comisión Femenil, was elected to the State Assembly in 1982, representing East Los Angeles and adjacent areas. Molina was the first Latina to win a seat in the state assembly. She made further inroads when she was subsequently elected to the Los Angeles City Council in 1987 and as Los Angeles County Supervisor in 1991, in which position she served for twenty-three years. As of 2022, two Mexican American women sit on the Los Angeles City Council, Eunisses Hernandez and Monica Rodriguez. Three Latinas, Kelly Gonez, Rocío Rivas, and Tanya Ortiz Franklin, sit on the Los Angeles School Board. At the county level, Hilda Solis was elected to the Los Angeles Supervisory Board in 2014 after having served four years as the Secretary of Labor in the Obama administration. In addition, there are ten Latinas serving as state senators, and nine Latina state assembly members. Ten of these women represent areas in or near the City of Angels.

Many of the issues that women faced in the pre-movement and Chicano insurgency eras remain with us today. In the current political climate, we have witnessed prolonged assaults on abortion rights and access to contraception, as well as continued debates about use of federal funding to terminate a pregnancy. We have witnessed the cruel and inhumane separation of families at the border, continued attacks on union organizing, and the defunding of public education, all of which affect Chicanas and Latinas disproportionately.

This epilogue began with a reiteration of Francisca Flores's political trajectory, which represents the cross-generational and activist nature of her political history. For Flores and the women profiled in this book, the adage from the women's liberation movement that the personal is political remained true. In addition to dedicating much of their time and effort to organizations as volunteers, these women participated in politics because their individual experiences in their own communities, be they college campuses or housing projects, called them to action. Their commitment to social justice was not unique to them; neither was the longevity of their activism. But their stories have remained unacknowledged. This is now changing. In 2018, for example, the Los Angeles County Board of Supervisors issued a formal apology to the women forcibly sterilized in state institutions and at Los Angeles County–University of Southern California Medical Center in the 1970s. The resolution, "Apologizing for Historical Coerced Sterilization Practices," specifically stated, "Regretfully, Los Angeles County also participated in questionable sterilization practices between 1968 and 1974. . . . It is significant and necessary to acknowledge the irreparable harm inflicted onto the women who were subjected to these coerced sterilizations at Los Angeles County+USC Medical Center and to their families. Every person's reproductive capacity should be controlled by themselves, and not by other individuals, institutions, or the state."[6] Although it took more than forty years for this acknowledgment and apology to be issued, it was Chicana activism and the bravery of women sterilized that forged the path. May their stories serve as an inspiration and as a testament to the power of women's organizing.

Notes

Introduction

1. Lilia Aceves, interview by the author, April 15, 2002, Alhambra, California. Cooperative nursery schools served as a site for emerging political consciousness for other mothers from the 1940s through the 1960s. See Robyn Muncy, "Cooperative Motherhood and Democratic Civic Culture in Postwar Suburbia, 1940–1965," *Journal of Social History* 38, no. 2 (2004): 285–310.

In a study that addresses ethnic, racial, and gender identity, terminology is a complicated terrain. The following terms, though not perfect, are used as appropriately as possible. When discussing the overall population of Mexican-origin peoples in the United States regardless of immigration or citizenship status, I use the terms *ethnic Mexican* and *Mexican-origin* interchangeably. The term *ethnic Mexicans*, following historian David G. Gutiérrez's usage, refers to those with Mexican ancestry or heritage who live in the United States. This term allows discussion of the combined groups, including Mexican Americans, Mexican immigrants, and Chicanos or Chicanas. The term *Mexican American* refers to those born in the United States of Mexican heritage. I also use this term when referring to people in the period before the Chicano movement, since it is what they would have called themselves for the most part. I use *Chicano* and *Chicana* in the spirit of those who identified themselves as such. The term was adopted during the 1960s and 1970s as a self-identification for a generation of Mexican immigrants and Mexican Americans who called for civil rights. In its original sense, *Chicano* or *Chicana* refers to a man or woman of Mexican origin born in the United States who also embraced the concepts of social justice and ethnic pride. Although in standard Spanish, using *Chicano* or *Chicanos* to refer to the entire population would be apropos, and there is a vibrant discussion regarding terminology and naming, I use *Chicana/o* as an inclusive term to denote the group as a whole. I realize that the current discussion challenges gender binaries in terminology, but the women and men about whom I am writing did not voice these issues, though they did voice issues regarding gender. *Mexican*, *Mexican immigrant*, and *mexicano* are used to refer to those born in Mexico and residing in the

United States who have not attained U.S. citizenship. See David G. Gutiérrez, "Significant to Whom? Mexican Americans and the History of the American West," *Western Historical Quarterly* (1993): 519–39, esp. note 1.

I use the term *Euro-American* to refer to persons of European origin who are classified as white Americans.

2. Corinne Sánchez, interview by the author, April 4, 2002, San Fernando, California.

3. The concept of bridging activism builds on previous scholarship concerning Chicanas. This includes the strategy of "gear shifting" defined by Chela Sandoval as well as "hidden insurgencies" as defined by Maylei Blackwell. See Chela Sandoval, *Methodology of the Oppressed* (Minneapolis: University of Minnesota Press, 2000), and Maylei Blackwell, *¡Chicana Power! Contested Histories of Feminism in the Chicano Movement* (Austin: University of Texas Press, 2011).

4. On the expansion of the Los Angeles County Hospital, known also as General Hospital, see Helen Eastman Martin, *The History of the Los Angeles County Hospital (1878–1968) and the Los Angeles County–University of Southern California Medical Center (1968–1978)* (Los Angeles: University of Southern California Press, 1979), chap. 30. During the period Aceves discusses, the expansion of the hospital could have been the construction of the Graduate Nurses' Residence or the Osteopathic Hospital. See ibid., 252.

5. On the Heights Cooperative Nursery School, see Mike Castro, "One of Oldest in City: Co-op Nursery School Struggling to Survive," *Los Angeles Times*, March 15, 1974, C1. On the Mexican American Political Association, see Ernesto Chávez, *"¡Mi Raza Primero!" (My People First!): Nationalism, Identity, and Insurgency in the Chicano Movement in Los Angeles, 1966–1978* (Berkeley: University of California Press, 2002), chap. 1; and David G. Gutiérrez, *Walls and Mirrors: Mexican Americans, Mexican Immigrants, and the Politics of Ethnicity* (Berkeley: University of California Press, 1995).

6. See Mario T. García, *The Chicano Generation: Testimonios of the Movement* (Oakland: University of California Press, 2015); Mario T. García, ed., *The Chicano Movement: Perspectives from the Twenty-First Century* (New York: Routledge, 2014); F. Arturo Rosales, *Chicano! The History of the Mexican American Civil Rights Movement* (Albuquerque, NM: Arte Público, 1997); David Montejano, *Quixote's Soldiers: A Local History of the Chicano Movement, 1966–1981* (Austin: University of Texas Press, 2010).

7. At this time, the more current way of thinking of the spectrum of gender identities was not in the mindset of the women featured in this study.

8. Corinne Sánchez, interview by the author.

9. See E. Chávez, *"¡Mi Raza Primero!"*; Lorena Oropeza, *¡Raza Sí! ¡Guerra No! Chicano Protest and Patriotism During the Viet Nam War Era* (Berkeley: University of California Press, 2005); Juan Gómez-Quiñones, *Chicano Politics: Reality and Promise, 1940–1990* (Albuquerque: University of New Mexico Press, 1994); Rodolfo Acuña, *Occupied America: A History of Chicanos* (New York: Harper and Row, 1988); Ignacio García, *Chicanismo: The Forging of a Militant Ethos Among Mexican Americans* (Tucson: University of Arizona Press, 1998); Ignacio García, *United We Win: The Rise and Fall of La Raza Unida Party* (Tucson: Mexican American Studies Research Center, University of Arizona Press, 1989); Edward J. Escobar, *Race, Police and the Making of a Political Identity: Mexican Americans and the Los Angeles Police Department, 1900–1945* (Berkeley: University of California Press, 1999); and Pablo Landeros, "AKA Frances: Francisca Flores and the Radical Roots

of Chicana Feminism in California," in *Latina Histories and Cultures: Feminist Readings and Recoveries of Archival Knowledge*, ed. Yolanda Padilla and Montse Feu (Houston: Arte Público, 2023), 229–48.

10. See Vicki L. Ruiz, *From Out of the Shadows: Mexican Women in Twentieth-Century America* (New York: Oxford University Press, 2008), 96–97, 101. Also see Mario T. García, *Mexican Americans: Leadership, Ideology, and Identity* (New Haven: Yale University Press, 1989), 164.

11. Gabriela Gónzalez, *Redeeming la Raza: Transborder Modernity, Race, Respectability, and Rights* (New York: Oxford University Press, 2018), 126.

12. See Cynthia Orozco, "Beyond Machismo, La Familia, and Ladies Auxiliaries: A Historiography of Mexican-Origin Women's Participation in Voluntary Associations and Politics in the United States, 1870–1990," *Perspectives on Mexican American Studies* 5 (1995): 1–34; Emma Pérez, *The Decolonial Imaginary: Writing Chicanas into History* (Bloomington: Indiana University Press, 1999); and Gabriela González, "Carolina Munguía and Emma Tenayuca: The Politics of Benevolence and Radical Reform," *Frontiers* (2003): 200–229.

13. Floya Anthias and Nira Yuval-Davis, *Racialized Boundaries: Race, Nation, Gender, Colour, Class and the Anti-Racist Struggle* (New York: Routledge, 1992), 27.

14. Dionne Espinoza, María Eugenia Cotera, and Maylei Blackwell, "Introduction: Movements, Movimientos, and Movidas," in *Chicana Movidas: New Narratives of Activism and Feminism in the Movement Era*, ed. Dionne Espinoza, María Eugenia Cotera, and Maylei Blackwell (Austin: University of Texas Press, 2018), 10.

15. Adelaida del Castillo, "Mexican Women in Organization," in *Mexican Women in the United States: Struggles Past and Present*, ed. Magdalena Mora and Adelaida del Castillo (Los Angeles: University of California, Chicano Studies Research Center, Occasional Paper 2, 1980), 10.

16. Sonia A. López, "The Role of the Chicana Within the Student Movement," in *Essays on La Mujer*, ed. Rosaura Sánchez (Los Angeles: UCLA Chicano Studies Center Publications, 1977), 22.

17. Blackwell, *¡Chicana Power!*, 92.

18. Ibid.

19. See Akasha (Gloria T.) Hull, Patricia Bell-Scott, and Barbara Smith, eds., *All the Women Are White, All the Men Are Black, But Some of Us Are Brave: Black Women's Studies* (Old Westbury, NY: Feminist Press, 1982); Beverly Guy-Sheftall, ed., *Words of Fire: A Black Feminist Anthology* (New York: New Press, 1995); Annelise Orleck, *Storming Caesar's Palace: How Black Mothers Fought Their Own War on Poverty* (Boston: Beacon, 2006); Anne Valk, *Radical Sisters: Second-Wave Feminism and Black Liberation in Washington, D.C.* (Urbana: University of Illinois Press, 2010); Chana Kai Lee, *For Freedom's Sake: The Life of Fannie Lou Hamer* (Champaign: University of Illinois Press, 2000); Barbara Ransby, *Ella Baker and the Black Freedom Movement* (Chapel Hill: University of North Carolina Press, 2005); Bettye Collier-Thomas, *Sisters in the Struggle: African-American Women in the Civil Rights–Black Power Movement* (New York: NYU Press, 2001); Kimberly Springer, *Living for the Revolution: Black Feminist Organizations, 1968–1980* (Durham, NC: Duke University Press, 2005); Erik S. McDuffie, *Sojourning for Freedom: Black Women, American Communism, and the Making of Black Left Feminism* (Durham, NC: Duke University Press, 2011); Sonia Shah, Yuri Kochiyama, and Karin Aguilar-San Juan, eds., *Dragon Ladies: Asian*

American Feminists Breathe Fire (Boston: South End, 1999); Benita Roth, *Separate Roads to Feminism: Black, Chicana, and White Feminist Movements in America's Second Wave* (New York: Cambridge University Press, 2003); Keisha N. Blain, *Set the World on Fire: Black Nationalist Women and the Global Struggle for Freedom* (Philadelphia: University of Pennsylvania Press, 2018); Keeanga-Yamahtta Taylor, ed., *How We Get Free: Black Feminism and the Combahee River Collective* (Chicago: Haymarket, 2017).

20. See, e.g., Ruth Rosen, *The World Split Open: How the Modern Women's Movement Changed America*, rev. ed. (New York: Penguin, 2006); Stephanie Gilmore and Sara Evans, eds., *Feminist Coalitions: Historical Perspectives on Second-Wave Feminism in the United States* (Champaign: University of Illinois Press, 2008); Sara Evans, *Personal Politics: The Roots of Women's Liberation in the Civil Rights Movement and the New Left* (New York: Vintage, 1980); and Alice Echols, *Daring to Be Bad: Radical Feminism in America, 1967–1975* (Minneapolis: University of Minnesota Press, 1989).

21. See T. Wilson Longmore and Homer L. Hitt, "A Demographic Analysis of First and Second Generation Mexican Population of the United States: 1930," *Southwestern Social Science Quarterly* 24, no. 2 (1943): 138–49; Population Reference Bureau, "Shifting Latino Ethnic and Racial Identity," https://www.prb.org/resources/shifting-latino-ethnic-and-racial-identity/; George J. Sánchez, *Becoming Mexican American: Ethnicity, Culture and Identity in Chicano Los Angeles, 1900–1945* (New York: Oxford University Press, 1993), 70–71, 90; Rodolfo F. Acuña, *A Community Under Siege: A Chronicle of Chicanos East of the Los Angeles River, 1945–1975* (Los Angeles: UCLA Chicano Studies Research Center, Monograph no. 11, 1984), 13; E. Chávez, *"¡Mi Raza Primero!,"* 10. For 1980, the number of Mexican-origin residents in Los Angeles is an approximation due to the methods of data gathering in the census. See "State of the Cities Data Systems (SOCDS)," Office of Policy Development and Research, https://socds.huduser.gov/Census/race.odb?newmsacitylist=31100%2A0600044000%2A1.0&msavar=1&metro=cbsa. The number cited is the "Total Hispanic (All Races)" figure for the city of Los Angeles. Countywide, the figure is approximately double, at 1,645,980. See Steven Ruggles, Sarah Flood, Sophia Foster, Ronald Goeken, Jose Pacas, Megan Schouweiler, and Matthew Sobek, IPUMS USA: Version 11.0, *1980 5%-State* (Minneapolis, MN: IPUMS, 2021). https://doi.org/10.18128/D010.V11.0.

22. G. Sánchez, *Becoming Mexican American*, introduction and chap. 3.

23. Mexican-American Study Project, "California Mexican-Americans Score Zero in State Legislature," *Mexican-American Study Project Progress Report* 9 (University of California, Los Angeles, May 1967), 3.

24. See G. Sánchez, *Becoming Mexican American*; Mario Garcia, *Mexican Americans: Leadership, Ideology and Identity, 1930–1960* (New Haven: Yale University Press, 1991); and D. Gutiérrez, *Walls and Mirrors*.

25. See Ruiz, *From out of the Shadows*, xiii. My father and mother arrived in the United States with their families as young children in the mid-1950s from Ciudad Juárez, Chihuahua, first crossing into El Paso, Texas, and then settling in Los Angeles. Their parents hoped that leaving their home country for the United States would provide their children with opportunities for better lives than they had known in Mexico. They grew up in downtown and East Los Angeles and were part of the select few ethnic Mexicans who graduated from high school in the 1960s and went on to college. In college, my parents immersed themselves in understanding their status in U.S. society and began their quest to change

the social and economic conditions of poor Mexican-origin people in their community through political activism. They practiced their own linked activism—they joined MEChA (Chicano Student Movement of Aztlán) and participated in the Committee to Free Los Tres and subsequently in El Centro de Acción Social Autónomo (Autonomous Center for Social Action).

26. Patricia Preciado Martin, *Songs My Mother Sang to Me: An Oral History of Mexican American Women* (Tucson: University of Arizona Press, 1992). Also see Diana Taylor, *The Archive and the Repertoire: Performing Cultural Memory in the Americas* (Durham: Duke University Press, 2003).

27. On the dynamics of "insider" status in academic research and oral history, see the foundational article by Maxine Baca Zinn, "Field Research in Minority Communities: Ethical, Methodological and Political Observations by an Insider," *Social Problems* 27, no. 2 (1979): 209–19. On conducting oral history with family, especially women, see Sally Alexander, "'Do Grandmas Have Husbands?' Generational Memory and Twentieth-Century Women's Lives," *Oral History Review* 36, no. 2 (2009): 159–76. Also see Julie Stephens, "Our Remembered Selves: Oral History and Feminist Memory," *Oral History* 38, no. 1 (Spring 2010): 81–90; and Kim Lacy Rogers, "Memory, Struggle, and Power: On Interviewing Political Activists," *Oral History Review* 15, no. 1 (1987): 165–84.

28. Alessandro Portelli, *The Death of Luigi Trastulli, and Other Stories: Form and Meaning in Oral History* (Albany: SUNY Press, 1991), 46.

29. Blackwell, *¡Chicana Power!*, 11.

Chapter 1. Bridging Activism

1. See Bill Flores, "Francisca Flores, 1913–1996," *Tonatiuh Quinto Sol* (June 1996): 2–4; Naomi H. Quiñonez, "Francisca Flores," in *Latinas in the United States: A Historical Encyclopedia*, ed. Vicki Ruiz and Virginia Sánchez Korrol (Bloomington: Indiana University Press, 2006), 264–65; and Marisela R. Chávez, "'We Have a Long, Beautiful History': Chicana Feminist Trajectories and Legacies," in *No Permanent Waves: Recasting U.S. Feminist History*, ed. Nancy Hewitt (New Brunswick: Rutgers University Press, 2010), 77–97. Bill Flores's eulogy also mentions that Flores participated in screening the blacklisted film *Salt of the Earth (1954)*. Although it screened for nine weeks at a theater in New York, no other theaters would screen it. It was not officially banned, per se. The ban was a de facto agreement in the industry. One of the most dramatic events during the production of the film was the arrest and subsequent deportation of one of its main stars, the Mexican actress Rosaura Revueltas, in 1953. There is no conclusive evidence of a connection between Flores and Revueltas. In *Chicano Communists* Enrique Buelna notes that his main source, Ralph Cuarón, and his wife Sylvia participated in the film. Although Flores and Cuarón had met during this time because they had both been CP members, there is no evidence that Flores had any direct connection with the film or with Revueltas. See Ellen R. Baker, *On Strike and on Film: Mexican American Families and Blacklisted Filmmakers in Cold War America* (Charlotte: University of North Carolina Press, 2007); Esteve Riambau and Casimiro Torreiro, "This Film Is Going to Make History," *Cineaste* 19, nos. 2/3 (December 1992) 50–51; and Enrique Buelna, *Chicano Communists and the Struggle for Social Justice* (Tucson: University of Arizona Press, 2019).

2. See Frances Flores, Federal Bureau of Investigation File 1228233-0 and 100-17204 (hereafter cited as Flores, FBI File). Also see Pablo Landeros, "AKA Frances: Francisca Flores and the Radical Roots of Chicana Feminism in California," in *Latina Histories and Cultures*, ed. Montse Feu and Yolanda Padilla (Houston: Arte Público, 2023), 229–48.

3. See, e.g., Dorothy Healey, *Dorothy Healey Remembers: A Life in the Communist Party* (New York: Oxford University Press, 1990); Robert W. Cherny, "The Communist Party in California, 1935–1940: From the Political Margins to the Mainstream and Back," *American Communist History* 9, no. 1 (2010): 3–33; Bob Blauner, *Resisting McCarthyism: To Sign or Not to Sign California's Loyalty Oath* (Palo Alto, CA: Stanford University Press, 2009); and Ellen Schrecker, *Many Are the Crimes: McCarthyism in America* (New York: Little, Brown, 1998).

4. For a more complete review of Francisca Flores's life prior to her arrival in Los Angeles, see Landeros, "AKA Frances."

5. Flores, FBI File. California Labor School, "Schedule of Classes, Winter Term 1949: January 24–April 1," "Schedule of Classes, Spring Term 1950: April 10–June 16," and "Schedule of Classes, Winter Term 1950: January 16–March 24," Comisión Femenil Mexicana Nacional Archives, Pablo Landeros Research on Francisca Flores, box 79, folder 1. There is some discrepancy among various sources regarding the founding year of the League of Mexican American Women. My documents date it from 1963, as do newspaper accounts in Rodolfo F. Acuña, *A Community Under Siege: A Chronicle of Chicanos East of the Los Angeles River* (Los Angeles: UCLA Chicano Studies Research Center, 1984), 122. A newer publication by Anna NietoGómez, however, puts the founding year at 1958. Since this is the latest publication, I have used this date. See Anna NietoGómez, "Francisca Flores, the League of Mexican American Women, and the Comisión Femenil Mexicana Nacional, 1958–1975," in *Chicana Movidas: New Narratives of Activism in the Movement Era*, ed. Dionne Espinoza, María Eugenia Cotera, and Maylei Blackwell, 36 (Austin: University of Texas Press, 2018), 36.

6. The periodicals and other works that these women published and contributed to were precursors to the print community that the scholar Maylei Blackwell identified in later Chicana feminist formations. See Maylei Blackwell, *¡Chicana Power! Contested Histories of Feminism in the Chicano Movement* (Austin: University of Texas Press, 2011).

7. Acuña, *Community Under Siege*.

8. George J. Sánchez, *Becoming Mexican American: Ethnicity, Culture and Identity in Chicano Los Angeles, 1900–1945* (New York: Oxford University Press, 1993), 73–74. In the early decades of the twentieth century Mexicans were mostly concentrated in the downtown, southern, and eastern areas of the city. As Sánchez tells us, "Mexicans lived in almost every part of the city, with close to 20 percent living beyond the east and central region. . . . By and large, however, the largest concentration of Mexicans were in the Plaza area, directly to the east of the Los Angeles River, in Boyle Heights, and outside the city limits in Belvedere" (ibid.) Some Mexicans also lived in various sections to the north and east of downtown Los Angeles.

9. Ricardo Romo, *East Los Angeles: History of a Barrio* (Austin: University of Texas Press, 1983), 81, 169.

10. See Ernesto Chávez, *¡Mi Raza Primero! (My People First!): Nationalism, Identity, and Insurgency in the Chicano Movement in Los Angeles, 1966–1978* (Berkeley: University of California Press, 2002), 10; and Fredric Gey, Cecilia Jiang, Jon Stiles, and Ilone

Einowski, *California Latino Demographic Handbook*, 3rd ed. (Berkeley: UC Data Archive and Technical Assistance, California Policy Research Center, 2004), 2–10.

11. Mexican-American Study Project, "California Mexican-Americans Score Zero in State Legislature," *Mexican-American Study Project Progress Report* no. 9 (University of California, Los Angeles, May 1967), 3.

12. See Flores, FBI report.

13. Fair Employment Practices Division, State of California, *Californians of Spanish Surname: Population, Education, Income, Employment* (1964; repr., San Francisco: Fair Employment Practice Commission, 1966), 16, 17, 40, 48. In 1960 the number of employed Spanish-surnamed people in California totaled 622,397, with 410,023 men and 212,374 women; "'Women' of Spanish Surname in the Los Angeles Metropolitan Area," *Carta Editorial*, October 26, 1963, 1.

14. Max Felker-Kantor, "'A Pledge Is Not Self-Enforcing': Struggles for Equal Employment Opportunity in Multiracial Los Angeles," *Pacific Historical Review* 82 (2013): 70. Also see Laura Pulido, *Black, Brown, Yellow and Left: Radical Activism in Los Angeles* (Berkeley: University of California Press, 2006).

15. Martha P. Cotera, *Diosa y Hembra: The History and Heritage of Chicanas in the U.S.* (Austin: Information Systems Development, 1976), 145. Material cited from U.S. Department of Health, Education and Welfare, *A Study of Selected Socio-Economic Characteristics of Ethnic Minorities Based on the 1970 Census*, vol. 1, *Americans of Spanish Origin* (Washington, DC: Government Printing Office, 1974), 35.

16. Dolores Sánchez, interview by the author, May 9, 2002, City of Commerce, California; Connie Pardo, interview by the author, March 29, 2002, Los Angeles, California.

17. "Women [of Spanish Surname,]" 2. The college attendance rate had wider gaps in this same age group—the percentage of Spanish-surnamed men and women who attended some college was less than half that of their white counterparts.

18. Ursula Vils, "Chicanas Stand Up and Speak Out," *Los Angeles Times*, June 26, 1980.

19. Fair Employment Practices Division, State of California, *Californians of Spanish Surname*, 11. In addition, the educational attainment of Spanish-surnamed people was below that of nonwhites in California. In younger groups, however, those aged twenty to twenty-four had a higher percentage of men (60 percent) and women (58 percent) that finished high school, reflecting new social programs in effect during this period.

20. Juan Gómez-Quiñones, *Chicano Politics: Reality and Promise, 1940–1990* (Albuquerque: University of New Mexico Press, 1994), 31.

21. Mario T. García, *Mexican Americans: Leadership, Ideology, and Identity* (New Haven: Yale University Press, 1989), 146.

22. G. Sánchez, *Becoming Mexican American*, 243. Also see Enrique Buelna, "Resistance from the Margins: Mexican American Radical Activism in Los Angeles, 1930–1970" (PhD diss., University of California, Irvine, 2007); Buelna, *Chicano Communists*; Douglas Monroy, *Rebirth: Mexican Los Angeles from the Great Migration to the Great Depression* (Berkeley: University of California Press, 1999); David Gutierrez, *Walls and Mirrors: Mexican Americans, Mexican Immigrants, and the Politics of Ethnicity* (Berkeley: University of California Press, 1995); Jeffrey M. Garcilazo, "McCarthyism, Mexican Americans, and the Los Angeles Committee for the Protection of the Foreign-Born, 1950–1954," *Western Historical Quarterly* 32, no. 3 (2001): 273–95; and Robin D. G. Kelley, *Hammer and Hoe: Alabama Communists During the Great Depression*, 25th anniv. ed. (Chapel Hill: Univer-

sity of North Carolina Press, 2015). For Mexican American women and labor unions, see Vicki L. Ruiz, *Cannery Women, Cannery Lives: Mexican Women, Unionization, and the California Food Processing Industry, 1930–1950* (Albuquerque: University of New Mexico Press, 1987).

23. Monroy, *Rebirth*, 252.

24. See Buelna, *Chicano Communists*; Emma Pérez, *The Decolonial Imaginary: Writing Chicanas into History* (Bloomington: Indiana University Press, 1999); Garcilazo, "McCarthyism"; M. García, *Mexican Americans*; and Juan Gómez-Quiñones, *Sembradores: Ricardo Flores Magón y el Partido Liberal Mexicano* (Los Angeles: UCLA Chicano Studies Research Center, 1973).

25. Justin Akers Chacón, *Radicals in the Barrio: Magonistas, Socialists, Wobblies, and Communists in the Mexican American Working Class* (Chicago: Haymarket, 2018), 494; Schrecker, *Many Are the Crimes*, 15.

26. See Buelna, *Chicano Communists*, 29; and Akers Chacón, *Radicals in the Barrio*, chap. 30.

27. Schrecker, *Many Are the Crimes*, 19.

28. Akers Chacón, *Radicals in the Barrio*, 494–95; Buelna, *Chicano Communists*, 5.

29. Garcilazo, "McCarthyism," 291.

30. Dorothy Ray Healey and Maurice Isserman, *Dorothy Healey Remembers: A Life in the American Communist Party* (New York: Oxford University Press, 1990), 73.

31. Buelna, *Chicano Communists*, 4.

32. Ibid., 7; original quotation in Zaragoza Vargas, "Tejana Radical: Emma Tenayuca and the San Antonio Labor Movement During the Great Depression," *Pacific Historical Review* 66, no. 4 (1997): 556. According to Vargas, Tenayuca remained in the Communist Party for only two years. She left after the Nazi-Soviet nonaggression pact.

33. In Flores's FBI File 1228233-0, a report dated May 24, 1945, states that on March 28, 1945, "Source A" showed an FBI agent a letter that referred to Louise Morena [Luisa Moreno] of the FTA [ATA] that stated, "Morena had dismissed subject [Flores] as an employee of ATA-CIO LA because of technical deficiencies and because she was not a bookkeeper." There seemed to be tensions surrounding Flores's dismissal because she was described as an important asset for the San Diego Communist Party, and there was some conflict because the letter also noted that "Morena [Moreno] knew of Lym's [Francisca Flores] limitations when she insisted she come to LA." A report dated March 30, 1945, noted that Flores had received a check for her services as an employee from the "Progress Books" store for work performed on separate occasions, but not as a regular employee. On Communist Party–affiliated bookstores, see Joshua Clark Davis, "The Forgotten World of Communist Bookstores," *Jacobin* (August 11, 2017), https://jacobin.com/2017/08/communist-party-cpusa-bookstore-fbi. Also see Landeros, "AKA Frances."

34. Vicki L. Ruiz, "Luisa Moreno and Latina Labor Activism," in *Latina Legacies: Identity, Biography, and Community*, ed. Vicki L. Ruiz and Virginia Sánchez Korrol (New York: Oxford University Press, 2005), 175.

35. Vicki L. Ruiz, "Una Mujer Sin Fronteras: Luisa Moreno and Latina Labor Activism," *Pacific Historical Review* 73, no. 1 (2004):10.

36. Ibid., 6, 9.

37. Eduardo Obregón Pagán, *Murder at the Sleepy Lagoon: Zoot Suits, Race, and Riot in Wartime L.A.* (Charlotte: University of North Carolina Press, 2003), 210.

38. Landeros, "AKA Frances," 241; Schrecker, *Many Are the Crimes*, 9.
39. Schrecker, *Many Are the Crimes*, 15.
40. M. García, *Mexican Americans*, 154.
41. Kelley, *Hammer and Hoe*, 13.
42. Buelna, *Chicano Communists*, 117.
43. Ibid., 131. Although the party did not allow separate organizations made up of single ethnic or racial groups such as Mexican Americans or African Americans, members established the Zapata Club in Los Angeles. For CP member Ralph Cuarón, Flores's compatriot, the Zapata Club served as a path to revisit "the Mexican question" itself as well as to push for the CP to take a new position on Mexicans as a group. See ibid., 126.
44. Frances Lym, "The Mexican Americans Organize," *Jewish Life*, May 1955, 22. Also see Buelna, "Resistance from the Margins"; Garcilazo, "McCarthyism"; and M. Garcia, *Mexican Americans*.
45. See M. García, *Mexican Americans*, 175–76, and Buelna, *Chicano Communists*, 102.
46. Healey and Isserman, *Dorothy Healey Remembers*, 164. Also see Buelna, *Chicano Communists*, 150.
47. See Flores, FBI File. There do not appear to be very many Mexican American women who participated in the CP as did Flores. Sylvia Cuarón, who was involved with the CP in Mexican American communities, also participated; she is not Mexican American, however, but Jewish, having arrived in Los Angeles via New York. Married to Ralph Cuarón, who was heavily involved in trade unions and the CP, she was immersed in Mexican American politics on the East Side. Her daughter Margarita (Mita) Cuarón was one of the main organizers of the high school walkouts in East Los Angeles in 1968. See Buelna, *Chicano Communists*, chs. 4 and 5. In addition to the CSO, organizations such as the Los Angeles Committee for Protection of the Foreign Born represented activists and others targeted by immigration authorities for deportation. Founded in 1950, this committee was not necessarily a Mexican American political organization, but it operated an office in East Los Angeles. It viewed immigration policies during the era as un-American and as flatly contradicting the U.S. constitution. While the CSO continued to function successfully throughout the 1960s, the LACPFB stopped functioning in the early 1960s.
48. D. Gutiérrez, *Walls and Mirrors*, 173.
49. Ibid., 170.
50. Shana Bernstein, *Bridges of Reform: Interracial Civil Rights Activism in Twentieth-Century Los Angeles* (New York: Oxford University Press, 2011), 140.
51. D. Gutiérrez, *Walls and Mirrors*, 170.
52. Margaret Rose, "Gender and Civic Activism in Mexican American Barrios: The Community Service Organization, 1947–1962," in *Not June Cleaver: Women and Gender in Postwar America, 1945–1960*, ed. Joanne Meyerowitz (Philadelphia: Temple University Press, 1994), 189.
53. Ibid., 179.
54. Linda M. Apodaca, "Mexican American Women and Social Change: The Founding of the Community Service Organization in Los Angeles, An Oral History" (Mexican American Studies and Research Center Working Paper Series 27, January 1999), 7; D. Gutiérrez, *Walls and Mirrors*, 168–69. By the 1950s the CSO had established chapters in San Jose and Stockton, where two of its best-known organizers, César Chávez and Dolores Huerta, met. Huerta began to work with the CSO in 1955, when she met Fred Ross in

Stockton. In the late 1950s, when Chavez became executive director of the CSO, he hired Huerta as an organizer but quickly believed her to be better at lobbying.

55. Grace Montañez Davis, interview by Phillip C. Castruita, July–September 1994, Grace Montañez Davis Personal Collection, Los Angeles, California.

56. Ibid.

57. See Arthur Eckstein, "The Hollywood Ten in History and Memory," *Film History* 16 (2004): 424–36.

58. Grace Montañez Davis, interview by Phillip C. Castruita.

59. [Maria] Linda Apodaca, "They Kept the Home Fires Burning: Mexican American Women and Social Change" (PhD diss., University of California, Irvine, 1994), 65, 79.

60. Grace Montañez Davis interview by Phillip C. Castruita.

61. Edward Roybal, introduction to Hope Mendoza Schechter, "Hope Mendoza Schechter: Activist in the Labor Movement, the Democratic Party, and the Mexican-American Community" (oral history interview, Regional Oral History Office, Bancroft Library University of California, Berkeley, 1979), v. Also see D. Gutiérrez, *Walls and Mirrors*, 168–69.

62. For more on Chester Holifield, see "Chester Holifield, 91, Congressman for 32 Years," *New York Times*, Obituaries, February 9, 1995.

63. See ibid. Holifield also served as the chair of the Joint Committee on Atomic Energy, the House Committee on Government Operations, and the House Subcommittee on Legislation and Military Operations. Holifield was also interested in atomic energy. In 1946 he was a key proponent of the creation of the Atomic Energy Commission, a civilian body. Originally from Kentucky, Holifield and his family settled in Montebello, California, first running a dry-cleaning business and then a men's clothing store.

64. Mendoza Schechter, *Activist in the Labor Movement*, 143.

65. D. Gutierrez, *Walls and Mirrors*, 161–62; Public Law 414, June 27, 1952, 204–7.

66. Linda Apodaca, "The Community Service Organization," in *Latinas in the United States: A Historical Encyclopedia*, ed. Vicki L. Ruiz and Virginia Sánchez Korrol (Bloomington Indiana University Press, 2006), 170–72.

67. E. Chávez, "¡Mi Raza Primero!," 34.

68. Rodolfo F. Acuña, *A Community Under Siege: A Chronicle of Chicanos East of the Los Angeles River, 1945–1975* (Los Angeles: Chicano Studies Research Center Publications, Monograph No. 11, 1984), 111.

69. Dolores Sánchez, interview by the author.

70. *The Southern California District of the Communist Party Structure—Objectives—Leadership. Hearings Before the Committee on Un-American Activities, House of Representatives*, 85th Congress (September 2 and 3, 1958) (Washington, DC: Government Printing Office, 1958); ibid., Investigation of Communist Infiltration and Propaganda Activities in Basic Industry. Delfino Varela, pt. 3, February 25, 1959, 284–85.

71. Dolores Sánchez, interview by the author. In *Voicing Chicana Feminisms: Young Women Speak Out on Sexuality and Identity* (New York: New York University Press, 2003), Aida Hurtado uses young women's stories about the women in their lives and families to articulate that while many young Latinas do not identify as feminists, much like Dolores Sánchez's mother, when asked about feminism the women responded with stories of strong females in their families. Hurtado therefore argues that these women experienced feminism through lived experience. Part of the hesitancy is the ownership of the word

feminism, what it is thought to imply, and what many women feel will be inferred by others by identification as a feminist. Thus, the idea that feminist behavior and feminist self-identification are different, when perhaps this is not so. Perhaps the bigger idea is that our notion of what feminism means needs to be broadened.

72. Dolores Sánchez, interview by the author.

73. Ibid.

74. Connie Pardo, interview by the author. The Francis De Pauw school in Los Angeles was located on Sunset Boulevard in Hollywood. A single-sex women's school, it "educated approximately 1,800 young Mexican women from 1900–1946." See Vicki L. Ruiz, *From Out of the Shadows: Mexican Women in Twentieth-Century America* (New York: Oxford University Press, 1998), 43.

75. Grace Montañez Davis, interview with Virginia Espino for the Center for Oral History Research, University of California, Los Angeles, August 26, 2008; September 5, 11, 19, and 26, 2008; October 1, 12, and 28, 2008; and November 10, 2008.

76. Lilia Aceves interview by the author.

77. Ibid.

78. On neighborhood associations, see, e.g., Robyn Muncy, "Cooperative Motherhood and Democratic Civic Culture in Postwar Suburbia, 1940–1965," *Journal of Social History* 38, no. 2 (2004): 285. Academic OneFile, http://link.galegroup.com.libproxy.csudh.edu/apps/doc/A128027043/AONE?u=csudh&sid=AONE&xid=dd786937.

79. Ibid.

80. Delfino Varela was a social worker originally from New Mexico who was involved with the Communist Party. In 1958 he was called before the Committee on Un-American Activities. See *Hearings Before the Committee on Un-American Activities, House of Representatives, 85th Congress*, (Washington, DC: Government Printing Office, 1958), 284–85.

81. Anna NietoGómez, "Francisca Flores, the League of Mexican American Women, and the Comisión Femenil Mexicana Nacional, 1958–1975," in *Chicana Movidas: New Narratives of Activism and Feminism in the Movement Era*, ed. *Dionne* Espinoza, María Eugenia Cotera, and Maylei Blackwell (Austin: University of Texas Press, 2018), 35; *Carta Editorial*, "Bon Voyage," January 25, 1967.

82. See Ruben Salazar, "Doubt Cast on Johnson Parley Here," *Los Angeles Times*, August 9, 1963; Ruben Salazar, "Johnson to Hear Plaint of Minority," *Los Angeles Times*, July 29, 1963.

83. NietoGómez, "Francisca Flores," 36. NietoGómez uses the same quotation from *Carta Editorial* in her article.

84. Francisca Flores and Delfino Varela, "Women and Dogs Not Allowed," *Carta Editorial*, 6 August 1963, 2.

85. See Cynthia E. Orozco, *No Mexicans, Women, or Dogs Allowed: The Rise of the Mexican American Civil Rights Movement* (Austin: University of Texas Press, 2009).

86. [Francisca Flores and Delfino Varela], "The Statistics of Discrimination," *Carta Editorial*, April 1, 1964, 4–5.

87. Daniel Hosang, "Race and the Mythology of California's Lost Paradise," *Boom: A Journal of California* 1 (2011): 37.

88. [Sal Montenegro], "Effects of the Initiative and Fair Housing Law on the Mexican American Community (Excerpts from an Address)," *Carta Editorial*, August 1, 1964: 1.

Also see Wendy Cheng, *The Changs Next Door to the Díazes: Remapping Race in Suburban California* (Minneapolis: University of Minnesota Press, 2013).

89. [Francisca Flores and Delfino Varela], "The Urban Reality," *Carta Editorial*, August 30, 1965, 4.

90. See D. Gutiérrez, *Walls and Mirrors*, 163; E. Chávez, *¡Mi Raza Primero!*; Mario T. García, *Memories of Chicano History: The Life and Narrative of Bert Corona* (Berkeley: University of California Press, 1994), 181–84; and Kelly Lytle Hernandez, *Migra! A History of the U.S. Border Patrol* (Berkeley: University of California Press, 2010), esp. sec. 3.

91. On the Bracero Program, see Mireya Loza, *Defiant Braceros: How Migrant Workers Fought for Racial, Sexual, and Political Freedom* (Chapel Hill: University of North Carolina Press, 2016); and Ronald L. Mize, *Consuming Mexican Labor: From the Bracero Program to NAFTA* (Toronto: University of Toronto Press, 2011).

92. Delfino Varela, "After the Bracero Program, Then What," *Carta Editorial*, October 5, 1963, 1. Also see Deborah Cohen, *Braceros: Migrant Citizens and Transnational Subjects in the Postwar United States and Mexico* (Chapel Hill: University of North Carolina Press, 2013); and Ana Elizabeth Rosas, *Abrazando el Espíritu: Bracero Families Confront the U.S.–Mexico Border* (Berkeley: University of California Press, 2014).

93. The earliest documents that I had access to are from 1963.

94. NietoGómez, "Francisca Flores," 38.

95. Lilia Aceves, interview by the author.

96. NietoGómez, "Francisca Flores," 38; Dolores Sánchez interview by the author. Also see Gómez-Quiñones, *Chicano Politics*, 68.

97. League of Mexican-American Women, "Aims and Purposes," (n.d.), 1, Comisión Femenil Mexicana Nacional Records, California Ethnic and Multicultural Archives, University of California, Santa Barbara (hereafter cited as CFMN Records); League of Mexican-American Women, "Achievement Awards," May 7, 1966, CFMN Records, Conferences Series, box 1, folder 1.

98. League of Mexican-American Women, "Aims and Purposes," (n.d.)1.

99. Ramona Morín, "Resume" [1970], CFMN Records, Conferences Series, box 1, folder 1.

100. League of Mexican-American Women to MACPF [Mexican American Community Programs Foundation], n.d., Lilia Aceves, personal collection, Alhambra, California.

101. For more on women and consumer education, see Erma Angevine, *History of the National Consumers' League, 1899–1979* (Washington, DC: National Consumers' League, 1979); Landon R. Y. Storrs, *Civilizing Capitalism: The National Consumers' League, Women's Activities, and Labor Standards in the New Deal Era* (Chapel Hill: University of North Carolina Press, 2000).

102. League of Mexican-American Women, "Consumer Education," October 23, 1969, Lilia Aceves, personal collection. Although this document refers to a member of the Federal Drug and Sanitation Administration, such an administration has never existed, so the reference may have been a mistake. This person may have been a staff member of the Food and Drug Administration.

103. Ibid.

104. Consumer Action Council, "Proposal for the Establishment of a Comprehensive Consumer Protection Project" [1969, 1970], 13, CFMN Records, box 11, folder 2.

105. Ibid., 14–15.

106. Ibid., 3–4. The Consumer Action Council's report cites Sturdivant's report quite extensively. Sturdivant's study incorporated control areas in order to compare various items for sale in various stores. For example, furniture and appliance price comparisons included twenty-four items in twenty-four stores, with the control area encompassing Culver City, Inglewood, and Lawndale. Sturdivant found that, on average, for purchases such as televisions, vacuums, and free-standing ranges, the average price was $51.03 higher in Mexican American neighborhoods than in white ones. In a study of car purchases in which a "Mexican American and an Anglo white" male went to eight local car dealers and provided identical work, background, and credit information, and were interested in the same cars with the same accessories, the average price for the Mexican American buyer was $150 above the average price for the white buyer, and the interest rate for the Mexican American buyer was 4 percent higher than for the white buyer.

107. League of Mexican-American Women to MACPF, n.d., Lilia Aceves, personal collection.

108. League of Mexican-American Women, "Meeting Minutes," April 12, 1969, Lilia Aceves, personal collection.

109. NietoGómez, "Francisca Flores," 38–39.

110. Dolores Sánchez interview by the author.

111. On the phrase "ethnic Mexicans," see the introduction to this volume, note 1.

112. [Francisca Flores and Delfino Varela], "Women's Banquet," *Carta Editorial*, May 2, 1966, 1.

113. See Peter Matthiessen, *Sal Si Puedes: Cesar Chavez and the New American Revolution* (New York: Dell, 1973); Richard W. Etulain, ed., *César Chávez: A Brief Biography with Documents* (Boston: Bedford/St. Martin's, 2002); Reies López Tijerina, *They Called Me "King Tiger": My Struggle for the Land and Our Rights* (Houston: Arte Público, 2001); Ernesto Vigil, *The Crusade for Justice: Chicano Militancy and the Government's War on Dissent* (Madison: University of Wisconsin Press, 1999); Rodolfo "Corky" Gonzales, *Message to Aztlán: Selected Writings* (Houston: Arte Público, 2001); and José Angel Gutiérrez, *The Making of a Chicano Militant: Lessons from Cristal* (Madison: University of Wisconsin Press, 1999). The National Farm Workers Association, the predecessor to the United Farm Workers Union, was founded in 1962.

114. Francisca Flores, "The Children Shall Lead Them," *Carta Editorial*, March 27, 1968, 1.

Chapter 2. Forging a Chicana Feminist Praxis

1. Mexican American women had organized politically before 1966, but not in terms of political representation for themselves as women. See Cynthia Orozco, "Beyond Machismo, La Familia, and Ladies Auxiliaries: A Historiography of Mexican-Origin Women's Participation in Voluntary Associations and Politics in the United States, 1870–1990," *Perspectives in Mexican American Studies* 5 (1995): 1–34; Emma Pérez, *The Decolonial Imaginary: Writing Chicanas into History* (Bloomington: Indiana University Press, 1999); and Gabriela González, "Carolina Munguía and Emma Tenayuca: The Politics of Benevolence and Radical Reform," *Frontiers* 24 (2003): 200–229.

2. Lilia Aceves, interview by the author, April 5, 2002, Monterey Park, California. Also see Anna NietoGómez, "Francisca Flores, the League of Mexican American Women, and

the Comisión Femenil Mexicana Nacional, 1958–1975," in *Chicana Movidas: New Narratives of Activism and Feminism in the Movement Era*, ed. Dionne Espinoza, María Eugenia Cotera, and Maylei Blackwell 44 (Austin: University of Texas Press, 2018). Josephine Valdez Banda's spouse, Joe Banda, was one of the organizers of the Mexican American National Issues Conference.

3. In California, Comisión Femenil chapters existed in Bakersfield, Berkeley, the Central Coast, Fresno, Kern County, Los Angeles, Loyola Marymount University, Merced, Modesto, Oakland, Orange County, Pasadena, Pomona, Rio Hondo, Sacramento, San Diego, San Francisco, Southeast Los Angeles, Visalia, and Watsonville. Chapters also existed in Albuquerque, Aurora (Illinois), Tempe/Phoenix, and Washington, DC.

4. Winifred Breines, *The Trouble Between Us: An Uneasy History of White and Black Women in the Feminist Movement* (New York: Oxford University Press, 2006), 113.

5. For a similar argument, see Margaret Rose, "Gender and Civic Activism in Mexican American Barrios: The Community Service Organization, 1947–1962," in *Not June Cleaver: Women and Gender in Postwar America, 1945–1960*, ed. Joanne Meyerowitz (Philadelphia: Temple University Press, 1994), 177–200.

6. Marcie Miranda-Arrizón, "Building Herman(a)dad: Chicana Feminism and the Comision Femenil Mexicana Nacional" (Master's thesis, University of California, Santa Barbara, 1999), 55. Because women established the organization at a national Mexican American conference, the founding of the Comisión Femenil echoes the circumstances under which women founded the National Organization for Women (NOW) in 1966 at the National Conference of State Commissions on the Status of Women. But whereas NOW's founders envisioned an organization for all American women, the Comisión Femenil saw itself as an organ only for Mexican American women because they believed that in the four years of NOW's existence it had not represented their interests.

7. NietoGómez, "Francisca Flores," 47.

8. "Resolution to Establish Comisión Femenil Mexicana Nacional, Inc.," Comisión Femenil Mexicana Nacional Records, CEMA 30, California Ethnic and Multicultural Archives, University of California, Santa Barbara (hereafter California Ethnic and Multicultural Archives). Also see NietoGómez, "Francisca Flores," 47–48, and Sonia R. García and Marisela Márquez, "The Comisión Femenil: La Voz of a Chicana Organization," *Aztlán* 36, no. 1 (Spring 2011): 155–56.

9. Frances Bojorquez, interview by Marcie Miranda-Arrizón, September 13, 1996, Thousand Oaks, California, Miranda (Marcy) Collection, CEMA 053, California Ethnic and Multicultural Archives.

10. Linda C. Delgado, "Polly Baca Barragán," in *Latinas in the United States: An Historical Encyclopedia*, ed. Vicki L. Ruiz and Virginia Sánchez Korrol (Bloomington: Indiana University Press, 2006), 75–76.

11. F. Arturo Rosales, "Graciela Olivares," in *Latinas in the United States: An Historical Encyclopedia*, ed. Vicki L. Ruiz and Virginia Sánchez Korrol (Bloomington: Indiana University Press, 2006), 537–38.

12. Gloria de la Torre Wycoff, interview by Marcie Miranda-Arrizon, November 30, 1996, Whittier, California, Miranda (Marcy) Collection, CEMA 053, California Ethnic and Multicultural Archives.

13. Lilia Aceves interview by the author.

14. Francisca Flores, "Regeneración," *Regeneración*, January 1970, n.p.

15. See Mario T. García, *Mexican Americans: Leadership, Ideology, and Identity, 1930–1960* (New Haven: Yale University Press, 1991); Juan Gómez-Quinones, *Chicano Politics: Reality and Promise, 1940–1990* (Albuquerque: University of New Mexico Press, 1990); Cynthia Orozco, *No Mexicans, Women or Dogs Allowed: The Rise of the Mexican American Civil Rights Movement* (Austin: University of Texas Press, 2009).

16. See Orozco, "Beyond Machismo."

17. *Quest for a Homeland*, episode 1 of *Chicano! History of the Mexican American Civil Rights Movement*, produced by Mylene Moreno and Hector Galán (1996: National Latino Communications Center), VHS.

18. Quoted in Enriqueta Longeaux y Vásquez, "The Women of La Raza," *La Raza*, July 1969, 7.

19. Maylei Blackwell, *¡Chicana Power! Contested Histories of Feminism in the Chicano Movement* (Austin: University of Texas Press, 2011), 140.

20. See Alma M. García, *Chicana Feminist Thought: The Basic Historical Writings* (New York: Routledge, 1997); Blackwell, *¡Chicana Power!*; Sonia E. López, "The Role of the Chicana Within the Student Movement," in *Essays on la Mujer*, ed. Rosaura Sánchez, 16–29. (Los Angeles: UCLA Chicano Studies Research Center, 1977); and Adelaida del Castillo and Magdalena Mora, eds., *Mexican Women in the United States: Struggles Past and Present* (Los Angeles: UCLA Chicano Studies Research Center Occasional Paper no. 2, 1980). Euro-American refers to persons of European origin who would be racially classified as white. On second-wave feminism, see Alice Echols, *Daring to Be Bad: Radical Feminism in America, 1967–1975* (Minneapolis: University of Minnesota Press, 1989); Sara Evans, *Personal Politics: The Roots of Women's Liberation in the Civil Rights Movement and the New Left* (New York: Knopf, 1979); Daniel Horowitz, *Betty Friedan and the Making of The Feminine Mystique: The American Left, the Cold War, and Feminism* (Amherst: University of Massachusetts Press, 1998); William Chafe, *The Paradox of Change: American Women in the 20th Century* (New York: Oxford University Press, 1991); Ruth Rosen, *The World Split Open: How the Modern Women's Movement Changed America* (New York: Penguin, 2000); and Flora Davis, *Moving the Mountain: The Women's Movement in America Since 1960* (New York: Simon and Schuster, 1991).

21. Elizabeth Martínez, "La Chicana," *Ideal*, September 5–20, 1972, 2. Reprinted in A. García, *Chicana Feminist Thought*, 32–33.

22. Ibid.

23. López, "Role of the Chicana," 23.

24. Longeaux y Vásquez, "Women of la Raza," 7. The article was reprinted in the newspaper *La Raza*. It had originally been printed in *El Grito del Norte*, a newspaper published in New Mexico and edited by Elizabeth "Betita" Martínez and Longeaux y Vásquez from 1968 through 1973.

25. Blackwell, *¡Chicana Power!*, 140.

26. See Dionne Espinoza, "Rethinking Cultural Nationalism and La Familia Through Women's Communities: Enriqueta Vasquez and Chicana Feminist Thought," in *Enriqueta Vasquez and the Chicano Movement: Writings from El Grito del Norte*, ed. Lorena Oropeza

and Dionne Espinoza (Albuquerque: Arte Público, 2006), 217; Ernesto Vigil, *The Crusade for Justice: Chicano Militancy and the Government's War on Dissent* (Madison: University of Wisconsin Press, 1999), 124; and *El Gallo*, June 1970, 10.

27. Espinoza, "Rethinking Cultural Nationalism," 217. Also see Lee Bebout, *Mythohistorical Interventions: The Chicano Movement and Its Legacies* (Minneapolis: University of Minnesota Press, 2011), 116.

28. Blackwell, *¡Chicana Power!*, 98. Also see Richard T. Rodriguez, *Next of Kin: The Family in Chicano/a Cultural Politics* (Durham: Duke University Press, 2009), 21.

29. Also see Bebout, *Mythohistorical Interventions*, and E. Pérez, *Decolonial Imaginary*.

30. See Blackwell, *¡Chicana Power!*, chap. 3, and Maxine Baca Zinn, "Political Familism: Toward Sex Role Equality in Chicano Families," *Aztlán* 6, no. 1 (Spring 1975): 13–26.

31. E. Pérez, *Decolonial Imaginary*, 33. Bebout, *Mythohistorical Interventions*.

32. Dione Espinoza, "Revolutionary Sisters: Women's Solidarity and Collective Identification Among Chicana Brown Berets in East Los Angeles, 1967–1970," *Aztlán* 26, no. 1 (Spring 2001): 41.

33. For the concept of women of color strategizing their use of distinct identities in different situations, see Chela Sandoval, *Methodology of the Oppressed* (Minneapolis: University of Minnesota Press, 2000).

34. Women's Workshop (National Mexican American Issues Conference), "Resolutions—Women's Workshop," (11 October 1970), CFMN Records, CEMA 30, California Ethnic and Multicultural Archives, box 1, folder 1. For more on heterosexism in the Chicano movement, see Rodriguez, *Next of Kin*.

35. "Educational Attainment," http://www.census.gov/population/www/socdemo/educ-attn.html; U.S. Census Bureau, *U.S. Census of Population, 1970 and 1980*, vol. 1; Current Population Reports P20–550, and earlier reports.

36. For a similar argument about women involved in the 1968 East Los Angles high school walkouts, see Dolores Delgado Bernal, "Grassroots Leadership *Reconceptualized*: Chicana Oral Histories and the 1968 East Los Angeles Blowouts," *Frontiers* 19 (1998): 113–43.

37. Yolanda Nava, interview by Michelle Moravec, July 17, 1989, Los Angeles, California, Oral History Archives, California State University, Long Beach; Yolanda Nava, interview by the author, September 19, 2003, Santa Fe, New Mexico.

38. Sandra Serrano Sewell, interview by Jackie Hunt, Center for Oral History Research, University of California, Los Angeles, April 4, 22, 2011, and May 23, 2011, https://oralhistory.library.ucla.edu/catalog/21198-zz0028td1g?counter=5.

39. Connie Pardo, interview by the author, March 29, 2002, Los Angeles, California.

40. Corinne Sánchez, interview by the author, April 4, 2002, San Fernando, California; Anna NietoGómez, interview by the author, June 1, 2002, Lakewood, California.

41. Anna NietoGómez, interview by Maylei Blackwell (interview 3), April 22, 1991, Oral History Archives, California State University, Long Beach; Leticia Hernandez, interview by Maylei Blackwell (interview 2), July 30, 1992, Oral History Archives, California State University, Long Beach; Anna NietoGómez interview by the author; and Corinne Sánchez interview by the author. Also see Blackwell, *¡Chicana Power!*.

42. "El Movimiento Estudiantil Chicano de Aztlán", or the "Chicano Student Movement of Aztlán," became the name of choice for many, if not most, Chicana/o student

organizations on college campuses throughout the nation after April 1969, when *El Plan de Santa Barbara* was formulated at the University of California, Santa Barbara.

43. Corinne Sánchez interview by the author.

44. Women's Bureau, U.S. Department of Labor Employment Standards Division, "Consultation for Spanish-Surnamed Women: List of Participants," March 25–26, 1972, CFMN Records, box 1, folder 4. In addition to Flores, other Comisión Femenil members in attendance included Gracia Molina de Pick and Corinne Sánchez. Although Richard Nixon was elected president in 1968, the programs that his predecessor Lyndon B. Johnson had put into place, specifically those stemming from the War on Poverty, were still in existence. In 1964 Congress passed the Economic Opportunity Act, and the Office of Economic Opportunity (OEO) was established to coordinate efforts. One of the OEO's aims was to lift citizens out of poverty by involving them in their own self-help through educational, job training, and community development programs.

45. "Hispano Women Meet in Phoenix," *La Luz*, May 1972, 47.

46. Ibid.

47. Lilia Aceves interview by the author; Grace Montañez Davis, interview by Phillip Castruita, July–September 1994, tape 7, p. 11, Grace Montañez Davis personal collection.

48. Gloria Moreno-Wycoff, ["Tribute to Francisca Flores"], February 10, 1982, 1, CFMN Records.

49. Also see Miranda-Arrizón, "Building Hermana(a)dad," 66; Grace Montañez Davis interview by Phillip Castruita, tape 7, p. 12.

50. Commission on the Status of Women, *Transcript of Public Hearing on the Status of Women in 1973*, Los Angeles, February 9 and 10, 1973, 1:304.

51. Chicana Service Action Center, "CSAC Fact Sheet," n.d. [1976], CFMN Records, box 2.

52. Yolanda Nava interview by the author; Yolanda Nava interview by Michelle Moravec; Gloria Molina and Carlos Vásquez, "Oral History Interview with Gloria Molina," Department of Special Collections, University of California, Los Angeles, 1990; Aceves interview by the author.

53. Carol Frances Cini, "Making Women's Rights Matter: Diverse Activists, California's Commission on the Status of Women, and the Legislative and Social Impact of a Movement, 1962–1976" (PhD diss., University of California, Los Angeles, 2007), 438. For a more robust description of the themes at the hearings, see 442–79. Also see "Hearings Scheduled on Status of Women," *Los Angeles Times*, February 4, 1973, F4.

54. Nancy Baltad, "Burbank Woman May Now Be in Position to Change Things," *Los Angeles Times*, April 11, 1973, SF8.

55. Cini, "Making Women's Rights Matter," 484.

56. Ibid.; Yolanda Nava interview by the author.

57. Comisión Femenil Mexicana Nacional, "[Resolutions and Registered Participants]," June 2, 1973, CFMN Records, box 1, folder 12; Miranda-Arrizón, "Building Herman(a)dad," 68. Also see "Mexican-Americans to Have Convention Roles," *Los Angeles Times*, May 31, 1973, SG4.

58. Sandra Serrano Sewell interview by Jackie Hunt.

59. Gloria Moreno-Wycoff interview by Marcie Miranda-Arrizon.

60. See Benita Roth, *Separate Roads to Feminism: Black, Chicana, and White Feminist Movements in America's Second Wave* (New York: Cambridge University Press, 2003). In a later article, Anna NietoGómez, who also attended the conference, categorized the two groups as "loyalists" and "feminists." See Anna NietoGómez, "La Femenista," *Encuentro Femenil* 1, no. 2 (1974): 34–47, 74.

61. Ibid.

62. Ibid.; Mirta Vidal, in *Chicanas Speak Out—Women: New Voice of La Raza* (New York: Pathfinder, 1971), 13–15.

63. Suzan Racho, Gloria Meneses, Socorro Acosta, and Chicki Quijano, "Houston Chicana Conference," *La Gente* (UCLA), May 31, 1971, 6–7; "National Chicanas Conference," *La Verdad*, July–August 1971, 15–17.

64. Blackwell, *¡Chicana Power!*, 162.

65. See Marta Cotera, "La Conferencia De Mujeres Por La Raza: Houston, Texas, 1971," in *Chicana Feminist Thought: The Basic Historical Writings*, ed. Alma García (New York: Routledge, 1977), 155–57, originally published in Marta Cotera, *Profile on the Mexican American Woman* (Austin: National Educational Library Publishers, 1976), 224–27; Francisca Flores, "Conference of Mexican Women in Houston—Un Remolino [A Whirlwind], in *Chicana Feminist Thought: The Basic Historical Writings* ed. Alma García (New York: Routledge, 1977), 157–61, originally published in *Regeneración* 1, no. 10 (1971): 1–5; Vicki L. Ruiz, *From out of the Shadows: Mexican Women in Twentieth-Century America* (New York: Oxford University Press, 1998), 108.

66. S. García and Márquez, "Comisión Femenil," 156.

67. This dynamic was not unique to the CFMN. See Espinoza, "Revolutionary Sisters."

68. Amelia Lorenzo Wilson, "Comisión Femenil Mexicana, Nacional," July 10, 1973, CFMN Records, box 1, folder 18.

69. Sandra Serrano Sewell, interview by the author, March 14, 2002, Los Angeles, California.

70. "Responsibilities of the Comision Femenil Mexicana Nacional, Inc.," n.d., CFMN Papers, box 1, folder 11.

71. "Executive Board Meeting of Comision Femenil Mexicana Nacional, Inc.," August 18, 1973, CFMN Records, box 1, folder 16.

72. Chicana Service Action Center, "CSAC Fact Sheet," n.d. [1976], CFMN Records, box 2.

73. Francisca Flores to Anita Ramos, November 21, 1974, CFMN Records, box 1, folder 31.

74. Jeannie De Portillo, "Comisión Femenil Mexicana National Board Meeting," January 18, 1975, CFMN Records, box 2, folder 1.

75. Ilbert Phillips to Chicana Service Action Center, February 1975, CFMN Records, box 28, folder 8. In his summary of the meeting Phillips notes that there were five groups present: the new board of directors that represented the new CSAC corporation, the former CSAC board of directors, representatives from the CFMN board, CSAC staff, and other interested parties. Records do not show the members of the old and new center board of directors.

76. Ibid.

77. Ilbert Phillips to Chicana Service Action Center, February 1975, 4, CFMN Records, box 2, folder 8.

78. Ilbert Phillips to Steven M. Porter, March 10, 1975, CFMN Records, box 2, folder 8.

79. Ilbert Phillips to Connie Muñoz [Pardo], March 10, 1975, 1, CFMN Records, box 2, folder 8.

80. Ilbert Phillips to Steven M. Porter, March 10, 1975, CFMN Records, box 2, folder 8.

81. Raoul Teilhet to Gloria Molina, July 30, 1976, CFMN Records, box 12, folder 9.

82. Rose Ungar to Gloria Molina, July 27, 1976, CFMN Records, box 12, folder 9.

83. Gloria Molina to Raoul Teilhet, n.d. [ca. August 1976], CFMN Records, box 12, folder 9.

84. [Gloria Molina], "President's Report [1975–1976]," July 30, 1977, 4, CFMN Records, box 2, folder 11.

85. "Day Care Workers Unionize," *Sin Fronteras*, August 1976, 2.

86. Ibid.

87. García and Márquez, "Comisión Femenil," 161.

Chapter 3. California Chicanas and International Women's Year

1. Celia Herrera Rodríguez, interview by the author, October 10, 2002, Oakland, California. On El Teatro Campesino, see Yolanda Broyles-González, *El Teatro Campesino: Theater in the Chicano Movement* (Austin: University of Texas Press, 1994); and Randy J. Ontiveros, *In the Spirit of a New People: The Cultural Politics of the Chicano Movement* (New York: NYU Press, 2013).

2. See Leila J. Rupp, *Worlds of Women: The Making of an International Women's Movement* (Princeton, NJ: Princeton University Press, 1997), 4; Virginia R. Allan, Margaret E. Galey, and Mildred E. Persinger, "World Conference of International Women's Year," in *Women, Politics, and the United Nations*, ed. Anne Winslow (Westport, CT: Greenwood, 1995), 29; and Estelle B. Freedman, *No Turning Back: The History of Feminism and the Future of Women* (New York: Ballantine, 2003), 107.

3. The conference was originally going to take place in Colombia, but in October 1974 Colombia declined and Mexico volunteered to serve as the conference host. See Jocelyn Olcott, *International Women's Year: The Greatest Consciousness-Raising Event in History* (New York: Oxford University Press, 2017), 55.

4. See Allan, Galey, and Persinger, "World Conference"; Olcott, *International Women's Year*."

5. For a discussion of foreign travel by activists in the Chicano movement, see Elizabeth Martínez, *De Colores Means All of Us: Latina Views for a Multi-Colored Century* (Cambridge, MA: South End, 1997).

6. Anna NietoGómez, interview by the author, June 1, 2002, Lakewood, California.

7. I use the term *Third World*, following the work of Cheryl Johnson-Odim, to mean the following: (1) to identify "underdeveloped" or "overexploited geopolitical entities" such as nations and regions and (2) to identify those who live in or come from said nations or regions. I use the term *women of color* to identify non-European or non-Euro-American

women who believed that race, gender, and class had a direct negative impact on their lives. *Women of color* is used with its appropriate national signifier, such as U.S. women of color. See Cheryl Johnson-Odim, "Common Themes, Different Contexts: Third World Women and Feminism," in *Third World Women and the Politics of Feminism*, ed. Chandra Talpade Mohanty, Ann Ruso, and Lourdes Torres (Bloomington: Indiana University Press, 1991), 314.

8. See Juan Gómez-Quiñones, *Chicano Politics: Reality and Promise, 1940–1990* (Albuquerque: University of New Mexico Press, 1990), esp. chap. 3, and Alan Eladio Gómez, *The Revolutionary Imaginations of Greater Mexico: Chicana/o Radicalism, Solidarity Politics, and Latin American Social Movements* (Austin: University of Texas Press, 2016), esp. chap. 2.

9. Rupp, *Worlds of Women*, 223–24, quotation on 224; Margaret E. Galey, "Promoting Nondiscrimination Against Women: The UN Commission on the Status of Women," *International Studies Quarterly* 23 (June 1979): 275. Galey's article points to 1947 as the founding year of the Commission on the Status of Women.

10. Dionne Espinoza, "La Raza en Canada: San Diego Chicana Activists, the Indochinese Women's Conference of 1971, and Third World Womanism," in *Chicana Movidas: New Narratives of Activism and Feminism in the Movement Era*, ed. Dionne Espinoza, Maria Eugenia Cotera, and Maylei Blackwell (Austin: University of Texas Press, 2018), 262. For additional information on the Indochinese Women's Conference, see Judy Tzu-Chun Wu, *Radicals on the Road: Internationalism, Orientalism, and Feminism During the Vietnam Era* (Ithaca, NY: Cornell University Press, 2013).

11. Espinoza, "La Raza en Canada," 271.

12. Ibid., 266.

13. See "International Women's Tribune Center," International Women's Tribune Center, https://www.iwtc.org/.

14. See Jane S. Jaquette, "Losing the Battle/Winning the War: International Politics, Women's Issues, and the 1980 Mid-Decade Conference," in *Women, Politics, and the United Nations*, ed. Anne Winslow (Westport, CT: Greenwood, 1995), 45–49; Estelle B. Freedman, *No Turning Back: The History of Feminism and the Future of Women* (New York: Ballantine, 2002), esp. chap. 5; Johnson-Odim, "Common Themes"; Angela Gilliam, "Women's Equality and National Liberation," in *Third World Women and the Politics of Feminism*, ed. Chandra Talpade Mohanty, Ann Ruso, and Lourdes Torres (Bloomington: Indiana University Press, 1991); and Ruth Rosen, *The World Split Open: How the Modern Women's Movement Changed America* (New York: Penguin, 2000), epilogue.

15. After 1995 there were no subsequent Women's World Conferences. Instead, between 2000 and 2020 the United Nations held five-year reviews of the Platform for Action from the Beijing Women's World Conference in 1995. In 2020 only one meeting of the Commission on the Status of Women was held due to the emergence of a worldwide pandemic. At this meeting, the CSW provided a platform for opening statements and approval of the draft "Political Declaration on the Occasion of the 25th Anniversary of the Fourth World Conference on Women." See "World Conferences on Women," UN Women, https://www.unwomen.org/en/how-we-work/intergovernmental-support/world-conferences-on-women; and "CSW64/Beijing+25 (2020)," UN Women, https://www.unwomen.org/en/csw/csw64-2020.

16. See Allan, Galey, and Persinger, "World Conference," 29, 34–39; Jaquette, "Losing the Battle/Winning the War," 56; and Margaret E. Galey, "The Nairobi Conference: The Powerless Majority," *Political Science* 19 (Spring 1986): 275.

17. Gisela Espinosa Damián, "The Fruitful and Conflictive Relationship Between Feminist Movements and the Mexican Left," *Social Justice* 42, no. 3/4 (2016): 74–75.

18. Sylvia Marcos, "Twenty-five Years of Mexican Feminisms," *Women's Studies International Forum* 22 (1999): 431.

19. See Eli Bartra, "El movimiento feminista en México y su vínculo con la academia," *Revista de estudios de género: La ventana* 1 (1999): 214–33; Espinosa Damián, "Fruitful and Conflictive Relationship"; Marta Lamas, "Del 68 a hoy: La movilización política de las mujeres," *Revista Mexicana de ciencias políticas y sociales* 234 (2018): 265–86; Elizabeth Maier, "Accommodating the Private into the Public Domain: Experiences and Legacies of the Past Four Decades," in *Women's Activism in Latin America and the Caribbean: Engendering Social Justice, Democratizing Citizenship*, ed. Elizabeth Maier and Nathalie Lebon, 24–46 (New Brunswick: Rutgers University Press and Tijuana, Mexico: El Colegio de la Frontera Norte AC, 2010); Marcos, "Twenty-five Years of Mexican Feminisms," 431–33.

20. Espinosa Damián, "Fruitful and Conflictive Relationship," 75.

21. See Bartra, "El movimiento feminista," 214; and Tim Hodgdon, "Fem: A Window onto the Cultural Coalescence of a Mexican Feminist Politics of Sexuality," *Mexican Studies* 16 (2000): 95.

22. See Maier, "Accommodating the Private," 36.

23. Sonia E. Alvarez, Elisabeth Jay Friedman, Ericka Beckman, et al., "Encountering Latin American and Caribbean Feminisms," *Signs* 28 (2003): 571.

24. Yolanda M. López, interview by the author, March 15, 2002, Los Angeles, California. The Chicano Federation was a San Diego–based coalition of various Chicano movement organizations. It was founded in 1969. See Jimmy Patiño, *Raza Sí, Migra No: Chicano Movement Struggles for Immigrant Rights in San Diego* (Chapel Hill: University of North Carolina Press).

25. Judy Klemesrud, "International Women's Year World Conference Opening in Mexico," *New York Times*, June 19, 1975, 1.

26. Connie Pardo, interview by the author, March 29, 2002, Los Angeles, California.

27. Sandra Serrano Sewell, interview by the author, March 14, 2002, Los Angeles, California.

28. Quoted in "Announcements," *Women's New Journal*, June 1975, 11.

29. Sheila Marie Contreras, "Blood Lines: Modernism, Indigenismo and the Construction of Chicana/o Identity" (PhD diss., University of Texas, Austin, 1998), 193, emphasis in original.

30. Organización Chicana of UCLA was a student group, the Comisión Femenil Mexicana Nacional was a political and economic empowerment organization for Chicanas, Poder Femenino was a chapter of the Comisión Femenil, La Raza Unida Party was the Chicano third party, and the Chicano Federation was a community organization in San Diego, California. Another group of women was featured in the Los Angeles Spanish-language daily newspaper, *La Opinión*. The paper mentioned that a group of eight women from the Hispanic Women's Council of Los Angeles had returned from the conference.

See Cristina Luisa, "Pot Pourri," *La Opinión*, July 6, 1975, sec. 2, p. 4; and Cristina Luisa, "Pot Pourri," *La Opinión*, August 3, 1975, sec. 2, p. 4.

31. The exact number of Chicanas who attended is impossible to ascertain. I have arrived at this number from a review of oral history interviews and what Chicanas have written about the conference, especially Bea Vásquez Robinson, "Are We Racist? Are We Sexist?," *Agenda* (Winter 1976): 23–24.

32. Barbara Cady, "Women's Year Conference in 3 Rings," IV, (9 July 1975); Adelaida R. Del Castillo, (16 January 1976), International Women's Year Conference Collection #58, UCLA Chicano Studies Research Library. This collection was established by the efforts of the women from Organización Chicana. The collection includes pamphlets and newspapers gathered at the conference, but no slides, videotape, or audiotape of the conference. A Chicana student group from California State University, Northridge, also attended, with the same goals in mind; however, there is no record of any materials from the conference at CSUN. Note also that Chicana scholar Adelaida Del Castillo, co-author of *Mexican Women in the United States: Struggles Past and Present* (Los Angeles: UCLA Chicano Studies Research Center Publications, 1980) and editor of *Between Borders: Essays on Mexicana/Chicana History* (Encino, CA: Floricanto, 1990), organized the group from Organización Chicana to attend the conference and was instrumental in creating the archival collection at UCLA regarding the conference. On using student financial aid or welfare funds, see Celia Herrera Rodríguez interview.

33. Sandra Serrano Sewell, interview by the author.

34. Judy Klemesrud, "Scrappy, Unofficial Women's Parley Sets Pace," no. 3 (29 June 1975), 1.

35. Galey, "Nairobi Conference," 256; Judy Klemesrud, "International Women's Year," 1.

36. Karen Garner, "World YWCA Leaders and the UN Decade for Women," *Journal of International Women's Studies* 9 (November 2007): 216.

37. Ibid., 219.

38. Ibid.

39. Cady, "Women's Year Conference in 3 Rings," IV, (9 July 1975), 1.

40. The total number of participants at the tribune varies from five thousand to six thousand, depending on the source. I use the figure five thousand because that is the figure cited by Allan, Galey, and Persinger, "World Conference," because Persinger was one of the chief organizers of the tribune.

41. Allan, Galey, and Persinger, "World Conference," 40.

42. Cady, "Women's Year Conference in 3 Rings," IV, (9 July 1975).

43. From oral history interviews and written accounts, I have concluded that approximately 100 to 150 Chicanas from California attended the conference. Vásquez Robinson states that from 250 to 300 women, mostly Chicanas, attended the National Chicana Foundation meeting at the tribune. An estimate of 100 to 150 attendees from California would allow for an approximately equal representation from Texas.

44. Virginia R. Allan, Margaret E. Galey, and Mildred E. Persinger, "World Conference of International Women's Year," *Women, Politics, and the United Nations* (1995), 40; Barbara Cady, "Women's Year Conference in 3 Rings," IV, (9 July 1975); Judy Klemesrud,

Notes to Chapter 3

"U.S. Group Assails Women's Parley: Feminists at Conference in Mexico Complain That It Ignores Real Issues," no. 4 (22 June 1975), 4.

45. "Calendar," no. 1 (20 June 1975), 7, 1. The tribune newspaper was named after the Aztec maize goddess, also known as "the hairy one," because her hair resembled the fibers on unshucked corn. The Aztecs worshiped Xilonen in order to secure a good harvest. She was married to the Aztec god Tezcatlipoca, also known as "smoking mirror," god of night, north, and temptation.

46. "Calendar," no. 1 (24 June 1975), 1. Two possible reasons for this shift in the conference structure are that it reflected the organization and agitation by members of the tribune and that it reflected simple logistics. Not many organizations signed up for presentations before the conference, but they did so at the conference. These presentations then took place on the fourth day.

47. James Sterba, "Equal Rights Vital, U.N. Chief Asserts," no. 1 (20 June 1975), 1.

48. Cady, "Women's Year Conference in 3 Rings," IV, (9 July 1975), 1.

49. Olcott, *International Women's Year*, 121.

50. Lilia Aceves, interview by the author, April 15, 2002, Alhambra, California.

51. Chicanas of La Raza Unida Party, "International Women's Year Conference: La Mujer Chicana," June 23, 1975, International Women's Year Conference Papers, Collection #58, UCLA Chicano Studies Research Center; "Calendar," *Xilonen*, June 24, 1975, 7. Also see Olcott, *International Women's Year*, 198.

52. Chicanas of La Raza Unida Party, "International Women's Year Conference," 2.

53. Ignacio García, *Chicanismo: The Forging of a Militant Ethos Among Mexican Americans* (Tucson: University of Arizona Press, 1998), 49. On the internal colonial model in Chicano/a history, see Mario Barrera, Carlos Muñoz, and Charles Ornelas, "The Barrio as Internal Colony," *Urban Affairs Annual Review* 6 (1972): 465–98; Tomás Almaguer, "Toward the Study of Chicano Colonialism," *Aztlán* 2 (Spring 1971): 7–20; and Gilbert González and Raul Fernández, "Chicano History: Transcending Cultural Models," *Pacific Historical Review* 63 (November 1994): 469–97.

54. "Notes on People," no. 1 (13 June 1975); Judy Klemesrud, "Americans Ease Stand At Women's Conference," no. 1 (25 June 1975); Judy Klemesrud, "International Women's Year World Conference Opening in Mexico," no. 1 (19 June 1975), 1. Originally, Parker had been named the sole head of the delegation because the State Department believed that a political contest would ensue at the conference and that Parker could best handle it. After various protests by U.S. women, however, Hutar was added to chair the committee; she also gave the U.S. keynote address.

55. Olcott, *International Women's Year*, 135.

56. Yolanda M. López, "A Chicana's Look at the International Women's Year Conference," (August 1975), 3, reprinted in Alma M. García, *Chicana Feminist Thought: The Basic Historical Writings* (New York: Routledge, 1997), 181–83.

57. Vásquez Robinson, "Are We Racist? Are We Sexist?," 2.

58. See Olcott, *International Women's Year*, 126.

59. Yolanda M. López, "A Chicana's Look at the International Women's Year Conference," (August 1975); Stanley Meisler, "Women's Parley Debate Pits Two U.S. Groups," I, no. 1 (22 June 1975), sec. 1, p. 1. Also see Olcott, *International Women's Year*, 131.

60. "Therefore We Demand," (1975?), Año Internacional de la Mujer Mexicana Collection, UCLA Chicano Studies Research Library; Jane S. Jaquette, *What Do Women Want?* (Womenfilming, 1975), videocassette.

61. Mujeres en Acción Solidaria, *¡Alerta!* (Mexico City, June 26, 1975), pamphlet, International Women's Year Conference Papers, Collection #58, UCLA Studies Research Library. The full text in Spanish reads: "1. El intercambio de experiencias y problemas que afectan a las mujeres en las diversas actividades en todo el mundo, profundizar en el análisis de la condición de la mujer y buscar la instrumentación adecuada para nuestra acción concreta y permanente. 2. Apoyar la posición de los países que dentro de la conferencia gubernamental relacionan la necesidad de los cambios estructurales a nivel interno e internacional para propiciar una efectiva transformación de la condicion de la mujer de todos los grupos sociales." In English it reads: "1. The exchange of experiences and problems which affect women in diverse activities all over the world, deepen the analysis of the woman's condition, and look for the adequate grouping of instruments for concrete and permanent action. 2. Support the position of countries in the governmental conference that espouse the need for structural changes on an internal and international level to propagate an effective transformation of the woman's condition in all social groups" (translation by the author).

62. Olcott, *International Women's Year*, 118.

63. Quoted in Judy Klemesrud, "U.S. Group Assails Women's Parley: Feminists at Conference in Mexico Complain That It Ignores Real Issues," no. 4 (22 June 1975), 4.

64. Barbara Cady, "Women's Year Conference in 3 Rings," IV, (9 July 1975), 1.

65. Angela Gilliam, "Women's Equality and National Liberation," 217.

66. Bea Vásquez Robinson, "Are We Racist? Are We Sexist?," (Winter 1976), 24. The meeting in question took place on Thursday, June 26, 1975, in room 6 of the National Medical Center.

67. Quoted in Paula Diehl and Guadalupe Saavedra, "Hispanas in the Year of the Woman," (Winter 1976): 18.

68. Quoted in ibid.

69. Betty Friedan, *Betty Friedan vs. the Third World* (Pacifica Radio Archives, 1975), cassette. There are differing accounts of the many times Friedan spoke at the conference. This instance differs from Jocelyn Olcott's narrative about the conference, in which Friedan discussed women of color as "'true initiators' of the feminist movement in favor of equality" and depicted women's inequality as a result of North American economic interests. See Olcott, *International Women's Year*, 124.

70. Yolanda López, interview by the author.

71. Connie Pardo, interview by the author.

72. Ibid.

73. Corinne Sánchez, interview by the author, April 4, 2002, San Fernando, California.

74. See Espinosa Damián, "Fruitful and Conflictive Relationship," 75, and Ana Lau, "El nuevo movimiento feminista mexicano a fines del milenio," in *Feminismo en México: Ayer y hoy*, ed. Eli Bartra, Anna M. Fernández Poncela, and Ana Lau (Mexico City: Universidad Autónoma Metropolitana, 2000), 23. Also see Olcott, *International Women's Year*, 58.

75. Mujeres en Acción Solidaria, "¡Alerta!"

76. Olcott, *International Women's Year*, 58.

Notes to Chapter 3

77. "Calendar," no. 1 (20 June 1975), 1. There were a total of two general tribune sessions per day, one at 10:00 a.m. and one at 1:00 p.m., from June 20 through June 27, 1975, as far as can be told from the calendar. Other topics addressed at the general sessions were "Building the Human," "Agriculture and Rural Development," "Education," "Women and Environment," "Population and Planned Parenthood," "Women in Public Life," and "Peace and Disarmament."

78. Corinne Sánchez, interview by the author.

79. Celia Herrera Rodríguez, interview by the author.

80. Quoted in Freedman, *No Turning Back*, 117. In *Let Me Speak* (New York: Monthly Review Press, 1978), Barrios de Chungara states that Betty Friedan accused her of being "manipulated by men" and of being too concerned with politics because of her positions on development and poverty. See Gilliam, "Women's Equality and National Liberation," 224.

81. Yolanda López, interview the by author.

82. Lilia Aceves, interview by the author.

83. Anna NietoGómez, interview by the author.

84. On police brutality against ethnic Mexicans, see Edward J. Escobar, *Race, Police, and the Making of a Political Identity: Mexican Americans and the Los Angeles Police Department, 1900–1945* (Berkeley: University of California Press, 1999); Ernesto Chávez, *¡Mi Raza Primero! (My People First!): Nationalism, Identity, and Insurgency in the Chicano Movement in Los Angeles, 1966–1978* (Berkeley: University of California Press, 2002); Lorena Oropeza, *¡Raza sí! ¡Guerra no! Chicano Protest and Patriotism During the Viet Nam War Era* (Berkeley: University of California Press, 2005); and Ian Haney-López, *Racism on Trial: The Chicano Fight for Justice* (Cambridge, MA: Belknap Press of Harvard University Press, 2003).

85. Anna NietoGómez, interview by the author.

86. Alan Eladio Gómez, *The Revolutionary Imaginations of Greater Mexico: Chicana/o Radicalism, Solidarity Politics, and Latin American Social Movements* (Austin: University of Texas Press, 2016), 50, 51.

87. Corinne Sánchez, interview by the author.

88. Anna NietoGómez, interview by the author.

89. Connie Pardo, interview by the author.

90. United Nations, "Report of the World Conference of the International Women's Year, Mexico City, 19 June–2 July 1975," (New York: United Nations Publications, 1976), 11. Also see Judith P. Zinsser, "From Copenhagen to Nairobi: The United Nations Decade for Women, 1975–1985," *Journal of World History* 13, no. 1 (2002): 147.

91. United Nations, "Report of the World Conference," 13.

92. Doreen J. Mattingly and Jessica L. Nare, "A Rainbow of Women: Diversity and Unity at the 1977 U.S. International Women's Year Conference," *Journal of Women's History* 26 (2014): 88.

93. Cecilia Burciaga, "The 1977 National Women's Conference in Houston," in *Chicana Feminist Thought*, ed. Alma García, 184; originally published in *La Luz*, November 1978, 8–9.

94. Cecilia Burciaga, "1977 National Women's Conference in Houston," 184; Mattingly and Nare, "Rainbow of Women," 91.

95. Diana Camacho to Pat Vásquez, "Chicanas Change Course of Texas IWY," n.d., Martha Cotera Papers, Benson Latin American Library, University of Texas, Austin, box 9, folder 3. Underline in original.

96. *The Spirit of Houston: The First National Women's Conference; An Official Report to the President, the Congress and the People of the United States* (Washington, DC. National Commission on the Observance of International Women's Year, Government Printing Office, 1978), 114.

97. Ibid., 156.

98. Ibid., 278.

99. Martha Cotera, "Mujeres Bravas: How Chicanas Shaped the Feminist Agenda at the National IWY Conference in Houston, 1977," in *Chicana Movidas: New Narratives of Activism and Feminism in the Movement Era*, ed. Dionne Espinoza, María Eugenia Cotera, and Maylei Blackwell (Austin: University of Texas Press, 2018), 56.

100. Sandra Serrano Sewell, interview by the author.

101. Sandra Serrano Sewell, "President's Report," September 17, 1977, Comisión Femenil Mexicana Nacional Records, California Ethnic and Multicultural Archives, University of California, Santa Barbara, 1–2.

102. *Spirit of Houston*, 298–99. The other Latina/Chicana organizations with official booths were the Chicana Caucus—National Women's Political Caucus; LULAC National Education Service Centers, Inc. (although this was not specifically woman-centered); and Puerto Rican Women, Cuban Women, Mexican Women.

103. Comisión Femenil Mexicana Nacional, *La Mujer: International Women's Year 1977*, brochure, Comisión Femenil Mexicana Nacional Records, California Ethnic and Multicultural Archives, University of California, Santa Barbara.

104. Cotera, "Mujeres Bravas," 52.

105. Lindsey Van Gelder, "Four Days That Changed the World: Behind the Scenes at Houston," *Ms.*, March 1978, 90.

106. Mattingly and Nare, "Rainbow of Women," 96–97.

107. Comisión Femenil, "Report of the Conference," *La Mujer*.

108. Sandra Serrano Sewell, interview by author.

109. Comisión Femenil, "Report of the Conference," *La Mujer*.

110. Marcie Miranda-Arrizon, "Building Herman(a)dad" (M.A. thesis, University of California, Santa Barbara, 1997), 73.

111. Sandra Serrano Sewell, interview by the author.

112. Ibid.

113. Blackwell, *¡Chicana Power!*, 161.

Chapter 4. Chicana Body Politics in Los Angeles

1. In 1949, what is now California State University, Long Beach, was first named Los Angeles-Orange County State College. In 1950 the name was changed to Long Beach State College due to its permanent location in Long Beach. The campus underwent another name change in the 1960s to California State College, Long Beach, before receiving its final name, California State University, Long Beach, in 1972. The Educational Opportunity Program was established at California State University, Long Beach, in 1967. See "CSULB Through the Years," https://www.csulb.edu/historical.

Notes to Chapter 4

2. Anna NietoGómez, interview with Maylei Blackwell, April 22, 1991, Oral History Archives, California State University, Long Beach.

3. Ibid.

4. Nadia Brown and Sarah Allen Gershon, "Body Politics," *Politics, Groups, and Identities* 5, no. 1 (2017): 1.

5. This belief about women's domesticity and bodies has been longstanding in the U.S. political landscape. See, e.g., Joanne Meyerowitz, ed., *Not June Cleaver: Women and Gender in Postwar America, 1945–1960* (Philadelphia: Temple University Press, 1994); Nancy A. Hewitt, ed., *No Permanent Waves: Recasting Histories of U.S. Feminism* (New Brunswick: Rutgers University Press, 2010); and Estelle Freedman, *No Turning Back: The History of Feminism and the Future of Women* (New York: Ballantine, 200).

6. Richard T. Rodríguez, *Next of Kin: The Family in Chicana/o Cultural Politics* (Durham: University of North Carolina Press, 2009), 21.

7. Maylei Blackwell, *¡Chicana Power! Contested Histories of Feminism in the Chicano Movement* (Austin: University of Texas Press, 2011), 98.

8. Laura Elisa Pérez, "El Desorden, Nationalism, and Chicana/o Aesthetics," in *Between Woman and Nation: Nationalisms, Transnational Feminisms, and the State*, ed. Caren Kaplan, Norma Alarcón, and Minoo Moallem (Durham, NC: Duke University Press, 1999), 25.

9. See Benita Roth, *Separate Roads to Feminism: Black, Chicana, and White Feminist Movements in America's Second Wave* (Cambridge: Cambridge University Press, 2004), chap. 4.

10. Elena R. Gutiérrez, *Fertile Matters: The Politics of Mexican-Origin Women's Reproduction* (Austin: University of Texas Press, 2008), chap. 2.

11. See Natalie Lira, *Laboratory of Deficiency: Sterilization and Confinement in California, 1900–1950s* (Berkeley: University of California Press, 2022).

12. Freedman, *No Turning Back*, 234.

13. Jennifer Nelson, *Women of Color and the Reproductive Rights Movement* (New York: NYU Press, 2003), 1–2.

14. See *No Más Bebés*, directed by Renee Tajima-Peña (Moon Canyon Films, 2015), DVD.

15. Nelson, *Women of Color*, 1–2.

16. The term *reproductive justice* was not coined until 1994. See Jael Silliman, Marlene Gerber Fried, Loretta Ross, and Elena Gutiérrez, *Undivided Rights: Women of Color Organizing for Reproductive Justice*, 2nd ed. (Chicago: Haymarket, 2016); and Jennifer Nelson, *Women of Color and the Reproductive Rights Movement* (New York: New York University Press, 2003).

17. See E. Gutiérrez, *Fertile Matters*; and Virginia Espino, "'Woman Sterilized as Gives Birth': Forced Sterilization and Chicana Resistance in the 1970s," in *Las Obreras: Chicana Politics of Work and Family*, ed. Vicki L. Ruiz (Los Angeles: UCLA Chicano Studies Research Center Publications, 2000), 65–81.

18. There is some discrepancy about the relation between these two documents. In the Comision Femenil Mexicana Report, vol. 1, no. 2, n.d., the resolutions to establish the Comisión Femenil are combined with what have designated resolutions from the Women's Workshop. The date for both is October 11, 1970. In other documents, as noted later, and on the landing page for archives of the Comisión Femenil Mexicana Nacional, Inc., at

the University of California, Santa Barbara, only the resolution to establish the Comisión Femenil is listed. See "Comisión Femenil Mexicana Nacional, Inc.," UC Santa Barbara Library, Special Research Collections, https://www.library.ucsb.edu/special-collections/cema/cfmn.

19. "Resolutions—Women's Workshop," October 11, 1970, Comisión Femenil Mexicana Nacional, Comisión Femenil Mexicana Nacional Records at the California Ethnic and Multicultural Archives, University of California, Santa Barbara (hereafter CFMN Records); Comisión Femenil Mexicana, "Resolution to Establish Comisión Femenil Mexicana Nacional, Inc.," October 10, 1970, CFMN Records. According to my notes, the "Resolution to Establish Comisión Femenil Mexicana Nacional, Inc.," is dated October 10, 1970. The "Comisión Femenil Mexicana Nacional, Inc." page for the UC Santa Barbara Special Research Collections site gives the date of October 17, 1970, for the same resolution. Also see Sonia R. García and Marisela Marquez, "The Comisión Femenil: La Voz of a Chicana Organization," *Aztlán* 36 (2011): 155. García and Marquez give October 10, 1970 as the date of the resolution.

20. Comisión Femenil Mexicana, "Resolution to Establish Comisión Femenil Mexicana Nacional, Inc.," CFMN Records.

21. See, e.g., the website for the CFMN records, http://cemaweb.library.ucsb.edu/cfmn_intro.html. Also see Francisca Flores, "Conference of Mexican Women: Un Remolino," *Regeneración* 1, no. 10 (1971): 3.

22. "[Notes from Women's Workshop at Mexican American National Issues Conference]," n.d. [1970], CFMN Records, box 9, folder 5.

23. Dolores Sánchez, interview by the author, City of Commerce, California, May 9, 2002.

24. Quoted in Espino, "'Woman Sterilized as Gives Birth,'" 70. The Brown Berets, a militant Chicano organization, established a health clinic in East Los Angeles through the efforts of women in the organization. See Dionne Espinoza, "Revolutionary Sisters: Women's Solidarity and Collective Identification Among Chicana Brown Berets," *Aztlán* 26, no. 1 (Spring 2001): 17–58, and Dionne Espinoza, "Pedagogies of Nationalism and Gender: Cultural Resistance in Selected Representational Practices of Chicana/o Movement Activists, 1967–1972" (PhD diss., Cornell University, 1996).

25. Francisca Flores, "Comisión Femenil Mexicana," *Regeneración* 2, no. 1 (1971): 6–7; also see Lilia Aceves, interview by the author, Alhambra, California, April 15, 2002.

26. María Cotera, Maylei Blackwell, and Dionne Espinoza, "Introduction: Movements, Movimientos, and Movidas," in *Chicana Movidas: New Narratives of Activism and Feminism in the Movement Era*, ed. Dionne Espinoza, María Eugenia Cotera, and Maylei Blackwell, 1–30 (Austin: University of Texas Press, 2018), 12.

27. Ibid., 14, 16.

28. Lee Bebout, *Mythohistorical Interventions: The Chicano Movement and Its Legacies* (Minneapolis: University of Minnesota Press, 2011), 3, 5; Blackwell, *¡Chicana Power!*, 97.

29. R. Rodríguez, *Next of Kin*, 24.

30. Anne McClintock, *Imperial Leather: Race, Gender and Sexuality in the Colonial Conquest* (New York: Routledge, 1995), 354.

31. *Con Safos: Reflections of Life in the Barrio* was published approximately twice per year between 1968 and 1972 in Los Angeles, California. See Maxine Browsky Junge and Con

Safos, *Voices from the Barrio: "Con Safos: Reflections of Life in the Barrio"* (Los Angeles: CreateSpace Independent Publishing Platform, 2016).

32. Oscar Zeta Acosta, "A Love Letter to the Girls of Aztlan," *Con Safos* no. 6, 1970, 29.

33. Yolanda O. Rodriguez, "Para 'Zeta' y para otros que piensan como el" (letter to the editor), *Con Safos* no. 7, 1971, 60.

34. Una Chicana de Pittsburg, "Pensamientos sobre 3 Cartas de Zeta—'A Love Letter to the Girls of Aztlan' Con Safos Magazine, no. 6" (letter to the editor), *Con Safos* no. 7, 1971, 60.

35. Zeta Acosta, "Love Letter."

36. See, e.g., *Sor Juana Inés de la Cruz: Selected Works* (New York: Norton, 2015); Theresa A. Yugar, *Sor Juana Inés de la Cruz: Feminist Reconstruction of Biography and Text* (Eugene, OR: Wipf and Stock, 2014); Octavio Paz, *Sor Juana: Or, the Traps of Faith* (Cambridge, MA: Harvard University Press, 1988); and Stephanie Kirk, *Sor Juana Inés de la Cruz and the Gender Politics of Knowledge in Colonial Mexico* (New York: Routledge, 2016).

37. Editors, "El Memo de Con Safos, Subtext: Brown Buffalo," *Con Safos* no. 8, 1972, 9.

38. Ian Haney-Lopez, *Racism on Trial: The Chicano Fight for Justice* (Cambridge: Belknap Press of Harvard University Press, 2003), 30. Also see Oscar Zeta Acosta, *Revolt of the Cockroach People* (1973; repr., New York: Vintage, 1989); Oscar Zeta Acosta, *Autobiography of a Brown Buffalo* (1972; repr., New York: Vintage, 1989); and Ilan Stavans, *Oscar "Zeta" Acosta: The Uncollected Works* (Houston: Arte Público, 1989).

39. These ideologies were not unique to the Chicano movement but were also prevalent in social movements across the United States.

40. Concerned Chicanas, "Genocide on the Chicano Family," *La Causa*, March 1970, 3.

41. E. Gutiérrez, *Fertile Matters*, 16, 18–19.

42. Ibid., 30.

43. Alexandra Minna Stern, "Sterilized in the Name of Public Health: Race, Immigration, and Reproductive Control in Modern California," *American Journal of Public Health* 95 (2005): 1135.

44. Ibid, 1128. Also see Lira, *Laboratory of Deficiency*.

45. Concerned Chicanas, "Genocide on the Chicano Family."

46. Loretta Ross and Rickie Solinger, *Reproductive Justice: An Introduction* (Berkeley: University of California Press, 2017), 9.

47. Anna NietoGómez, "Response to Chapter Two: Chicana Print Culture and Chicana Studies; A Testimony to the Development of Chicana Feminist Culture," in *Chicana Feminisms: A Critical Reader*, ed. Gabriela Arredondo, Aída Hurtado, Norma Klahn, Olga Nájera-Ramírez, and Patricia Zavella (Durham, NC: Duke University Press, 2003), 94.

48. Sylvia Delgado, "Young Chicana Speaks Up on Problems Faced by Young Girls," *Regeneración* 1, no. 10 (1971): 6, 7.

49. Sylvia Delgado, "Chicana: The Forgotten Woman," *Regeneración* 2, no. 1 (1971): 3.

50. Anna NietoGómez, "La Femenista," *Encuentro Femenil* 1 (1974), reprinted in Alma M. García, *Chicana Feminist Thought: The Basic Historical Writings* (New York: Routledge, 1997), 91.

51. Blackwell, *¡Chicana Power!*, 146.

52. Sandra Ugarte, "Chicana Regional Conference," *Hijas de Cuauhtémoc* (1971): 1–3.

53. Suzan Racho, Gloria Meneses, Socorro Acosta, and Chicki Quijano, "Houston Chicana Conference," *La Gente* (UCLA), May 31, 1971, 6–7; "National Chicanas Conference," *La Verdad*, July–August 1971, 15–17.

54. Vidal, *Chicanas Speak Out*, 14.

55. Beverly Padilla, "Chicanas and Abortion," *Militant*, February 18, 1972, 4.

56. Ibid.

57. Nelson, *Women of Color*, 2.

58. Gloria Arellanes, interview by Virginia Espino for the Center for Oral History Research, University of California, Los Angeles, transcript, 91. Also see Espinoza, "Revolutionary Sisters," 35.

59. Gloria Arellanes interview by Virginia Espino, 91. In fact, Arellanes notes that the free clinic had received funding support from the Catholic Church but that because the clinic provided abortion counseling, the Catholic Church discontinued its funding.

60. Ibid., 26–27. Also see Ernesto Chávez, *¡Mi Raza Primero! (My People First!): Nationalism, Identity, and Insurgency in the Chicano Movement in Los Angeles, 1966–1978* (Berkeley: University of California Press, 2002), 43–45. Young Citizens for Community Action eventually became Young Chicanos for Community Action. Eventually, YCCA opened a coffee house called La Piranya in East Los Angeles. Over time, YCCA and La Piranya became a central meeting place for these youth. The meeting place also attracted the attention of the Los Angeles County Sheriffs. As events unfolded, this unwanted attention led to YCCA protests at the local sheriff's station. In 1968 YCCA changed its name to the Brown Berets.

61. For more on the Brown Berets, see E. Chávez, "*¡Mi Raza Primero!*, chap. 2.

62. Ibid., 55.

63. See Espinoza, "Revolutionary Sisters," 34–37.

64. Gloria Arellanes interview by Virginia Espino, 95.

65. Rona Marcia Fields, "The Brown Berets: A Participant Observation Study of Social Action in the Schools of Los Angeles" (PhD diss., University of Southern California, 1970), 154–59.

66. Virginia Espino, "Women Sterilized as They Give Birth: Population Control, Eugenics, and Social Protest in the Twentieth-Century United States" (PhD diss., Arizona State University, 2007), 219, 224–27. On the Bar Sinister, see Laura Pulido, *Black, Brown, Yellow, and Left: Radical Activism in Los Angeles* (Berkeley: University of California Press, 2006).

67. See E. Chávez, *¡Mi Raza Primero!*, 98–107.

68. Ibid., 104.

69. Espino, "Women Sterilized as They Give Birth," 219, 224–27. Pat Córdova, an activist highlighted in Espino's dissertation, is Patricia Córdova Vellanoweth, who also became part of the organizations The Committee to Free Los Tres and El Centro de Acción Social Autónomo. Patricia Córdova Vellanoweth, interview by the author, Montebello, California, March 12, 1996.

70. "Central Committee Report of the Retreat of December 21 and 22 of 1974," El Centro de Acción Social Autónomo (CASA) Collection, M0325, Department of Special Collections, Stanford University, box 1, folder 7.

71. Kathy Proppe, "Socialist Feminism in Practice," *L.A. Women's Union Newsletter*, December 1974, 2. At that time, Isabel Chávez used the surname of her partner. She

stopped using Chávez as a surname in the late 1970s and prefers to be known as Isabel H. Rodríguez.

72. Ibid., 12–13.

73. Cheryl Diehm, "Committee to Stop Forced Sterilization Splits over Tactics," *Sister*, February 1975, 3; Gini Faller, "Letter to the editor," *Sister*, February 1975, 10. Also see Espino, "Woman Sterilized as Gives Birth."

74. Espino, "Women Sterilized as They Give Birth," 246. Also see Alice Echols, *Daring to Be Bad: Radical Feminism in America, 1967–1975* (Minneapolis: University of Minnesota Press, 1989), 291; Isabel H. Rodríguez, interview by the author, March 11 and 17, 1996, Los Angeles, California; Patricia Vellanoweth interview by the author. For work on the forced sterilization of ethnic Mexican women in Los Angeles see Espino, "'Woman Sterilized as Gives Birth,'" 65–82; and Elena Gutiérrez, "The Racial Politics of Reproduction: The Social Construction of Mexican-Origin Women's Fertility" (PhD diss., University of Michigan, 1999).

75. Espino, "Women Sterilized as They Give Birth," 225–27.

76. See E. Gutiérrez, *Fertile Matters*, 36.

77. Espino, "'Woman Sterilized as Gives Birth,'" 75.

78. E. Gutiérrez, "Racial Politics of Reproduction," chap. 6.

79. Ibid., 248.

80. Ibid., 261. Also see Sally Andrade, "Family Planning Practices of Mexican Americans," and Maria Luisa Urdaneta, "Chicana Use of Abortion," both in *Twice a Minority: Mexican American Women*, ed. Margarita Melville (St. Louis: Mosby, 1980).

81. Espino, "'Woman Sterilized as Gives Birth,'" 69.

82. For a very similar argument about Puerto Ricans in the United States and reproductive rights, see Jennifer A. Nelson, "'Abortions Under Community Control': Feminism, Nationalism, and the Politics of Reproduction Among New York City's Young Lords," *Journal of Women's History* 13, no. 1 (Spring 2001): 157–80.

83. Jael Silliman, Marlene Gerber Fried, Loretta Ross, and Elena Gutiérrez, *Undivided Rights: Women of Color Organizing for Reproductive Justice*, 2nd ed. (Chicago: Haymarket, 2016), viii.

84. James Trussell, Jane Menken, Barbara L. Lindheim, and Barbara Vaughn, "The Impact of Restricting Medicaid Financing for Abortion," *Family Planning Perspectives* 12 (May–June 1980): 120; "Suit Challenges Medi-Cal Curbs on Abortion," *Los Angeles Times*, August 10, 1978, e4. Both of these laws would face legal challenges, but ultimately the ban on using government funds to pay for abortions was upheld.

85. Comisión Femenil Mexicana Nacional Issues Conference, "Resolution on Reproductive Freedom," April 22–23, 1978, CFMN Records, Conferences Series, box 1, folder 8; Comisión Femenil Mexicana Nacional, "CFMN Newsletter," May 1978, CFMN Records, box 54, folder 6.

86. Evelyn Martínez, "Comisión Femenil de Los Angeles Chapter Report," October 20, 1978, CFMN Records, box 2, folder 27.

87. Sandra Salazar, "Minutes[,] Meeting of the Board of Directors," September 29, 1979, 9, CFMN Records, box 3, folder 6.

88. "Report on Progress of Implementation of CFMN Resolutions," n.d., [1979], CFMN Records, box 2, folder 30.

89. "Minutes of the CFMN Transitional Board of Directors Meeting," August 15, 1981, CFMN Records, box 4, folder 16.

90. Hortensia Amaro and Maria Rodríguez, "Latinas and Abortion: Legal and Social Issues," November 16, 1981, CFMN Records, box 4, folder 19. Amaro went on to a career in academia. She is currently a distinguished university professor and senior scholar on community health at the Herbert Wertheim College of Medicine and Robert Stemple College of Public Health and Social Work at Florida International University. Maria Rodríguez passed away in 2009 after a long legal career. After serving as the director of the Chicana Rights Project at the Mexican American Legal Defense and Educational Fund, she went into private practice before serving as a senior counsel for the legal department of Kaiser Permanente.

91. Ibid.; Hortensia Aviaro [Amaro], "Latina Attitudes Towards Abortion," *Nuestro*, August/September 1981, 43–44; Hortensia Amaro, "Women in the Mexican American Community: Religion, Culture, and Reproductive Attitudes and Experiences," *Journal of Community Psychology* 16 (1988): 6–20.

92. Amaro and Rodríguez, "Latinas and Abortion," 6.

93. Ibid.

94. Ibid.

95. Hortensia Amaro, interview by the author, Los Angeles, California, October 20, 2003.

96. CFMN Board of Directors Meeting, Minutes, November 21, 1981, CFMN Records.

97. Nelson, *Women of Color*, 1–2.

98. See Epinoza, "Revolutionary Sisters," 37.

Epilogue

1. Francisca Flores, "Editorial," *Regeneración* 1, no. 10 (1971): n.p., emphasis in original.

2. Gloria Anzaldúa and Cherríe Moraga, introduction to *This Bridge Called My Back: Writings by Radical Women of Color*, ed. Cherríe Moraga and Gloria Anzaldúa (New York: Kitchen Table, 1981), xxiii.

3. Cherríe Moraga, "Catching Fire: Preface to the Fourth Edition," in *This Bridge Called My Back: Writings by Radical Women of Color*, ed. Gloria Anzaldúa and Cherríe Moraga (Albany: SUNY Press, 2015), xix.

4. Dionne Espinoza, María Eugenia Cotera, and Maylei Blackwell, introduction to *Chicana Movidas: New Narratives of Activism and Feminism in the Movement Era*, ed. Dionne Espinoza, María Eugenia Cotera, and Maylei Blackwell (Austin: University of Texas Press, 2018), 5–6.

5. See California Latinas for Reproductive Justice, "Herstory," https://californialatinas.org/about-us/herstory/.

6. Sheila Kuehl and Hilda L. Solis, "Apologizing for Historical Coerced Sterilization Practices," August 7, 2018, http://file.lacounty.gov/SDSInter/bos/supdocs/124712.pdf.

Bibliography

Archival Sources

MANUSCRIPTS AND SPECIAL COLLECTIONS

Chicano Resource Center, East Los Angeles County Library.
Colección Tloque Nahuaque Pamphlet Collection, University of California, Santa Barbara.
Comisión Femenil Mexicana Nacional Records, CEMA 30, California Ethnic and Multicultural Archives, University of California, Santa Barbara.
Devra Weber Collection, Chicano Studies Research Center Library, University of California, Los Angeles.
El Centro de Acción Social Autónomo (CASA) Collection, M0325, Department of Special Collections, Stanford University.
Feminist Collection, Oral History Archives, California State University, Long Beach.
International Women's Year Conference Papers, Collection #58, Chicano Studies Research Center, University of California, Los Angeles.
Joan Robins Collection, Southern California Library for Social Studies and Research, Los Angeles.
Marcie Miranda Collection, California Ethnic and Multicultural Archives, CEMA 053, University of California, Santa Barbara.
Martha Cotera Papers, Benson Latin American Library Collection, University of Texas at Austin.
Personal papers of Lilia Aceves, Alhambra, California.
Personal papers of Grace Montañez Davis, Los Angeles, California.

GOVERNMENT DOCUMENTS AND PUBLICATIONS

California Commission on the Status of Women. *Transcript of Public Hearing on the Status of Women in 1973: February 9 and 10, 1973*, vol. 1. Sacramento: Comission, [1973].
"Educational Attainment," http://www.census.gov/population/www/socdemo/educ-attn.html.

Fair Employment Practices Division, State of California. *Californians of Spanish Surname: Population, Education, Income, Employment.* San Francisco: Fair Employment Practices Commission, State of California, Division of Fair Employment Practices, 1964; repr., 1966.

Fair Employment Practices Division, State of California. *Californians of Spanish Surname: Population, Education, Income, Employment: A Summary of Changes Between 1960 and 1970—Based on U.S. Census of Population.* San Francisco: Fair Employment Practices Commission, State of California, Agriculture and Services Agency, Department of Industrial Relations, June 1976.

Hearings Before the Committee on Un-American Activities House of Representatives, 85th Congress. Washington, DC: Government Printing Office, 1958.

The Southern California District of the Communist Party Structure—Objectives—Leadership. Hearings Before the Committee on Un-American Activities, House of Representatives, 85th Cong., September 2 and 3, 1958. Washington, DC: Government Printing Office, 1958.

The Spirit of Houston: The First National Women's Conference; An Official Report to the President, the Congress and the People of the United States. Washington, DC: National Commission on the Observance of International Women's Year, Government Printing Office, 1978.

U.S. Bureau of the Census. *Statistical Abstract of the United States: 2010.* 129th ed. Washington, DC: Government Printing Office, 2009.

U.S. Bureau of the Census. *United States Census of Population,* 1970 and 1980, vol. 1. Current Population Reports P20-550.

U.S. Congress. House. A Bill to Amend the Immigration and Nationality Act, and for Other Purposes. 93rd Cong., H.R. 981, 1973.

U.S. Congress. House. A Bill to Amend the Immigration and Nationality Act, and for Other Purposes. 93rd Cong., H.R. 982, 1973.

U.S. Congress. House. Subcommittee Number One of the Committee on the Judiciary. *Hearing Before Subcommittee Number One of the Committee on the Judiciary, House of Representatives, on H.R. 981.* 93rd Cong., 1973.

U.S. Department of Health, Education, and Welfare. *A Study of Selected Socio-Economic Characteristics of Ethnic Minorities Based on the 1970 Census,* vol. 1, *Americans of Spanish Origin.* Washington, DC: Government Printing Office, 1974.

U.S. Department of Justice, Federal Bureau of Investigation. Frances Flores File, 1228233-0 and 100-17204.

NEWSPAPERS AND PERIODICALS

Agenda
Capirotada
Caracol
El Fuego de Aztlán
El Grito del Norte
Encuentro Femenil
La Gente
La Raza
La Razón Mestiza

La Verdad
Las Hijas de Cuauhtémoc
L.A. Women's Union Newsletter
The Los Angeles Times
Magazín
The Militant
The New York Times
Regeneración
Sin Fronteras
Sister (Los Angeles)
Xilonen (Mexico City)

INTERVIEWS

Aceves, Lilia. Interview by the author. Tape recording. Alhambra, California. April 15, 2002.

Amaro, Hortensia. Interview by the author. Tape recording. Los Angeles, California. October 20, 2003.

Arellanes, Gloria. Interview by Virginia Espino for the Center for Oral History Research, University of California, Los Angeles. September 26; October 3, 11, 17, and 24; and December 13, 2011. https://oralhistory.library.ucla.edu/catalog/21198-zz002cftg9.

Bojorquez, Frances. Interview by Marcie Miranda-Arrizon. Tape recording. Thousand Oaks, California. September 13, 1996. Miranda (Marcy) Collection, CEMA 053, California Ethnic and Multicultural Archives, University of California, Santa Barbara.

Davis, Grace Montañez. Interview by the author. Tape recording. Los Angeles, California. August 13, 2003.

Davis, Grace Montañez. Interview by Phillip C. Castruita. July–September 1994. Grace Montañez Davis personal collection, Los Angeles, California.

Davis, Grace Montañez. Interview by Virginia Espino for the Center for Oral History Research, University of California, Los Angeles. August 26, September 5, 11, 19, and 26, October 1, 13, and 28, and November 10, 2008. https://oralhistory.library.ucla.edu/catalog/21198-zz001d0pc1.

de la Torre-Wycoff, Gloria. Interview by Marcie Miranda. Tape recording. Whittier, California. November 30, 1996. Miranda (Marcy) Collection, CEMA 053, California Ethnic and Multicultural Archives, University of California, Santa Barbara.

Hernández, Leticia. Interview by Maylei S. Blackwell. Tape Recording. July 8 and August 21, 1992. Chicana Feminism Collection, Oral History Archive, California State University, Long Beach.

Herrera Rodríguez, Celia. Interview by the author. Tape recording. Los Angeles, California. October 10, 2002.

López, Yolanda M. Interview by the author. Tape recording. Los Angeles, California. March 15, 2002.

Márquez, Evelina. Interview by the author. Tape recording. Santa Fe, New Mexico, February 21, 1997.

Molina, Gloria, interview by Carlos Vásquez. Oral History Interview with Gloria Molina. Department of Special Collections, University of California, Los Angeles, 1990.

Nava, Yolanda. Interview by the author. Tape recording. Santa Fe, New Mexico. September 19, 2003.
Nava, Yolanda. Interview by Marcie Miranda-Arrizón. Tape recording. August 22, 1996. Marcie Miranda-Arrizón Collection, California Ethnic and Multicultural Archives, University of California, Santa Barbara.
Nava, Yolanda. Interview by Michelle Moravec. Tape recording. July 17, 1989. Chicana Feminism Collection, Oral History Archive, California State University, Long Beach.
NietoGómez, Anna. Interview by the author. Tape recording. Lakewood, California. June 1, 2002.
NietoGómez, Anna. Interviews by Maylei S. Blackwell. Tape recordings. April 7, 18, 22, and 29, 1991. Chicana Feminism Collection, Oral History Archive, California State University, Long Beach.
Pardo, Connie. Interview by the author. Tape recording. Los Angeles, California. March 29, 2002.
Rodríguez, Isabel H. Interview by the author. Tape recordings. Los Angeles, California. March 11 and 17, 1996.
Sánchez, Corinne. Interview by the author. Tape recording. San Fernando, California. April 4, 2002.
Sánchez, Dolores. Interview by the author. Tape recording. City of Commerce, California. May 9, 2002.
Sánchez, Dolores. Interview by Virginia Espino for the Center for Oral History Research. University of California, Los Angeles. August 9, September 27, October 11, and November 1, 2013; January 3 and 17, March 7, and April 11, 2014. https://oralhistory.library.ucla.edu/catalog/21198-zz002k7q92.
Schechter, Hope Mendoza. *Hope Mendoza Schechter: Activist in the Labor Movement, the Democratic Party, and the Mexican-American Community*. Regional Oral History Office, Bancroft Library, University of California, Berkeley, 1980.
Sewell, Sandra Serrano. Interview by the author. Tape recording. Los Angeles, California. March 14, 2002.
Sewell, Sandra Serrano. Interview by Marcie Miranda-Arrizón. Tape recording. July 10, 1996. Marcie Miranda-Arrizón Collection, California Ethnic and Multicultural Archives, University of California, Santa Barbara.
Sewell, Sandra Serrano. Interview by Jackie Hunt for the Center for Oral History Research. University of California, Los Angeles. April 4 and 22, May 23, 2011. https://oralhistory.library.ucla.edu/catalog/21198-zz0028td1g.
Vellanoweth, Patricia Córdova. Interview by the author. Tape recording. Montebello, California. March 12, 1996.

Other Sources

Acosta, Teresa Palomo, and Ruthe Weingarten, eds. *Las Tejanas: 300 Years of History*. Austin: University of Texas Press, 2003.
Acuña, Rodolfo A. *A Community Under Siege: A Chronicle of Chicanos East of the Los Angeles River, 1945–1975*. Los Angeles: Chicano Studies Research Center Publications, University of California, 1984.

Bibliography

Acuña, Rodolfo. *Occupied America: A History of Chicanos.* 3rd ed. New York: Harper and Row, 1988.

Aguirre, Lydia. "The Meaning of the Chicano Movement." *Social Casework* (May 1971): 259–61.

Akers Chacón, Justin. *Radicals in the Barrio: Magonistas, Socialists, Wobblies, and Communists in the Mexican American Working Class.* Chicago: Haymarket, 2018.

Alexander, Sally. "'Do Grandmas Have Husbands?' Generational Memory and Twentieth-Century Women's Lives." *Oral History Review* 36, no. 2 (2009): 159–176.

Allan, Virginia R., Margaret E. Galey, and Mildred E. Persinger. "World Conference of International Women's Year." In *Women, Politics, and the United Nations*, edited by Anne Winslow, 25–44. Westport, CT: Greenwood, 1995.

Almaguer, Tomás. "Toward the Study of Chicano Colonialism." *Aztlán* 2, no. 1 (Spring 1971): 7–20.

Alvarez, Rodolfo. "The Psycho-Historical and Socioeconomic Development of the Chicano Community." *Social Science Quarterly* 53, no. 4 (1973): 920–42.

Alvarez, Sonia E., Elisabeth Jay Friedman, Ericka Beckman, et al., "Encountering Latin American and Caribbean Feminisms," *Signs* 28, no. 2 (2003): 537–79.

Amaro, Hortensia. "Women in the Mexican American Community: Religion, Culture, and Reproductive Attitudes and Experiences." *Journal of Community Psychology* 16 (1988): 6–20.

Anderson, Benedict. *Imagined Communities: Reflections on the Origin and Spread of Nationalism.* London: Verso, 1991.

Andrade, Sally. "Family Planning Practices of Mexican Americans." In *Twice a Minority: Mexican American Women*, edited by Margarita Melville, 17–32. St. Louis: Mosby, 1980.

Angevine, Erma. *History of the National Consumers' League, 1899–1979.* Washington, DC: National Consumers' League, 1979.

Anthias, Floya, and Nira Yuval-Davis. *Racialized Boundaries: Race, Nation, Gender, Colour and Class and the Anti-Racist Struggle.* New York: Routledge, 1992.

Anzaldúa, Gloria, and Cherríe Moraga. Introduction to *This Bridge Called My Back: Writings by Radical Women of Color*, ed. Cherrie Moraga and Gloria Anzaldúa. New York: Kitchen Table, 1981.

Apodaca, Linda [Maria]. "The Community Service Organization." In *Latinas in the United States: A Historical Encyclopedia*, edited by Vicki L. Ruiz and Virginia Sánchez Korrol, 170–72. Bloomington: Indiana University Press, 2006.

Apodaca, Linda M. "Mexican American Women and Social Change: The Founding of the Community Service Organization in Los Angeles; An Oral History." Tucson: University of Arizona, Mexican American Studies and Research Center Working Paper Series 27, January 1999.

Aviaro [Amaro], Hortensia. "Latina Attitudes Towards Abortion." *Nuestro* (August/September 1981): 43–44.

Baker, Ellen R. *On Strike and on Film: Mexican American Families and Blacklisted Filmmakers in Cold War America.* Charlotte: University of North Carolina Press, 2007.

Barrera, Mario, Carlos Muñoz, and Charles Ornelas. "The Barrio as Internal Colony." *Urban Affairs Annual Review* 6 (1972): 465–98.

Barrios de Chungara, Domitila. *Let Me Speak.* New York: Monthly Review Press, 1978.

Bartra, Eli. "El movimiento feminista en México y su vínculo con la academia." *Revista de estudios de género: La ventana* 1 (1999): 214–33.

Basso, Sister Teresita. "The Emerging Chicana." *Review for Religious* 30, no. 6 (1971): 1019–28. Reprinted in Alma García, ed., *Chicana Feminist Thought: The Basic Historical Writings.* New York: Routledge, 1997, 58–65.

Bebout, Lee. *Mythohistorical Interventions: The Chicano Movement and Its Legacies.* Minneapolis: University of Minnesota Press, 2011.

Berkeley, Kathleen C. *The Women's Liberation Movement in America.* Westport, CT: Greenwood, 1999.

Bernstein, Shana. *Bridges of Reform: Interracial Civil Rights Activism in Twentieth-Century Los Angeles.* New York: Oxford University Press, 2011.

Blackwell, Maylei. *¡Chicana Power! Contested Histories of Feminism in the Chicano Movement.* Austin: University of Texas Press, 2011.

Blackwell, Maylei. "Contested Histories: Las Hijas de Cuauhtémoc, Chicana Feminisms, and Print Culture in the Chicano Movement." In *Chicana Feminisms: A Critical Reader,* edited by Gabriela Arredondo, Aida Hurtado, Norma Klahn, Olga Najera-Ramírez, and Patricia Zavella, 59–89. Durham, NC: Duke University Press, 2003.

Blain, Keisha N. *Set the World on Fire: Black Nationalist Women and the Global Struggle for Freedom.* Philadelphia: University of Pennsylvania Press, 2018.

Blauner, Bob. *Resisting McCarthyism: To Sign or Not to Sign California's Loyalty Oath.* Palo Alto, CA: Stanford University Press, 2009.

Bloom, Alexander, ed. *Long Time Gone: Sixties America Then and Now.* New York: Oxford University Press, 2001.

Bonaparte, Ronald. "The Rodino Bill: An Example of Prejudice Towards Mexican Immigration to the United States." *Chicano Law Review* 2, no. 1 (Summer 1975): 40–50.

Brave Bird, Mary, and Richard Erdoes. *Lakota Woman.* New York: HarperPerennial, 1991.

Breines, Winifred. *The Trouble Between Us: An Uneasy History of White and Black Women in the Feminist Movement.* New York: Oxford University Press, 2006.

Brown, Elaine. *A Taste of Power: A Black Woman's Story.* New York: Pantheon, 1992.

Brown, Nadia, and Sarah Allen Gershon. "Body Politics." *Politics, Groups, and Identities* 5, no. 1 (2017): 1–3.

Browsky Junge, Maxine, and Con Safos. *Voices from the Barrio: "Con Safos: Reflections of Life in the Barrio."* Los Angeles: CreateSpace Independent Publishing Platform, 2016.

Broyles-González, Yolanda. *El Teatro Campesino: Theater in the Chicano Movement.* Austin: University of Texas Press, 1994.

Buelna, Enrique. *Chicano Communists and the Struggle for Social Justice.* Tuscon: University of Arizona Press, 2019.

Burciaga, Cecilia. "The 1977 National Women's Conference in Houston." In *Chicana Feminist Thought,* edited by Alma García, 184; originally published in *La Luz* (November 1978): 8–9.

Chabram-Dernersesian, Angie. "I Throw Punches for My Race, but I Don't Want to Be a Man: Writing Us—Chica-nos (Girl, Us)/Chicanas—into the Movement Script." In *Cultural Studies,* edited by Lawrence Grossberg, Cary Nelson, and Paula Treichler, 81–95. New York: Routledge, 1992.

Chafe, William. *The Paradox of Change: American Women in the 20th Century*. New York: Oxford University Press, 1991.
Chávez, Ernesto. *¡Mi Raza Primero! (My People First!): Nationalism, Identity and Insurgency in the Chicano Movement in Los Angeles*. Berkeley: University of California Press, 2002.
Chávez, John R. *The Lost Land: The Chicano Image of the Southwest*. Albuquerque: University of New Mexico Press, 1982.
Chávez, Marisela R. "Pilgrimage to the Homeland: California Chicanas and International Women's Year, Mexico City, 1975." In *Memories and Migrations: Mapping Boricua and Chicana Histories*, edited by Vicki L. Ruiz and John R. Chávez, 170–95. Urbana: University of Illinois Press, 2008.
Chávez, Marisela R. "Rooted in Community: The Scholarship of Chicana Political Leadership and Activism." In *Suffrage at 100: Women in American Politics Since 1920*, edited by Stacie Taranto and Leandra Zarnow. Baltimore, MD: Johns Hopkins University Press, 2020.
Chávez, Marisela R. "'We Lived and Breathed and Worked the Movement': The Contradictions and Rewards of Chicana/Mexicana Activism in El Centro de Acción Social Autónomo, Los Angeles, 1975–1978." In *Las Obreras: Chicana Politics of Work and Family*, edited by Vicki L. Ruiz, 83–105. Los Angeles: Chicano Research Center Publications, University of California, 2000.
Chávez, Marisela R. "'We Have a Long, Beautiful History': Chicana Feminist Trajectories and Legacies." In *No Permanent Waves: Recasting U.S. Feminist History*, edited by Nancy Hewitt, 77–97. New Brunswick: Rutgers University Press, 2010.
Chávez-García, Miroslava. "The Interdisciplinary Project of Chicana History: Looking Back, Moving Forward." *Pacific Historical Review* 82, no. 4 (2013): 551.
Chávez Leyva, Yolanda. "Listening to the Silences in Latina/Chicana Lesbian History." In *Living Chicana Theory*, edited by Carla Trujillo, 429–34. Berkeley, CA: Third Woman, 1998.
Cheng, Wendy. *The Changs Next Door to the Díazes: Remapping Race in Suburban California*. Minneapolis: University of Minnesota Press, 2013.
Cherny, Robert W. "The Communist Party in California, 1935–1940: From the Political Margins to the Mainstream and Back." *American Communist History* 9, no. 1 (2010): 3–33.
Churchill, Ward, and Jim Vander Wall. *Agents of Repression: The FBI's Secret Wars Against the Black Panther Party and the American Indian Movement*. Boston: South End, 1990.
Cleaver, Kathleen. "Women, Power and Revolution." In *Liberation, Imagination and the Black Panther Party: A New Look at the Panthers and Their Legacy*, edited by Kathleen Cleaver and George Katsifiacas, 123–27. New York: Routledge, 2001.
Cohen, Deborah. *Braceros: Migrant Citizens and Transnational Subjects in the Postwar United States and Mexico*. Chapel Hill: University of North Carolina Press, 2013.
Cohen, Robert. *When the Old Left Was Young: Student Radicals and America's First Mass Student Movement, 1929–1941*. New York: Oxford University Press, 1993.
Collier-Thomas, Bettye, and V. P. Franklin, eds. *Sisters in the Struggle: African American Women in the Civil Rights–Black Power Movement*. New York: NYU Press, 2001.
Collins, Patricia Hill. *Black Feminist Thought: Knowledge, Consciousness, and the Politics of Empowerment*. New York: Routledge, 1991.

Córdova, Teresa. "Roots and Resistance: The Emergent Writing of Twenty Years of Chicana Feminist Struggle." In *Handbook of Hispanic Cultures in the United States: Sociology*, edited by Felix Padilla, 175–202. Houston: Arte Público, 1993.

Cotera, María Eugenia, Maylei Blackwell, and Dionne Espinoza. "Introductions: Movement, Movimientos, and Movidas." In *Chicana Movidas: Narratives of Activism and Feminism in the Movement Era*, edited by Dionne Espinoza, María Eugenia Cotera, and Maylei Blackwell, 1–30. Austin: University of Texas Press, 2018.

Cotera, Martha. "Mujeres Bravas: How Chicanas Shaped the Feminist Agenda at the National IWY Conference in Houston, 1977." In *Chicana Movidas: New Narratives of Activism and Feminism in the Movement Era*, edited by Dionne Espinoza, María Eugenia Cotera, and Maylei Blackwell, 51–75. Austin: University of Texas Press, 2018.

Cotera, Martha. *The Chicana Feminist*. Austin: Information Systems Development, 1977.

Cotera, Martha. *Diosa y Hembra: The History and Heritage of Chicanas in the United States*. Austin: Information Systems Development, 1976.

Cotera, Martha. "Feminism: The Chicana and Anglo Versions." In *Twice a Minority: Mexican American Women*, ed. Margarita B. Melville, 217–34. St. Louis: Mosby, 1980.

Cotera, Martha. *Profile on the Mexican-American Woman*. Austin: National Educational Laboratory, 1976.

Cott, Nancy F. *The Grounding of Modern Feminism*. New Haven: Yale University Press, 1987.

Davis, Flora. *Moving the Mountain: The Women's Movement in America Since 1960*. New York: Simon and Schuster, 1991.

De la Cruz, Juana Inés. *Sor Juana Inés de la Cruz: Selected Works*. New York: Norton, 2015.

Del Castillo, Adelaida, ed. *Between Borders: Essays on Mexicana/Chicana History*. Encino, CA: Floricanto, 1990.

Del Castillo, Adelaida, and Magdalena Mora, eds. *Mexican Women in the United States: Struggles Past and Present*. Los Angeles: UCLA Chicano Studies Research Center Publications, 1980.

Delgado, Linda C. "Polly Baca Barragán." In *Latinas in the United States: An Historical Encyclopedia*, edited by Vicki L. Ruiz and Virginia Sánchez Korrol, 75–76. Bloomington: Indiana University Press, 2006.

Delgado Bernal, Dolores. "Grassroots Leadership Redefined: Chicana Oral Histories and the 1968 East Los Angeles High School Blowouts," *Frontiers* 19, no. 2 (1998): 113–42.

Diehl, Paula, and Guadalupe Saavedra. "Hispanas in the Year of the Woman." *Agenda* (Winter 1976): 18.

Diehm, Cheryl. "Committee to Stop Forced Sterilization Splits over Tactics." *Sister* 5, no. 10 (February 1975): 3.

Dionne, Kim Yi, Darin Dewitt, Michael Stone, and Michael Suk-Young Chwe. "The May 1 Marchers in Los Angeles: Overcoming Conflicting Frames, Bilingual Women Connectors, English-Language Radio, and Newly Politicized Spanish Speakers." *Urban Affairs Review* 51, no. 4 (2015): 533–62.

Dunbar, Roxanne. "Marxist Feminism." In *Reader's Companion to U.S. Women's History*. Edited by Gwendolyn Mink, Wilma Mankiller, Marysa Navarro, Barbara Smith, and Gloria Steinem, 214–15. New York: Houghton Mifflin Harcourt, 1998.

Echols, Alice. *Daring to Be Bad: Radical Feminism in America, 1967–1975*. Minneapolis: University of Minnesota Press, 1989.

Eckstein, Arthur. "The Hollywood Ten in History and Memory." *Film History* 16 (2004): 424–36.

Enck-Wanzer, Darrel, Iris Morales, and Denise Oliver-Velez, eds. *The Young Lords: A Reader*. New York: New York University Press, 2010.

Escobar, Edward J. *Race, Police and the Making of a Political Identity: Mexican Americans and the Los Angeles Police Department, 1900–1945*. Berkeley: University of California Press, 1999.

Espino, Virginia. "'Woman Sterilized as Gives Birth': Forced Sterilization and Chicana Resistance in the 1970s." In *Las Obreras: Chicana Politics of Work and Family*, edited by Vicki L. Ruiz, 65–81. Los Angeles: UCLA Chicano Studies Research Center Publications, 2000.

Espinosa Damian, Gisela. "The Fruitful and Conflictive Relationship Between Feminist Movements and the Mexican Left." *Social Justice* 42 (2016): 74–88.

Espinoza, Dionne. "La Raza en Canada: San Diego Chicana Activists, the Indochinese Women's Conference of 1971, and Third World Womanism." In *Chicana Movidas: New Narratives of Activism and Feminism in the Movement Era*, edited by Dionne Espinoza, Maria Eugenia Cotera, and Maylei Blackwell, 261–75. Austin: University of Texas Press, 2018.

Espinoza, Dionne. "Rethinking Cultural Nationalism and La Familia Through Women's Communities: Enriqueta Vasquez and Chicana Feminist Thought," in *Enriqueta Vasquez and the Chicano Movement: Writings from El Grito del Norte*, ed. Lorena Oropeza and Dionne Espinoza, 205–31. Albuquerque: Arte Público, 2006.

Espinoza, Dionne. "Revolutionary Sisters: Women's Solidarity and Collective Identification Among Chicana Brown Berets." *Aztlán* 26, no. 1 (Spring 2001): 17–58.

Espinoza, Dionne, María Eugenia Cotera, and Maylei Blackwell, eds. *Chicana Movidas: New Narratives of Activism and Feminism in the Movement Era*. Austin: University of Texas Press, 2018.

Etulain, Richard W., ed. *César Chávez: A Brief Biography with Documents*. Boston: Bedford/St. Martin's, 2002.

Evans, Sara. *Born for Liberty: A History of Women in America*. New York: Free Press, 1997.

Evans, Sara. *Personal Politics: The Roots of Women's Liberation in the Civil Rights Movement and the New Left*. New York: Knopf, 1979.

Faller, Gini. Letter to the editor. *Sister* 5, no. 10 (February 1975): 10.

Farber, David, and Beth Bailey. *The Columbia Guide to America in the 1960s*. New York: Columbia University Press, 2001.

Farber, David, and Eric Foner, eds. *The Age of Great Dreams: America in the 1960s*. New York: Hill and Wang, 1994.

Felker-Kantor, Max. "'A Pledge Is Not Self-Enforcing': Struggles for Equal Employment Opportunity in Multiracial Los Angeles." *Pacific Historical Review* 82, no. 1 (2013): 63–94.

Fernández, Johanna. *The Young Lords: A Radical History*. Chapel Hill: University of North Carolina Press, 2020.

Flores, Bill. "Francisca Flores, 1913–1996." *Tonatiuh Quinto Sol* (June 1996): 2–4.

Freedman, Estelle. *No Turning Back: The History of Feminism and the Future of Women*. New York: Ballantine, 2002.

Friedan, Betty. *It Changed My Life: Writings on the Women's Movement*. New York: Random House, 1976.
Fundamentals of Marxism-Leninism: Manual. Moscow: Foreign Languages Publishing House, 1961.
Gabin, Nancy Felice. *Feminism in the Labor Movement: Women and the United Auto Workers, 1935–1975*. Ithaca: Cornell University Press, 1990.
Galey, Margaret E. "The Nairobi Conference: The Powerless Majority." *Political Science* 19, no. 2 (Spring 1986): 255–65.
Galey, Margaret E. "Promoting Nondiscrimination Against Women: The UN Commission on the Status of Women." *International Studies Quarterly* 23, no. 2 (June 1979): 273–302.
García, Alma M., ed. *Chicana Feminist Thought: The Basic Historical Writings*. New York: Routledge, 1997.
García, Alma M. "The Development of Chicana Feminist Discourse." In *Unequal Sisters: A Multicultural Reader in U.S. Women's History*, 2nd ed., edited by Vicki L. Ruiz and Ellen Carol DuBois, 531–44. New York: Routledge, 1994.
García, Ignacio M. *Chicanismo: The Forging of a Militant Ethos Among Mexican Americans*. Tucson: University of Arizona Press, 1998.
García, Ignacio M. *United We Win: The Rise and Fall of La Raza Unida Party*. Tucson: University of Arizona Press, 1989.
García, Mario T. *The Chicano Generation: Testimonios of the Movement*. Berkeley: University of California Press, 2015.
García, Mario T., ed. *The Chicano Movement: Perspectives from the Twenty-First Century*. New York: Routledge, 2014.
García, Mario T. *Memories of Chicano History: The Life and Narrative of Bert Corona*. Berkeley: University of California Press, 1994.
García, Mario T. *Mexican Americans: Leadership, Ideology and Identity*. New Haven: Yale University Press, 1989.
García, Sonia R., and Marisela Marquez. "The Comisión Femenil: La Voz of a Chicana Organization," *Aztlán* 36, no. 1 (2011): 149–69.
Garcilazo, Jeffrey M. "McCarthyism, Mexican Americans, and the Los Angeles Committee for the Protection of the Foreign-Born, 1950–1954." *Western Historical Quarterly* 32, no. 3 (2001): 273–95.
Garner, Karen. "World YWCA Leaders and the UN Decade for Women." *Journal of International Women's Studies* 9, no. 1 (November 2007): 212–33.
Gey, Fredric, Cecilia Jiang, Jon Stiles, and Ilone Einowski. *California Latino Demographic Handbook*, 3rd ed. Berkeley: UC Data Archive and Technical Assistance, California Policy Research Center, 2004.
Giddings, Paula. *When and Where I Enter: The Impact of Black Women on Race and Sex in America*. New York: Morrow, 1984.
Gilliam, Angela. "Women's Equality and National Liberation." In *Third World Women and the Politics of Feminism*, edited by Chandra Talpade Mohanty, Ann Ruso, and Lourdes Torres, 215–36. Bloomington: Indiana University Press, 1991.
Gilmore, Stephanie, and Sara Evans, eds. *Feminist Coalitions: Historical Perspectives on Second-Wave Feminism in the United States*. Champaign: University of Illinois Press, 2008.

Gitlin, Todd. *The Sixties: Years of Hope, Days of Rage*. New York: Bantam, 1981.
Glessing, Robert J. *The Underground Press in America*. Bloomington: Indiana University Press, 1970.
Gómez, Alan Eladio. *The Revolutionary Imaginations of Greater Mexico: Chicana/o Radicalism, Solidarity Politics, and Latin American Social Movements*. Austin: University of Texas Press, 2016.
Gómez-Quiñones, Juan. *Chicano Politics: Reality and Promise, 1940–1990*. Albuquerque: University of New Mexico Press, 1994.
Gómez-Quiñones, Juan. *Sembradores: Ricardo Flores Magón y el Partido Liberal Mexicano*. Los Angeles: Chicano Studies Research Center Publications, 1973.
Gómez-Quiñones, Juan, and Irene Vásquez. *Making Aztlán: Ideology and Culture of the Chicana and Chicano Movement, 1966–1977*. Albuquerque: University of New Mexico Press, 2014.
González, Deena J. *Refusing the Favor: The Spanish-Mexican Women of Santa Fe*. New York: Oxford University Press, 1999.
González, Gabriela. "Carolina Munguía and Emma Tenayuca: The Politics of Benevolence and Radical Reform." *Frontiers* 24, no. 2/3 (2003): 200–229.
Gónzalez, Gabriela. *Redeeming la Raza: Transborder Modernity, Race, Respectability, and Rights*. New York: Oxford University Press, 2018.
González, Gilbert, and Raul Fernández. "Chicano History: Transcending Cultural Models." *Pacific Historical Review* 63 (November 1994): 469–97.
Gonzales, Rodolfo "Corky." *I Am Joaquin*. Santa Barbara: La Causa, 1967.
Gonzales, Rodolfo "Corky." *Message to Aztlán: Selected Writings*. Houston: Arte Público, 1999.
Grebler, Leo, Joan Moore, and Ralph Guzmán. *The Mexican-American People: The Nation's Second Largest Minority*. New York: Free Press, 1970.
Gutiérrez, David G. "CASA in the Chicano Movement: Ideology and Organizational Politics in the Chicano Movement, 1968–1978." Stanford, CA: Stanford Center for Chicano Research, Working Papers Series 5, Stanford University, 1984.
Gutiérrez, David G. "Significant to Whom? Mexican Americans and the History of the American West." *Western Historical Quarterly* 24, no. 4 (1993): 519–39.
Gutiérrez, David G. *Walls and Mirrors: Mexican Americans, Mexican Immigrants, and the Politics of Ethnicity*. Berkeley: University of California Press, 1995.
Gutiérrez, Elena R. *Fertile Matters: The Politics of Mexican-Origin Women's Reproduction*. Austin: University of Texas Press, 2008.
Gutiérrez, José Angel. *The Making of a Chicano Militant*. Madison: University of Wisconsin Press, 1999.
Gutiérrez, Ramón. "Community, Patriarchy and Individualism: The Politics of Chicano History and the Dream of Equality." *American Quarterly* 45, no. 1 (March 1993): 44–72.
Guy-Sheftall, Beverly, ed. *Words of Fire: A Black Feminist Anthology*. New York: New Press, 1995.
Haney-Lopez, Ian. *Racism on Trial: The Chicano Fight for Justice*. Cambridge, MA: Belknap Press of Harvard University Press, 2003.
Harrison, Cynthia Ellen. *On Account of Sex: The Politics of Women's Issues, 1945–1968*. Berkeley: University of California Press, 1988.

Hartmann, Heidi. "The Unhappy Marriage of Marxism and Feminism: Towards a More Progressive Union." In *Women and Revolution,* edited by Lydia Sargent, 2–4. Boston: South End, 1981.

Healey, Dorothy. *Dorothy Healey Remembers: A Life in the Communist Party.* New York: Oxford University Press, 1990.

Hernandez, Kelly Lytle. *Migra! A History of the U.S. Border Patrol.* Berkeley: University of California Press, 2010.

Hodgdon, Tim. "Fem: A Window onto the Cultural Coalescence of a Mexican Feminist Politics of Sexuality." *Mexican Studies* 16, no. 1 (2000): 79–104.

Horowitz, Daniel. *Betty Friedan and the Making of* The Feminine Mystique: *The American Left, the Cold War, and Feminism.* Amherst: University of Massachusetts Press, 1998.

Hosang, Daniel. "Race and the Mythology of California's Lost Paradise." *Boom* 1, no. 1 (2011): 36–49.

Hull, Gloria T., Patricia Bell Scott, and Barbara Smith, eds. *All the Women Are White, All the Blacks Are Men, But Some of Us Are Brave: Black Women's Studies.* Old Westbury, NY: Feminist Press, 1982.

Hurtado, Aída. *Voicing Chicana Feminisms: Young Women Speak out on Sexuality and Identity.* New York: NYU Press, 2003.

Ikas, Karin. *Chicana Ways: Conversations with Ten Chicana Writers.* Reno: University of Nevada Press, 2001.

Isserman, Maurice, and Michael Kazin. *America Divided: The Civil War of the 1960s.* New York: Oxford University Press, 2000.

Jaquette, Jane S. "Losing the Battle/Winning the War: International Politics, Women's Issues, and the 1980 Mid-Decade Conference." In *Women, Politics and the United Nations,* edited by Anne Winslow, 45–59. Westport, CT: Greenwood, 1995.

Johnson-Odim, Cheryl. "Common Themes, Different Contexts: Third World Women and Feminism." In *Third World Women and the Politics of Feminism,* edited by Chandra Talpade Mohanty, Ann Ruso, and Lourdes Torres, 314–27. Bloomington: Indiana University Press, 1991.

Jones, Charles E., ed. *The Black Panther Party Reconsidered.* Baltimore: Black Classic, 1998.

Kaplan, Judy, and Linn Shapiro, eds. *Red Diapers: Growing up in the Communist Left.* Urbana: University of Illinois Press, 1998.

Kelley, Robin D. G. *Hammer and Hoe: Alabama Communists During the Great Depression.* 25th anniv. ed. Chapel Hill: University of North Carolina Press, 2015.

Kessler, Lauren. *The Dissident Press: Alternative Journalism in American History.* Beverly Hills: Sage, 1984.

Kirk, Stephanie. *Sor Juana Inés de la Cruz and the Gender Politics of Knowledge in Colonial Mexico.* New York: Routledge, 2016.

Lamas, Marta. "Del 68 a hoy: La movilización política de las mujeres." *Revista Mexicana de ciencias políticas y sociales* 234 (2018): 265–86.

Landeros, Pablo. "AKA Frances: Francisca Flores and the Radical Roots of Chicana Feminism in California." In *Latina Histories and Cultures: Feminist Readings and Recoveries of Archival Knowledge,* edited by Montse Feu and Yolanda Padilla, 229–45. Houston: Arte Público, 2023.

Lau, Ana. "El nuevo movimiento feminista mexicano a fines del milenio." In *Feminismo en México: Ayer y hoy*, edited by Eli Bartra, Anna M. Fernández Poncela, and Ana Lau, 11–42. Mexico City: Universidad Autónoma Metropolitana, 2000.

Lee, Chana Kai. *For Freedom's Sake: The Life of Fannie Lou Hamer*. Champaign: University of Illinois Press, 2000.

Limón, José. *Mexican Ballads, Chicano Poems: History and Influence in Mexican-American Social Poetry*. Berkeley: University of California Press, 1992.

Ling, Peter J., and Sharon Monteith, eds. *Gender in the Civil Rights Movement*. New York: Garland, 1999.

Lira, Natalie. *Laboratory of Deficiency: Sterilization and Confinement in California, 1900–1950s*. Berkeley: University of California Press, 2022.

Longeaux y Vásquez, Enriqueta. "The Mexican American Woman." In *Sisterhood Is Powerful: An Anthology of Writings from the Women's Liberation Movement*, edited by Robin Morgan, 426–32. New York: Vintage, 1970.

Longmore, T. Wilson, and Homer L. Hitt. "A Demographic Analysis of First and Second Generation Mexican Population of the United States: 1930." *Southwestern Social Science Quarterly* 24, no. 2 (1943): 138–49.

López, Sonia A. "The Role of the Chicana Within the Student Movement." In *Essays on la Mujer*, edited by Rosaura Sánchez, 16–29. Los Angeles: Chicano Studies Research Center Publications, 1977.

Loza, Mireya. *Defiant Braceros: How Migrant Workers Fought for Racial, Sexual, and Political Freedom*. Chapel Hill: University of North Carolina Press, 2016.

Lym, Frances [Francisca Flores]. "The Mexican Americans Organize." *Jewish Life* 9, no. 7 (May 1955): 22–26.

Macedo, Stephen, ed. *Reassessing the Sixties: Debating the Political and Cultural Legacy*. New York: Norton, 1997.

Maier, Elizabeth. "Accommodating the Private into the Public Domain: Experiences and Legacies of the Past Four Decades." In *Women's Activism in Latin America and the Caribbean: Engendering Social Justice, Democratizing Citizenship*, edited by Elizabeth Maier and Nathalie Lebon, 24–46. New Brunswick, N.J. and Tijuana, Mexico: Rutgers University Press and the El Colegio de la Frontera Norte AC, 2010.

Marcos, Sylvia. "Twenty-five Years of Mexican Feminisms." *Women's Studies International Forum* 22, no. 4 (1999) 431–33.

Marín, Marguerite. *Social Protest in an Urban Barrio: A Case Study of the Chicano Movement, 1966–1974*. Lanham, MD: University Press of America, 1991.

Martínez, Elizabeth. "Colonized Women: The Chicana." In *Sisterhood Is Powerful: An Anthology of Writings from the Women's Liberation Movement*, edited by Robin Morgan, 423–25. New York: Vintage, 1970.

Martínez, Elizabeth. *De Colores Means All of Us: Latina Views for a Multi-Colored Century*. Cambridge, MA: South End, 1997.

Matthiessen, Peter. *Sal Si Puedes: Cesar Chavez and the New American Revolution*. New York: Dell, 1973.

Mattingly, Doreen J., and Jessica L. Nare. "A Rainbow of Women: Diversity and Unity at the 1977 U.S. International Women's Year Conference." *Journal of Women's History* 26, no. 2 (2014): 88–112.

Mazón, Mauricio. *Zoot-Suit Riots: The Psychology of Symbolic Annihilation*. Austin: University of Texas Press, 1984.

McClintock, Anne. *Imperial Leather: Race, Gender and Sexuality in the Colonial Conquest*. New York: Routledge, 1995.

McDuffie, Erik S. *Sojourning for Freedom: Black Women, American Communism, and the Making of Black Left Feminism*. Durham, NC: Duke University Press, 2011.

Mexican-American Study Project. "California Mexican-Americans Score Zero in State Legislature." *Mexican-American Study Project Progress Report* no. 9. Los Angeles: UCLA, May 1967.

Millett, Kate. *Sexual Politics*. Garden City, NY: Doubleday, 1970.

Minh-Ha, Trinh T. "Not You/Like You: Postcolonial Women and the Interlocking Questions of Identity and Difference." In *Dangerous Liaisons: Gender, Nation and Postcolonial Perspectives*, edited by Anne McClintock, Aamir Mufti, and Ella Shohat, 415–19. Minneapolis: University of Minnesota Press, 1997.

Mirandé, Alfredo, and Evangelina Vigil. *La Chicana: The Mexican-American Woman*. Chicago: University of Chicago Press, 1979.

Mize, Ronald L. *Consuming Mexican Labor: From the Bracero Program to NAFTA*. Toronto: University of Toronto Press, 2011.

Monroy, Douglas. *Rebirth: Mexican Los Angeles from the Great Migration to the Great Depression*. Berkeley: University of California Press, 1999.

Montejano, David. *Quixote's Soldiers: A Local History of the Chicano Movement, 1966–1981*. Austin: University of Texas Press, 2010.

Moraga, Cherríe. "Catching Fire: Preface to the Fourth Edition," in *This Bridge Called My Back: Writings by Radical Women of Color*, ed. Gloria Anzaldúa and Cherríe Moraga. Albany: SUNY Press, 2015.

Moreno, Dorinda, ed. *La Mujer en Pie de Lucha—Y la Hora es Ya*. Mexico City: Espina del Norte, 1975.

Morgan, Edward P. *The 60s Experience: Hard Lessons About Modern America*. Philadelphia: Temple University Press, 1991.

Morgan, Robin, ed. *Sisterhood Is Powerful: An Anthology of Writings from the Women's Liberation Movement*. New York: Vintage, 1970.

Muncy, Robyn. "Cooperative Motherhood and Democratic Civic Culture in Postwar Suburbia, 1940–1965." *Journal of Social History* 38, no. 2 (2004): 285–310.

Muñoz, Carlos. *Youth, Identity, Power: The Chicano Movement*. New York: Verso, 1989.

Navarro, Armando. *Mexican American Youth Organization: Avant-Garde of the Chicano Movement in Texas*. Austin: University of Texas Press, 1995.

Nelson, Jennifer A. "'Abortions Under Community Control': Feminism, Nationalism, and the Politics of Reproduction Among New York City's Young Lords." *Journal of Women's History* 13, no. 1 (Spring 2001): 157–80.

Nelson, Jennifer A. *Women of Color and the Reproductive Rights Movement*. New York: NYU Press, 2003.

NietoGómez, Anna. "Francisca Flores, the League of Mexican American Women, and the Comisión Femenil Mexicana Nacional, 1958–1975." In *Chicana Movidas: New Narratives of Activism and Feminism in the Moement Era*, edited by Dionne Espinoza, Maria Cotera, and Maylei Blackwell, 33–50. Austin: University of Texas Press, 2018.

NietoGómez, Anna. "La Femenista." *Encuentro Femenil* 1, no. 2 (1974): 34–47, 74.

NietoGómez, Anna. "Response to Chapter Two: Chicana Print Culture and Chicana Studies; A Testimony to the Development of Chicana Feminist Culture." In *Chicana Feminisms: A Critical Reader*, ed. Gabriela Arredondo, Aída Hurtado, Norma Klahn, Olga Nájera-Ramírez, and Patricia Zavella, 94. Durham: Duke University Press, 2003.

Olcott, Jocelyn. *International Women's Year: The Greatest Consciousness-Raising Event in History*. New York: Oxford University Press, 2017.

Ontiveros, Randy J. *In the Spirit of a New People: The Cultural Politics of the Chicano Movement*. New York: NYU Press, 2013.

Orleck, Annelise. *Rethinking American Women's Activism*. New York: Routledge, 2014.

Orleck, Annelise. *Storming Caesar's Palace: How Black Mothers Fought Their Own War on Poverty*. Boston: Beacon, 2006.

Oropeza, Lorena. *¡Raza Sí! ¡Guerra No! Chicano Protest and Patriotism During the Viet Nam War Era*. Berkeley: University of California Press, 2005.

Oropeza, Lorena, Dionne Espinoza, Enriqueta Vasquez, and John Nichols. *Enriqueta Vasquez and the Chicano Movement: Writings from el Grito del Norte*. Houston: Arte Público, 2005.

Orozco, Cynthia. "Beyond Machismo, La Familia, and Ladies Auxiliaries: A Historiography of Mexican-Origin Women's Participation in Voluntary Associations and Politics in the United States, 1870–1990." *Perspectives in Mexican American Studies* 5 (1995): 1–34.

Orozco, Cynthia. *No Mexicans, Women, or Dogs Allowed: The Rise of the Mexican American Civil Rights Movement*. Austin: University of Texas Press, 2009.

Pagán, Eduardo Obregón. *Murder at the Sleepy Lagoon: Zoot Suits, Race, and Riot in Wartime L.A.* Chapel Hill: University of North Carolina Press, 2003.

Patiño, Jimmy. *Raza Sí, Migra No: Chicano Movement Struggles for Immigrant Rights in San Diego*. Chapel Hill: University of North Carolina Press, 2017.

Paz, Octavio. *The Labyrinth of Solitude: Life and Thought in Mexico*. New York: Grove, 1961.

Peck, Abe. *Uncovering the Sixties: The Life and Times of the Underground Press*. New York: Pantheon, 1985.

Pérez, Emma. *The Decolonial Imaginary: Writing Chicanas into History*. Bloomington: Indiana University Press, 1999.

Pérez, Laura Elisa. "El Desorden, Nationalism, and Chicana/o Aesthetics." In *Between Woman and Nation: Nationalisms, Transnational Feminisms, and the State*, edited by Karen Kaplan, Norma Alarcón, and Minoo Moallen. Durham: Duke University Press, 1999.

Portelli, Alessandro. *The Death of Luigi Trastulli, and Other Stories: Form and Meaning in Oral History*. Albany: SUNY Press, 1991.

Proppe, Kathy. "Socialist Feminism in Practice." *L.A. Women's Union Newsletter* 1, no. 5 (December 1974): 2

Pulido, Laura. *Black, Brown, Yellow and Left: Radical Activism in Los Angeles*. Berkeley: University of California Press, 2006.

Quiñonez, Naomi H. "Francisca Flores." In *Latinas in the United States: A Historical Encyclopedia*, edited by Vicki Ruiz and Virginia Sánchez Korrol, 264–65. Bloomington: Indiana University Press, 2006.

Ramírez, Catherine S. "Crimes of Fashion: The Pachuca and Chicana Style Politics." *Meridians* 2 no. 2 (2002): 1–35.

Ransby, Barbara. *Ella Baker and the Black Freedom Movement*. Chapel Hill: University of North Carolina Press, 2005.

Riambau, Esteve, and Casimiro Torreiro. "This Film Is Going to Make History: An Interview with Rosaura Revueltas." *Cineaste* 19, nos. 2/3 (December 1992): 50–51.

Riddell, Adaljiza Sosa. "Chicanas and El Movimiento." *Aztlán* 5, nos. 1–2 (1974): 155–65.

Robnett, Belinda. *How Long? How Long? African-American Women in the Struggle for Civil Rights*. New York: Oxford University Press, 1997.

Rodriguez, Richard T. *Next of Kin: The Family in Chicano/a Cultural Politics*. Durham, NC: Duke University Press, 2009.

Rogers, Kim Lacy. "Memory, Struggle, and Power: On Interviewing Political Activists." *Oral History Review* 15, no. 1 (1987): 165–84.

Romo, Ricardo. *East Los Angeles: History of a Barrio*. Austin: University of Texas Press, 1983.

Rosales, Francisco A[rturo]. *Chicano! A History of the Mexican American Civil Rights Movement*. Houston: Arte Público, 1996.

Rosales, F[rancisco] Arturo. "Graciela Olivares." In *Latinas in the United States: An Historical Encyclopedia*, edited by Vicki L. Ruiz and Virginia Sánchez Korrol, 537–38. Bloomington: Indiana University Press, 2006.

Rose, Margaret. "Gender and Civic Activism in Mexican American Barrios in California: The Community Service Organization, 1947–1962." In *Not June Cleaver: Women and Gender in Postwar America, 1945–1960*, edited by Joanne Meyerowitz, 177–99. Philadelphia: Temple University Press, 1994.

Rosen, Gerald Paul. *Political Ideology and the Chicano Movement: A Study of the Political Ideology of Activists in the Chicano Movement*. San Francisco: R & E Research Associates, 1975.

Rosen, Ruth. *The World Split Open: How the Modern Women's Movement Changed America*, rev. ed. New York: Penguin, 2006.

Ross, Loretta, and Rickie Solinger. *Reproductive Justice: An Introduction*. Berkeley: University of California Press, 2017.

Roth, Benita. *Separate Roads to Feminism: Black, Chicana, and White Feminist Movements in America's Second Wave*. New York: Cambridge University Press, 2003.

Rothschild, Mary Aickin. *A Case of Black and White: Northern Volunteers and the Southern Freedom Summers, 1964–1965*. Westport, CT: Greenwood, 1982.

Ruggles, Steven, Sarah Flood, Sophia Foster, Ronald Goeken, Jose Pacas, Megan Schouweiler, and Matthew Sobek. IPUMS USA: Version 11.0, *1980 5%-State*. Minneapolis, MN: IPUMS, 2021. https://doi.org/10.18128/D010.V11.0.

Ruiz, Vicki L. *From out of the Shadows: Mexican Women in Twentieth-Century America*. New York: Oxford University Press, 1998.

Ruiz, Vicki L. "Luisa Moreno and Latina Labor Activism." In *Latina Legacies: Identity, Biography, and Community*, edited by Vicki L. Ruiz and Virginia Sánchez Korrol, 175–92. New York: Oxford University Press, 2005.

Ruiz, Vicki L. "Una Mujer Sin Fronteras: Luisa Moreno and Latina Labor Activism." *Pacific Historical Review* 73, no. 1 (2004): 1–20.

Rupp, Leila J. *Worlds of Women: The Making of an International Women's Movement*. Princeton, NJ: Princeton University Press, 1997.

Sánchez, George J. *Becoming Mexican American: Ethnicity, Culture and Identity in Chicano Los Angeles, 1900–1945*. New York: Oxford University Press, 1993.

Sánchez, Rosaura. "The History of Chicanas: A Proposal for a Materialist Perspective." In *Between Borders: Essays on Mexicana/Chicana History*, edited by Adelaida R. Del Castillo, 1–29. Encino, CA: Floricanto, 1990.

Sandoval, Chela. *Methodology of the Oppressed*. Minneapolis: University of Minnesota Press, 2000.

Sargent, Lydia. *Women and Revolution: A Discussion of the Unhappy Marriage of Marxism and Feminism*. Boston: South End, 1981.

Schrecker, Ellen. *Many Are the Crimes: McCarthyism in America*. New York: Little, Brown, 1998.

Shah, Sonia, Yuri Kochiyama, and Karin Aguilar-San Juan, eds. *Dragon Ladies: Asian American Feminists Breathe Fire*. Boston: South End, 1999.

Silliman, Jael, Marlene Gerber Fried, Loretta Ross, and Elena Gutiérrez. *Undivided Rights: Women of Color Organizing for Reproductive Justice*, 2nd ed. Chicago: Haymarket, 2016.

Soares, Kristie. "Joy, Rage, and Activism: The Gendered Politics of Affect in the Young Lords Party." *Signs* 46, no. 4 (2021): 939–62.

Springer, Kimberly. *Living for the Revolution: Black Feminist Organizations, 1968–1980*. Durham, NC: Duke University Press, 2005.

Steiger, David. *The Sixties and the End of Modern America*. New York: St. Martin's, 1995.

Stephens, Julie. "Our Remembered Selves: Oral History and Feminist Memory." *Oral History* 38, no. 1 (Spring 2010): 81–90.

Stern, Alexandra Minna. "Sterilized in the Name of Public Health: Race, Immigration, and Reproductive Control in Modern California." *American Journal of Public Health* 95, no. 7 (2005): 1128–38.

Storrs, Landon R. Y. *Civilizing Capitalism: The National Consumers' League, Women's Activities, and Labor Standards in the New Deal Era*. Chapel Hill: University of North Carolina Press, 2000.

Streitmatter, Rodger. *Voices of Revolution: The Dissident Press in America*. New York: Columbia University Press, 2001.

Strom, Sharon Hartman. "Challenging 'Woman's Place': Feminism, the Old Left, and Industrial Unionism in the 1930s." *Feminist Studies* 9, no. 2 (1983): 359–86.

Taylor, Keeanga-Yamahtta, ed. *How We Get Free: Black Feminism and the Combahee River Collective*. Chicago: Haymarket, 2017.

Tijerina, Reies López. *They Called Me "King Tiger": My Struggle for the Land and Our Rights*. Houston: Arte Público, 2001.

Tischler, Barbara, ed. *Sights on the Sixties*. New Brunswick, NJ: Rutgers University Press, 1992.

Trujillo, Carla, ed. *Chicana Lesbians: The Girls Our Mothers Warned Us About*. Berkeley: Third Woman, 1991

Trussell, James, Jane Menken, Barbara L. Lindheim, and Barbara Vaughn. "The Impact of Restricting Medicaid Financing for Abortion." *Family Planning Perspectives* 12, no. 3 (May–June 1980): 120–30.

Tucker, Robert C., ed. *The Lenin Anthology*. New York: Norton, 1975.

United Nations. "Report of the World Conference of the International Women's Year, Mexico City, 19 June–2 July 1975." New York: United Nations Publications, 1976.

Urdaneta, Maria Luisa. "Chicana Use of Abortion." In *Twice a Minority: Mexican American Women*, edited by Margarita Melville. St. Louis: Mosby, 1980.

Valk, Anne. *Radical Sisters: Second-Wave Feminism and Black Liberation in Washington, D.C.* Urbana: University of Illinois Press, 2010.

Van Gelder, Lindsey. "Four Days That Changed the World: Behind the Scenes at Houston." *Ms.* (March 1978): 67.

Vargas, Zaragosa. "Tejana Radical: Emma Tenayuca and the San Antonio Labor Movement During the Great Depression." *Pacific Historical Review* 66, no. 4 (1997): 553–80.

Vásquez Robinson, Bea. "Are We Racist? Are We Sexist?" *Agenda* (Winter 1976): 23.

Vidal, Mirta. *Chicanas Speak Out: Women; New Voice of La Raza*. New York: Pathfinder, 1971.

Vidal, Mirta. "New Voice of La Raza: Chicanas Speak Out." *International Socialist Review* 32, no. 9 (October 1971): 7–9.

Vigil, Ernesto. *The Crusade for Justice: Chicano Militancy and the Government's War on Dissent*. Madison: University of Wisconsin Press, 1999.

Weber, Devra. *Dark Sweat, White Gold: California Farm Workers, Cotton, and the New Deal*. Berkeley: University of California Press, 1994.

Wu, Judy Tzu-Chun. *Radicals on the Road: Internationalism, Orientalism, and Feminism During the Vietnam Era*. Ithaca, NY: Cornell University Press, 2013.

Young, Iris. "Beyond the Unhappy Marriage: A Critique of the Dual Systems Theory." In *Women and Revolution*, edited by Lydia Sargent, 43–69. Boston: South End, 1981.

Yugar, Theresa A. *Sor Juana Inés de la Cruz: Feminist Reconstruction of Biography and Text*. Eugene, OR: Wipf and Stock, 2014.

Yuval-Davis, Nira, and Floya Anthias, eds. *Woman-Nation-State*. London: Macmillan, 1989.

Zavella, Patricia. *Women's Work and Chicano Families: Cannery Workers of the Santa Clara Valley*. Ithaca: Cornell University Press, 1987.

Zetkin, Clara. "My Recollections of Lenin (An Interview on the Woman Question)." In *The Emancipation of Women: From the Writings of V.I. Lenin*. New York: International, 1966.

Zinn, Maxine Baca. "Field Research in Minority Communities: Ethical, Methodological and Political Observations by an Insider." *Social Problems* 27 no. 2 (1979): 209–19.

Zinsser, Judith P. "From Copenhagen to Nairobi: The United Nations Decade for Women, 1975–1985," *Journal of World History* 13 no. 1 (2002): 139–68.

VIDEO RECORDINGS

Galán, Hector, dir. *Quest for a Homeland*. Episode 1 of *Chicano! The History of the Mexican American Civil Rights Movement*. Videocassette. Los Angeles: National Latino Communications Center, 1996.

Jaquette, Jane S. *What Do Women Want?* Produced by Jane S. Jaquette. Videocassette. Womenfilming, 1975.

Tajima-Peña, Renee, dir. *No Más Bebés*. DVD. Los Angeles: Moon Canyon Films, 2015.

AUDIO RECORDINGS

Friedan, Betty. *Betty Friedan vs. the Third World*. Audiocassette. Studio City, CA: Pacifica Radio Archives, 1975.

TELEVISION BROADCASTS

Linea Abierta: The Emerging Role of the Mexican American Woman. Community Television of Southern California, February 3, 1969. Transcript.

INTERNET SOURCES

Acosta, Teresa Palomo. "Chicano Literary Renaissance." In *Handbook of Texas Online*. Texas State Historical Association. https://www.tshaonline.org/handbook/entries/chicano-literary-renaissance.

California Ethnic and Multicultural Archives. Comisión Femenil Mexicana Nacional. http://cemaweb.library.ucsb.edu/cfmn_intro.html.

California Latinas for Reproductive Justice. "Herstory." https://californialatinas.org/about-us/herstory/.

"CSULB Through the Years." https://www.csulb.edu/historical.

"CSW64/Beijing+25 (2020)," UN Women. https://www.unwomen.org/en/csw/csw64-2020.

Dunbar, Roxanne. "Marxist Feminism." In *Online Reader's Companion to U.S. Women's History*, ed. Wilma Mankiller. Boston: Houghton Mifflin, 1994. http://college.hmco.com/history/readerscomp/women/html/wh_013115_marxistfemin.htm.

Gottlieb, Robert, and Peter Dreier. "A History of the Progressive Movement in Los Angeles." http://www.progressivela.org/history/fifties.htm (site discontinued).

International Women's Tribune Center. "International Women's Tribune Center." https://www.iwtc.org/.

Kuehl, Sheila, and Hilda L. Solis. "Apologizing for Historical Coerced Sterilization Practices." August 7, 2018. http://file.lacounty.gov/SDSInter/bos/supdocs/124712.pdf.

National Council of La Raza. "Formation of Southwest Council of La Raza." http://www.nclr.org/section/about/history/history_formation_swclr/. Now under History of UnidosUS. https://www.unidosus.org/about/history/.

Office of Policy Development and Research. "State of the Cities Data Systems (SOCDS)." https://socds.huduser.gov/Census/race.odb?newmsacitylist=31100%2A0600044000%2A1.0&msavar=1&metro=cbsa

Population Reference Bureau. "Shifting Latino Ethnic and Racial Identity." December 27, 2010. https://www.prb.org/resources/shifting-latino-ethnic-and-racial-identity/.

Venceremos Brigade. *Who We Are and What We Do*. http://www.venceremosbrigade.org/aboutVB.htm. Site discontinued. Now under https://vb4cuba.com/about-the-venceremos-brigade/.

UN Women. "World Conferences on Women." https://www.unwomen.org/en/how-we-work/intergovernmental-support/world-conferences-on-women.

UNPUBLISHED SOURCES

Apodaca, [Maria] Linda. "They Kept the Home Fires Burning: Mexican American Women and Social Change." PhD diss., University of California, Irvine, 1994.

Cini, Carol Frances. "Making Women's Rights Matter: Diverse Activists, California's Commission on the Status of Women, and the Legislative and Social Impact of a Movement, 1962–1976." PhD diss., University of California, Los Angeles, 2007.

Espino, Virginia. "Women Sterilized as They Give Birth: Population Control, Eugenics, and Social Protest in the Twentieth-Century United States." PhD diss., Arizona State University, 2007, 219, 224–27.

Espinoza, Dionne. "Pedagogies of Nationalism and Gender: Cultural Resistance in Selected Representational Practices of Chicana/o Movement Activists, 1967–1972." PhD diss., Cornell University, 1996.

Fields, Rona Marcia. "The Brown Berets: A Participant Observation Study of Social Action in the Schools of Los Angeles." PhD diss., University of Southern California, 1970.

Gutiérrez, Elena R. "The Racial Politics of Reproduction: The Social Construction of Mexican-Origin Women's Fertility." PhD diss., University of Michigan, 1999.

Landeros, Pablo Eduardo. "The Birth of Her Causa: The Construction, Development, and Ideology of Comisión Femenil Mexicana Nacional, Inc., 1973–1993." PhD diss., University of California, Santa Barbara, 2012.

Miranda-Arrizón, Marcie. "Building Herman(a)dad: Chicana Feminism and Comisión Femenil Mexicana Nacional." M.A. thesis, University of California, Santa Barbara, 1998.

Rose, Margaret. "Women in the United Farm Workers: A Study of Chicana and Mexicana Participation in a Labor Union, 1950–1980." PhD diss., University of California, Los Angeles, 1988.

Index

abortion, 52, 73, 95–100, 103–9, 114–19, 123, 125–26
Abzug, Bella, 90, 92–93
Aceves, Lilia, 31–32; background of, 1, 31–32, 43, 46, 55; bridging activism and, 3–5, 6; California Commission on the Status of Women and, 58–59; CFMN and, 47, 53, 54, 55, 57–58, 67; Chicana Service Action Center and, 57–58; entrance into Los Angeles Mexican American political scene, 1, 2; Heights Co-op Nursery School and, 3, 31; IWY Conference (Mexico City, 1975) and, 79, 86–88; League of Mexican American Women and, 3–4, 35–39, 40, 46; Los Angeles Human Relations Commission and, 3, 31; Mexican American Political Association and, 3, 31, 46; Wabash Coordinating Council and, 3, 31
African Americans: Black Power movement, 7, 87; civil rights movement, 7, 87; Coalition of Unrepresented Women and, 81–84; Combahee River Collective, 45; commonalities of Chicanas and African American women, 9; Communist Party and, 22–23, 27; consumer protection programs and, 37–38; deaths from abortion, 117; IWY Conference (Mexico City, 1975) and, 81–84
Agency for International Development, 80
Aguirre, Edward, 57
Akers-Chacón, Justin, 20

Alatorre, Richard, 59, 60
La Alianza Federal de Mercedes (The Federal Alliance of Land Grants), 40
Amaro, Hortensia, 116–18
American Civil Liberties Union (ACLU), 116
American Federation of Labor-Congress of Industrial Organizations (AFL-CIO), 55–56, 67; Congress of Industrial Organizations (CIO), 20, 21
American GI Forum, 27, 36–37
Andrade v. Los Angeles County, 111–12
Anthias, Floya, 7–8
antidraft/antiwar movement, 7, 11, 47, 60, 62, 72, 88–89, 92
Anzaldúa, Gloria, 124
Arellanes, Gloria, 109–11; background of, 109; El Barrio Free Clinic, East Los Angeles, 109–11, 118–19
Arizona: Consultation for Spanish-Speaking Women (Phoenix, 1972), 57–60; Mexican American state representatives, 10; oral histories of Mexican American women in, 12
Asociación Nacional México-Americana (Mexican American National Association), 16, 24, 48
Aztec (Mexica) cultural heritage, 7–8, 40, 100–102
Aztlán (common homeland), 39–40, 51, 52, 62, 96, 100–101

Baca, Polly, 46–47
Banda, Josephina "Jo," 58–59
Banda, Manuel, 43
El Barrio Free Clinic (EBFC), East Los Angeles, 109–11, 118–19
Barrios de Chungara, Domitila, 86
Bar Sinister Legal Collective, 111–12
Bebout, Lee, 100–102
Benítez, Celeste, 92
Berkeley Free Speech Movement, 7
Bernstein, Shana, 25
birth control/family planning, 60–62, 95–98, 103–9, 114–15, 118, 125
Black Panthers, 87
Blackwell, Maylei, 49, 50, 51, 61–62, 94, 96, 100, 101, 107; ¡Chicana Power!, 8–9; theory of "retrofitted memory," 12
body politics. *See* Chicana body politics in Los Angeles (1969–1981)
Bojorquez, Frances, 46, 52–53
Bojorquez Gjurich, Gilda, 80
Borrell, George W., 34
Bracero Program (1942–1964), 34–35
Bread and Roses Guerrilla Theatre, Los Angeles Women's Union, 112
Breines, Winifred, 45
bridging activism, 2–6, 14, 15–41, 90–91, 93–94, 121–26; *Carta Editorial*, 16, 24–25, 32–35, 39–41, 43, 47–48; Chicana feminist praxis in, 2–6, 16–17, 19–32, 53–56; Communist Party and, 15–16, 19–32; Community Service Organization and, 16, 19–20, 25–29, 36; cross-generational experiences in, 2–5, 125–26; ideological approaches in changing conditions in community, 3; League of Mexican American Women and, 3–4, 13, 16, 35–39; Mexican American Political Association and, 3, 16, 17, 19–20, 28–32, 36; as modality shaped by historical circumstances, 3; nature of, 2, 16–17; participation in multiple organizations across lifespan, 3, 5; political journeys beginning in local community, 2–3; reproductive rights and, 98–100, 108, 109–11, 113; sexism and identities of Chicana women, 3, 105–6; by the women of the CFMN, 53–56, 98–100
Brooks, Homer, 23
Brown, Nadia, 96
Brown Berets, 11, 51–52, 98; El Barrio Free Clinic, East Los Angeles, 109–11, 118–19; *La Causa*, 104; emergence, 110; precursor organizations, 109–10; pro-natalist position, 114
Buelna, Enrique, 20, 21, 23
Burciaga, Cecilia, 90

Cady, Barbara, 82
California: abortion funding and Medi-Cal, 115–16; forced sterilization program, 104–5; Los Angeles (*see* Los Angeles)
California Commission on Human Relations, 34
California Commission on the Status of Women (CCSW), 58–60
California Federation of Teachers (CFT), 66–67, 68
California Labor School, 16
California Latinas for Reproductive Justice, 124–25
California Population Study Commission (1966), 104
California State University, Long Beach, 1, 2, 5, 51, 56, 95–96, 106, 107, 123, 152n1
California State University, Los Angeles, 46, 52–53
California State University, Northridge, 56
California State University, Sacramento, 69
California Un-American Activities Committee, 6
Camacho, Diane, 90
Carrillo, Elvina, 27
Carta Editorial (Editorial Letter), 16, 24–25, 32–35, 39–41, 43, 47–48; housing issues and, 33–34; immigration issues and, 34–35
Carter, Jimmy, 90
Catholic Church, 61–62, 107, 110
Caurón, Ralph, 21
La Causa (Brown Beret newspaper), 104
Cedillos, Alice, 116
Center for Law and Justice (Los Angeles), 114
El Centro de Niños, 45, 60, 66–67, 68
CFMN. *See* Comisión Femenil Mexicana Nacional (National Mexican Women's Commission) (CFMN)
Chávez, Cesar, 40, 114
Chávez, Ernesto, 29
Chicana activism/liberation movement: backlash against, 8–9; body politics and (*see* Chicana body politics in Los Angeles); bridging activism and, 2–6 (*see also* bridging activism); Chicana, as term and, 44, 47, 127–28n1; Chicanas in the

Index

Chicano movement, 1–2, 4–9, 11–12, 13, 56, 70–71, 95–98; Chicanx queer activists, 124; CP and (*see* Communist Party); CSO and (*see* Community Service Organization); "double discrimination" and, 6–7; gender as framework of analysis in, 4, 6, 33, 35–39; higher education and leaders of, 1–2, 5, 11–12, 19, 26–27, 46–47, 54–56, 95–96; ideologies of, 3, 47–48; MAPA (*see* Mexican American Political Association); methodology of study, 12–13, 16–17, 98; Mexican American women in Los Angeles politics, 10–11, 19–32; positionality of author and, 11–12, 130–31n25; positionality of ethnic Mexican women and, 9; self-determination and, 51, 52; types of oppression, 49–50

Chicana body politics in Los Angeles (1969–1981), 95–119; abortion, 52, 73, 95–100, 103–9, 114–19, 123, 125–26; El Barrio Free Clinic, East Los Angeles, 109–11, 118–19; body politics, defined, 96; California Latinas for Reproductive Justice, 124–25; CFMN and, 95, 98–100, 101, 104, 107, 111, 114–18, 119; Chicana writings on, 101–9; Chicano movement/nationalism and, 95–98, 100–103, 109–11; contraception/family planning, 60–62, 95–98, 103–9, 114–15, 118, 125; forced sterilization, 96–98, 104–5, 109, 111–18; gendered body politics and, 95–98; self-determination/bodily autonomy and, 52, 97–99, 101, 105–6, 108, 114–15, 118–19, 123, 124–25

Chicana feminism, 4; body politics and (*see* Chicana body politics in Los Angeles); bridging activism praxis, 2–6, 16–18, 19–32, 53–56 (*see also* bridging activism); Chicana, as term, 44, 47, 127–28n1; Coalition of Unrepresented Women and, 81–84; consciousness about feminist ideas and identities, 9; Euro-American feminists vs., 7, 9, 49–50, 78–84, 88, 92–94, 108–9, 118, 124, 128n1, 141n20; pursuit of higher education and, 1–2, 5, 11–12, 19, 26–27, 46–47, 54–56, 95–96. *See also* Comisión Femenil Mexicana Nacional (National Mexican Women's Commission, CFMN); International Women's Year (IWY) Conference and Tribune

Chicana Movidas (D. Espinoza et al.), 100, 124

¡*Chicana Power!* (Blackwell), 8–9

Chicana Service Action Center (CSAC), 5, 11, 45, 53, 56–58, 63–66, 68, 74–76, 107, 123

Chicana Welfare Rights Organization, 11, 111, 113

Chicanismo, 39–40, 122

Chicano Federation (San Diego), 74, 76

Chicano Moratorium (1970), 11, 47, 89

Chicano movement: Brown Berets and, 11, 51–52, 98, 104, 109–11, 118–19; CFMN and, 47–48; Chicana activists in, 1–2, 4–9, 11–12, 13, 56, 70–71, 95–98; Chicanismo and, 39–40, 122; Chicano, as term, 127–28n1; cross-generational relationships and, 4–5; emergence of, 39–41; expansion of, 10, 40–41; gendered roles and erasure of women in, 8–9, 46, 50–52, 75, 76, 86, 110; as ideology of Chicana activism, 3; law enforcement and, 87–88, 110, 111–12; organizations in, 40–41; patriarchal structures and gendered roles in, 8, 95–96, 108–9; politics and professional experiences of women in, 4–5; and *La Raza*, 5; La Raza Unida Party, 11, 47, 48, 61, 76, 78, 79, 123; representation in state and federal governments, 10; reproductive rights/family and, 95–98, 100–103, 109–11; self-determination and, 7, 97; student organizations/movement in, 8–9, 40; of the Vietnam War era, 1–2, 10–11

Chicano nationalism: Aztec (Mexica) cultural heritage, 7–8, 40, 100–102; Aztlán (common homeland) and, 39–40, 51, 52, 62, 96, 100–102

Chicano Studies Research Center (UCLA), 76

Chicano Youth Liberation Conferences (Denver, 1969 and 1970), 48–51; Crusade for Justice, 40, 48; El Plan Espiritual de Aztlán, 100–102

Chicanx queer activists, 124

Circulo Cultural "Isabel la Católica" (Cultural Circle "Isabel the Catholic"), 7

Civil Rights Congress, 11

civil rights movement, 7, 87

Coalition of Unrepresented Women (CUW), 81–84

Cold War era, 15, 28–29

Colorado: Chicano Youth Liberation Conferences (Denver, 1969 and 1970), 40, 48–51, 100–102; Crusade for Justice and, 40, 48; Mexican American state representative, 10

Combahee River Collective, 45
Comisión Femenil Mexicana Nacional (National Mexican Women's Commission) (CFMN), 43–68; archival collection, 12; base of operations in Los Angeles, 52–53, 56, 70, 94, 115–16, 122; becomes an NGO with the United Nations, 94; El Centro de Niños, 45, 60, 66–67, 68; challenges faced by, 44–45, 61–66; chapters in California, 52–53, 140n3; Chicana Service Action Center, 5, 11, 45, 53, 56–58, 63–66, 68, 74–76, 107, 123; developing national organization, 47, 58–61, 62–66, 67, 68; formation of Comisión Femenil Mexicana, 11, 13, 16, 43–44, 45–53, 57, 67, 98–100, 122; goals of, 44–45, 52, 68; Health Committee, 115–16; IWY Conference (Mexico City, 1975) and, 74–76, 80; naming of, 47; National Women's Conference (Houston, 1977) and, 89–94, 123; as outgrowth of the League of Mexican American Women, 13; reproductive justice and, 95, 98–100, 101, 104, 107, 111, 114–18, 119, 153n16; women of, 41, 43–44, 46–47, 53–56
Commission on the Status of Women (CSW): formation, 52, 73; naming of, 47; of the United Nations, 70–73, 77, 80, 146n15
Committee to Free Los Tres (Committee to Free the Three, CTFLT), 98, 111–13
Committee to Stop Forced Sterilizations (CSFS), 112–13
communism: anti-communism forces and, 6, 21, 26–30; as ideology of Chicana activism, 3, 15–17, 19–32, 40, 43, 55, 69, 70. *See also* Communist Party (CP)
Communist Party (CP), 13, 15–32, 41, 121–22; anti-communism and, 6, 21, 26–30; Chicana feminist involvement in, 3, 15–17, 19–32, 40, 43, 55, 69, 70, 131n1; Cold War legislation and, 28–29; Congress of Industrial Organizations and, 20, 21; decline in the U.S., 28; FBI and, 21, 134n33, 135n47; founding of Communist Party USA, 20; House Un-American Activities Committee and, 6, 26–30; International Bookstore, 21; Mexican American Commission, 23; Mexican American membership in the 1950s, 20–21; Popular Front era/New Deal, 20, 22–23; Progressive Bookstore, 21; of the Soviet Union, 24; Young Communist League, 20

Community Service Organization (CSO), 10–11, 13, 19–20, 41, 122; deportation and, 28–29; expansion across the Southwest, 25; founding, 16, 18, 25, 27; gender disparities in leadership, 25–26, 27, 36; Los Angeles women active in, 16, 25–29
Comprehensive Employment and Training Act (1973), 64–65
"Concerned Chicanas": "Genocide on the Chicano Family," 104–6, 107
Concilio Mujeres (San Francisco), 75
Conferencia de Mujeres por La Raza (Houston, 1971), 61–62, 107, 108
El Congreso de Pueblos de Habla Española (the Spanish-Speaking People's Congress), 22; founding, 1, 6–7, 48; women's committee and "double discrimination," 6–7
Congress of Industrial Organizations (CIO), 20, 21
Con Safos (literary magazine), 101–3
Consultation for Spanish-Speaking Women (CSSW) (Phoenix, 1972), 57–60
consumer education and protection, 37–38
contraception/family planning, 60–62, 95–98, 103–9, 114–15, 118, 125
Contracongreso a través del Frente de Mujeres contra el Año Internacional de la Mujer (Countercongress by the Women's Front Against International Women's Year), 85–86
Contreras, Sheila, 75–76
Córdova, Patricia, 112
Costanza, Midge, 90
Cotera, María, 8, 100
Cotera, Martha, 90, 92, 123–24
Crusade for Justice, 40, 48
Cruz, Ricardo, 111–12
CSAC. *See* Chicana Service Action Center (CSAC)
cultural nationalism, 6, 8, 44, 50, 93, 95, 96–97, 101, 104, 105, 108, 118–19, 123

De la Cruz, Sor Juana, 102–3
De la Torre-Wycoff, Gloria (Gloria Moreno-Wycoff), 60–61
Del Castillo, Adelaida, 8, 123
Delgado, Sylvia, 105–7
Democratic Party, 17, 27–28, 60; Democratic National Committee, 46–47; gender issues and, 36–37
De Saram, Carole, 82

"double discrimination," 6–7
Dressmakers' strike (1943), 10
Du Bois, W. E. B., 27
Duran, Maria, 27

EBCF. *See* El Barrio Free Clinic (EBCF), East Los Angeles
Encuentro Femenil (journal), 107, 123
Encuentros, 73–74
Equal Rights Amendment, 58
Escalante, Alicia, 111
Espino, Virginia, 113
Espinoza, Dionne, 8, 51–52, 72, 100
Espinoza Damián, Gisela, 73
ethnic Mexican, as term, 127–28n1
eugenics, 104–5
Euro-American feminist movement, 7, 9, 49–50, 78–84, 88, 92–94, 108–9, 118, 124, 128n1, 141n20

Family Planning Services and Research Act (1970), 104
Federal Bureau of Investigation (FBI), 6, 15, 21, 29, 55, 87, 134n33, 135n47
feminism: Euro-American feminist movement, 7, 9, 49–50, 78–84, 88, 92–94, 108–9, 118, 124, 128n1, 141n20; historical (neofeminism), 73; as ideology of Chicana activism, 3 (*see also* Chicana feminism); popular, 73. *See also* international feminism
Fernández, Juan, 111
Filipino Americans, farm worker labor movements, 7
Flores, Francisca, 15–25; and the Asociación Nacional México-Americana (Mexican American National Association), 16, 24, 48; background of, 15–16, 18, 19, 28, 41, 46, 54; at the California Labor School, 16; *Carta Editorial* (Editorial Letter) and, 16, 24–25, 32–35, 39–41, 43, 47–48; changing with the times and, 4; Chicana feminism and, 4, 18, 121; and the Chicana Service Action Center, 57–58, 64; as co-founder of the CFMN, 11, 13, 16, 41, 43–48, 53–54, 56–59, 67, 99–100, 106, 121 (*see also* Comisión Femenil Mexicana Nacional); as co-founder of the Community Service Organization, 16; as co-founder of the League of Mexican American Women, 16, 46; as co-founder of the Mexican American Political Association, 16; in the Communist Party, 15–16, 20, 21–25, 43, 121, 131n1, 134n33, 135n47; at the Consultation for Spanish-Speaking Women (Phoenix, 1972), 57–60; in the Food, Tobacco, Agricultural, and Allied Workers union, 16, 21, 22; Hermanas de la Revolución Mexicana (Sisters of the Mexican Revolution) and, 24; and the International Union of Mine, Mill and Smelter Workers, 24; *Jewish Life* article, 23–24; League of Mexican American Women and, 35–39, 41, 43; loss of personal papers of, 12, 15–16; as Frances Lym, 21, 23–24, 134n33; in the Mexican American Political Association, 43, 46, 121; move to Los Angeles (1945), 15, 21, 22, 23; political trajectory of, 121, 125–26; *Regeneración* (Regeneration) and, 16, 47–48, 99–100, 106, 121; in a San Diego tuberculosis sanatorium, 15, 24, 46; Women's Workshop and, 99–100, 105
Food, Tobacco, Agricultural, and Allied Workers (FTA) union (formerly the United Cannery, Agricultural, Packing, and Allied Workers of America), 16, 21, 22
forced sterilization. *See* sterilization programs
Freedman, Estelle, 97
Friedan, Betty, 83–84, 88

García, Mario T., 6, 20, 23
García, Soledad, 38
García, Sonia R., 68
Garcilazo, Jeffrey, 20–21
"Genocide on the Chicano Family" ("Concerned Chicanas"), 104–6, 107
Gershon, Sarah Allen, 96
Gilliam, Angela, 82
Girls Athletic Association, 2
Goldsmith, Romero, 47
Gómez, Alan, 88
Gonez, Kelly, 125
Gonzales, Rodolfo "Corky," 40
González, Gabriela, 6, 7
Great Depression, deportation of Mexicans during, 10
El Grito del Norte (newspaper), 49, 51
Gutiérrez, Angel, 40
Gutiérrez, David G., 25, 28, 127–28n1
Gutiérrez, Elena R., 97, 114

Haney-Lopez, Ian, 103
Harris, Rosalind, 77–78

Healey, Dorothy, 21, 26–27
Heights Co-op Nursery School, 3
Hermanas de la Revolución Mexicana (Sisters of the Mexican Revolution), 24
Hernández, Antonia, 114, 116
Hernandez, Eunisses, 125
Herrera Rodríguez, Celia: background of, 69–70; IWY Conference (Mexico City, 1975) and, 74–76, 84–85, 86
heteropatriarchy, 51–52
High School Blowouts (1968), 11
Las Hijas de Cuauhtémoc (California State University, Long Beach), 51, 56, 107, 123
Holifield, Chester "Chet," 27–28, 136n63
Hosang, Daniel, 34
House Un-American Activities Committee (HUAC), 6, 26–30
housing, 33–34
Huerta, Dolores, 40
Hutar, Patricia, 80
Hyde Amendment, 115

immigration: deportation and, 10, 17, 28–29, 34–35, 97; eugenics and, 104–5; racist practices in, 6, 29, 34–35, 104–5
Immigration and Nationality Act/McCarran-Walter Act (1952), 28–29
imperialism, resistance to, 23, 47, 72, 79, 113
indigenous people: Aztec (Mexica) cultural heritage, 7–8, 40, 100–101; Aztlán (common homeland), 39–40, 51, 52, 62, 96, 100–102; commonalities of Chicanas and African American women with, 9; indigenous feminism, 73; positionality of ethnic Mexican women and, 9
Indochinese Women's Conference (Vancouver, 1971), 72
Industrial Areas Foundation, 25
Internal Security Act (1950), 28
international feminism: historical context of, 71–74; historical feminism (neofeminism) vs. popular feminism, 73; Indochinese Women's Conference (Vancouver, 1971), 72; International Women's Conference (Copenhagen, 1980), 93, 94; National Women's Conference (Houston, 1977), 89–94, 123 (*see also* International Women's Year Conference and Tribune); Third World womanism and, 72–73, 88–89
International Ladies' Garment Workers' Union (ILGWU), 27, 30, 31
International Social Service, 77

International Union of Mine, Mill and Smelter Workers (Mine Mill), 24
International Women's Conference (Copenhagen, 1980), 93, 94
International Women's Year (IWY) Conference and Tribune (Mexico City, 1975), 14, 68, 69–90, 123; Coalition of Unrepresented Women, 81–84; Decade for Women launch and, 72–73, 89; Declaration of Mexico adoption, 77; events leading to, 74–78; First World/Third World schism and, 73, 78–84; historical context of international feminism and, 71–74; impact of conference, 93–94; International Women's Tribune Center, 72–73; National Chicana Coalition, 78, 82–83; political fault lines, 73, 78–84; tribune attendees, 70–89; UN approval of inaugural conference, 70; "underground conference"/boycott by Mexican feminists, 85–86; World Plan of Action adoption, 74, 77, 83, 89

Jewish Life, 23–24
Johnson, Lady Bird, 33
Johnson, Lyndon B., 33

Kelley, Robin D. G., 23
Khrushchev, Nikita, 24
Korean War era, 1

law enforcement: Brown Berets and, 110; Chicano movement and, 87–88, 110, 111–12; Committee to Free Los Tres (Committee to Free the Three), 98, 111–13; Federal Bureau of Investigation, 6, 15, 21, 29, 55, 87, 134n33; police brutality, 6, 29, 87, 110
League of Mexican American Women (LMAW), 3–4, 35–39, 41, 46, 50, 52, 122; founding, 13, 16, 17, 35–36, 43; Sixth Annual Awards Banquet, 40; as women-only Latina political organization, 13, 36, 39
League of United Latin American Citizens, 27, 48
Long Beach State College, 95–96, 106, 152n1. *See also* California State University, Long Beach
Longeaux y Vásquez, Enriqueta, 50
López, Sonia, 8, 50
López, Yolanda, 74, 84, 86, 88
López Tijerina, Reies, 40
Los Angeles: as base of operations for CFMN, 52–53, 56, 70, 94, 115–16, 122; Chicana body politics (*see* Chicana body

Index

politics in Los Angeles); Chicana liberation movement and, 2–3, 10 (*see also* Chicana activism/liberation movement; Chicana feminism); Chicano movement and, 4, 10–11 (*see also* Chicano movement; Chicano nationalism); demographic trends and, 10–11, 18–19; as the epicenter of Mexican American politics, 2; exclusion of ethnic Mexicans from local politics, 10; founding as Spanish settlement, 10; Mexican Americans under siege in (1945–1975), 17–19; Mexican American women in politics of, 10–11, 19–32

Los Angeles Committee for the Protection of the Foreign Born, 11, 17

Los Angeles County–University of Southern California Medical Center (LAC+USC), 111, 112, 115–16, 118, 126

Los Angeles Human Relations Commission, 3, 31

Lym, Frances, 21, 23–24, 134n33. *See also* Flores, Francisca

Lym, La Verne, 21

Madrigal v. Quilligan, 115–16
Marcos, Sylvia, 73
Márquez, Marisela, 68
Martínez, Elizabeth, 49
Marxist-Leninism, 3, 22, 111
Mattingly, Doreen J., 89, 92
Mayor's Latin American Advisory Council, 36–37
McCarran-Walter Act/Immigration and Nationality Act (1952), 28–29
McClintock, Anne, 101
McCrae v. Califano, 116
MEChA (El Movimiento Estudiantil Chicano de Aztlán, Chicano Student Movement of Aztlán), 5, 46, 48, 52–53, 56
Mendoza Schechter, Hope, 16–17; Central Labor Council Committee on Political Education and, 28; and the Community Service Organization (CSO), 27–28; Democratic Party and, 27–28; ULGWU and, 27
methodology of study, 12–13, 16–17, 98
Mexican American Education Conference Committee, 33
Mexican American Legal Defense and Education Fund (MALDEF), 116
Mexican American National Issues Conference (Sacramento, 1970), 43–44; formation of Comisión Femenil Mexicana, 11, 13, 16, 43–44, 45–53, 57, 67, 98–100, 122; Women's Workshop, 99–100, 105

Mexican American Political Association (MAPA), 3, 16, 17, 19–20, 28–32, 36–37, 41, 43, 46, 48, 121, 122

Mexican Americans: farm worker labor movements, 7, 40, 114; gender issues among, 4, 6–7, 17–18, 33, 35–39; as representatives and state and local governments, 10, 18; as under siege in Los Angeles (1945–1975), 17–19; terminology for, 44, 47, 127–28n1

Mexican-American Youth Leadership Conference (Los Angeles Commission on Human Relations), 109

Mexican American Youth Organization (Texas), 40

Mexican Revolution (1910–1920), 20, 24, 51

Mexican Student Movement (1968), 85

Molina, Gloria: California Commission on the Status of Women and, 58–59; CFMN and, 58–59, 67, 114, 125; as elected representative, 125

Molina de Pick, Gracia, 53, 90
Monroy, Douglas, 20
Montañez Davis, Grace: background of, 26–27, 28, 43; CFMN and, 53, 54, 91; changing with the times and, 4; Chicana feminism and, 4; Community Service Organization and, 26, 31; education of, 19, 26–27; Hollywood Ten and, 26–27; and the Mexican American Political Association, 31; in the U.S. Department of Labor, 57
Montenegro, Sal, 34
Montes, Phil, 59
Montoya, Alfredo, 24
Mora, Magdalena, 123
Moraga, Cherríe, 124
Moreno, Dorinda, 75
Moreno, Luisa: background of, 21–22; in El Congreso de Pueblos de Habla Española (the Spanish-Speaking People's Congress), 22; at the Food, Tobacco, Agricultural, and Allied Workers union, 16, 21, 22
Moreno-Wycoff, Gloria (Gloria De la Torre-Wycoff), 60–61
Morín Ramona, 16–17; background of, 36–37; consumer education and protests and, 37–38; League of Mexican American Women and, 35–39
El Movimiento Estudiantil Chicano de Aztlán (MEChA, Chicano Student Movement of Aztlán), 5, 46, 48, 52–53, 56

Las Mujeres de California, 91–92
Mujeres en Acción Solidaria (MAS), 81–82, 85
Muñoz, Connie. *See* Pardo, Connie (Muñoz)
Muñoz, Frank, 30–31, 75

Nare, Jessica L., 89, 92
National Association of Cuban Women, 92
National Chicana Coalition, 78, 82–83
National Commission on the Observance of International Women's Year, 90
National Commission on Women, 90
National Council of Jewish Women, 116
National Hispanic Feminist Conference (1980), 116
National Organization for Women (NOW), 82, 116, 140n6
National Women's Conference (Houston, 1977), 89–94, 123
Nava, Julian, 18
Nava, Yolanda: background of, 55; California Commission on the Status of Women and, 58–59; CFMN and, 54, 55, 65
Nelson, Jennifer, 97, 108, 118
New Left, 7
New Mexico: La Alianza Federal de Mercedes (The Federal Alliance of Land Grants), 40; Crusade for Justice and, 40, 48; *El Grito del Norte*, 49, 51; Mexican American state representatives, 10
NietoGómez, Anna, 32, 33, 36, 45–46, 62; background of, 55–56; CFMN and, 53, 54, 70–71, 107; and the Educational Opportunity Program, Long Beach State College, 95–96, 106; as founding member of Hijas de Cuauhtémoc at California State University, Long Beach, 107; IWY Conference (Mexico City, 1975) and, 70–71, 84–88
Nixon, Richard, 90
NOW Minority Women's Conference, 116

Obama, Barack, 125
Olcott, Jocelyn, 79
Olivares, Graciela, 46–47
Operation Wetback (1954), 29, 34–35
La Opinion (newspaper), 54–55
Organización Chicana (UCLA), 76, 147–48n30
Orona, Carolyn, 59
Ortiz, Alberto, 111

Ortiz Franklin, Tanya, 125

Padilla, Beverly, 108
Pardo, Connie (Muñoz), 16–17; background of, 19, 30–31, 43, 46, 55; CFMN and, 53, 74–75; Chicana Service Action Center and, 65, 74–75; ILGWU and, 31; IWY Conference (Mexico City, 1975) and, 84–85, 87, 89; Mexican American Political Association and, 30–31, 46
Parker, Daniel, 80
Partido Liberal Mexicano (Mexican Liberal Party), 20, 51
patriarchy: Chicano movement and, 8, 95–96, 108–9; double standard in relation to sexuality, 73, 103, 105–6; gendered body politics and, 95–98; heteropatriarchy, 51–52
Peace and Freedom Party, 60
Peña, Ada, 83
Perera, Ana Maria, 92
Pérez, Emma, 51–52
Pérez, Laura Elisa, 96
Persinger, Mildred, 77–78
Phillips, Ilbert, 65
El Plan Espiritual de Aztlán, 100–102
Poder Femenino, 76
police brutality, 6, 29, 87, 110
Population Conference (Bucharest, 1974), 70
Population Study Commission, 104
Portelli, Alessandro, 12
Porter, Steven, 65
Preciado Martin, Patricia, 12
Pro Choice Coalition, 116
Progressive Party, 55
Proposition 14 (California), 34

Quezada, Leticia, 68, 116

racial discrimination: housing and, 33–34; immigration and, 6, 29, 34–35, 104–5
Railroad Workers Association, 55–56
La Raza (Chicano newspaper), 5
La Raza Unida Party (Chicano third party), 11, 47, 48, 61, 76, 78, 79, 123
Reagan, Ronald, 59
Realtors for Fair Housing, 34
Las Redondillas (*A Philosophical Satire*), 103
Regeneración (Regeneration), 16, 47–48, 99–100, 106, 121
retrofitted memory (Blackwell), 12
Revolutionary Student Brigade, 113

Revolutionary Union, 113
Rivas, Rocío, 125
Robeson, Paul, 27
Rodríguez, Isabel Chávez, 112
Rodríguez, Maria, 116, 118
Rodriguez, Monica, 125
Rodríguez, Richard T., 96, 101
Rodriguez, Yolanda O., "Una Chicana de Pittsburg," 101–3, 104
Roe v. Wade (1973), 95, 97
Romero, Frances, 69–70, 76
Romero Goldsmith, Simmie: as co-founder of the CFMN, 13, 43–44, 47–48, 53; Mexican American National Issues Conference (Sacramento, 1970) and, 43–44
Romo, Ricardo, 18
Rose, Margaret, 25–26
Ross, Loretta, 105
Roybal, Edward, 10, 18, 25, 27, 30
Ruiz, Vicki L., 6, 11, 22
Rumford Fair Housing Act (California, 1963), 34
Rupp, Leila, 71–72

Sánchez, Corinne: athletic activities and, 2, 5; background of, 1–2, 55–56; bridging activism and, 3, 5–6; at California State University, Long Beach, 1, 2, 5; CFMN and, 53; changing with the times and, 4; at the Chicana Service Action Center, 5; entrance into Los Angeles Mexican American political scene, 1–2; at *La Raza*, 5; Third-World women and, 88–89; and the United Mexican American Students/ El Movimiento Estudiantil Chicano de Aztlán, MEChA/Hijas de Cuauhtémoc, 5
Sánchez, Dolores, 16–17; background of, 19, 29–30, 43, 55; CFMN and, 53, 54, 99; ILGWU and, 30; League of Mexican American Women and, 36, 38–39; Mexican American Political Association and, 30
Sánchez, George J., 20
Sánchez, Rodolfo, 111
Schrecker, Ellen, 20, 22
self-determination: Chicana activism and, 51, 52; Chicana bodily autonomy and, 52, 97–99, 101, 105–6, 108, 114–15, 118–19, 123, 124–25; Chicano movement/nationalism and, 7, 97
Serrano Sewell, Sandra, 54, 75, 84; background of, 55; CFMN and, 91, 92–93; identification as Chicana, 60

sexualism (Gilliam), 82
Sleepy Lagoon incident and trial, 10–11, 15, 22, 28
Socialist Workers Party, 108
Solidarity Band, 112
Solinger, Rickie, 105
Solis, Hilda, 125
Songs My Mother Sang to Me (Preciado Martin), 12
Stalin, Joseph, 22–24
sterilization programs, 96–98, 104–5, 109, 111–18; formal apology for, 126; at the University of Southern California–Los Angeles County Medical Center (USC-LACMC), 111, 112, 115–16, 118, 126
Stern, Alexandra Minna, 104
Students for a Democratic Society, 7
Sturdivant, Frederick, 38, 139n106

Teamsters, 37
El Teatro Campesino, 69
Tenayuca, Emma, 21, 23
Texas: Communist Party in, 23; Conferencia de Mujeres por La Raza (Houston, 1971), 61–62, 107, 108; Mexican American state representatives, 10; Mexican American Youth Organization, 40; National Women's Conference (Houston, 1977), 89–94, 123
third-worldism: First World/Third World schism and, 73, 78–84; as ideology of Chicana activism, 3; IWY Conference (Mexico City, 1975) and, 84–89; "Third World womanism," 72–73, 88–89; U.S. colonialism and, 71, 72
This Bridge Called My Back (Anzaldúa and Moraga), 124
Tovar, Irene, 38

Ugarte, Sandra, 107
Undivided Rights (Silliman et al.), 115
Ungar, Rose, 67
unionism: AFL-CIO, 20, 21, 55–56, 67; California Federation of Teachers and, 66–67, 68; of farm workers, 7, 40, 114; FTA and, 16, 21, 22; as ideology of Chicana activism, 3, 55–56; ILGWU and, 27, 30, 31; Mine Mill, 24; Teamsters, 37
United Cannery, Agricultural, Packing, and Allied Workers of America (later Food, Tobacco, Agricultural, and Allied Workers [FTA] union), 16, 21, 22

United Farm Workers Union, 40, 114
United Mexican American Students/El Movimiento Estudiantil Chicano de Aztlán, MEChA/Hijas de Cuauhtémoc, 5, 46, 48, 52–53, 56
United Nations: CFMN becomes NGO with, 94; Commission on the Status of Women, 70–73, 77, 80, 146n15; Food Conference (Rome, 1974), 70; International Women's Conference (Copenhagen, 1980), 93, 94; nongovernmental organizations and, 70, 77–78, 94; Population Conference (Bucharest, 1974), 70. *See also* International Women's Year (IWY) Conference and Tribune
United States–Mexican War (1846–1848), 23–24, 79
University of California, Los Angeles, 26–27; CFMN archival collection, 12; Chicano Studies Research Center, 76; Organización Chicana, 76, 147–48n30
University of California, San Diego, 74
University of California, Santa Barbara, CFMN archival collection, 12
University of Southern California–Los Angeles County Medical Center (USC-LACMC), 111, 112, 115–16, 118, 126
U.S. Census, 18, 54
U.S. Civil Rights Commission, 59
U.S. Department of Health, Education and Welfare: Hyde Amendment (Medicaid-funded abortion), 115; Office of Population Affairs, 104
U.S. Department of Labor: Women's Bureau, 57–58; Women's Commission, 47

Valdez Banda, Josephine: CFMN and, 53; Mexican American National Issues Conference (Sacramento, 1970), 43–44
Van Gelder, Lindsey, 92
Varela, Delfino, 30; *Carta Editorial* and, 24–25, 32–35, 39–41

Vargas, Zaragoza, 21
Vásquez Robinson, Bea, 80–81, 82–83
Vietnam War era, 1–2, 7, 10–11, 47, 62, 72, 87, 88–89
Villaescusa, Henrietta, 27
Voice of Women, 72

Wabash Coordinating Council, 3, 31
Waters, Maxine, 91
Women's Bureau (U.S. Department of Labor), 57–58
Women's Commission (U.S. Department of Labor), 47
Women Strike for Peace, 72
Women's Workshop, 99–100, 105
Women's World Conference (Beijing, 1995), 73, 146n15
World Plan of Action, 74, 77, 83, 89
World War I era, 70
World War II era, 6, 10, 22–23, 28, 31, 35, 48, 88

Xilonen (newspaper), 78

Young Chicanos for Community Action (YCCA), 110, 156n60
Young Citizens for Community Action, 109, 156n60
Young Women's Christian Association (YWCA), 36–37, 61–62; World YWCA, 77–78
Yucatán Feminist Congress, 51
Yuval-Davis, Nira, 7–8

Zapata, Carmen, 60
Zeta Acosta, Oscar: *Autobiography of a Brown Buffalo,* 103; "Love Letter to the Girls of Aztlan," 101–3
Zoot Suit–Sailor Riots, 28

MARISELA R. CHÁVEZ is a professor of Chicana and Chicano studies at California State University, Dominguez Hills.

The University of Illinois Press
is a founding member of the
Association of University Presses.

University of Illinois Press
1325 South Oak Street
Champaign, IL 61820–6903
www.press.uillinois.edu